Journalism in Iran

From mission to profession

Hossein Shahidi

Routledge
Taylor & Francis Group

LONDON AND NEW YORK

First published 2007
by Routledge
2 Park Square, Milton Park, Abingdon, Oxon, OX14 4RN

Simultaneously published in the USA and Canada
by Routledge
270 Madison Ave, New York NY 10016

*Routledge is an imprint of the Taylor & Francis Group,
an informa business*

Transferred to Digital Printing 2010

© 2007 Hossein Shahidi

Typeset in Times New Roman by
Newgen Imaging Systems (P) Ltd, Chennai, India

British Library Cataloguing in Publication Data
A catalogue record for this book is available
from the British Library

Library of Congress Cataloging in Publication Data
A catalog record for this book has been requested

ISBN10: 0–415–42573–5 (hbk)
ISBN10: 0–415–58316–0 (pbk)
ISBN10: 0–203–96196–X (ebk)

ISBN13: 978–0–415–42573–5 (hbk)
ISBN13: 978–0–415–58316–9 (pbk)
ISBN13: 978–0–203–96196–4 (ebk)

Journalism in Iran

Journalism in Iran charts the development of the profession in Iran since the 1979 Revolution that replaced the monarchy with an Islamic Republic.

The book is aimed at finding out the extent to which journalism in Iran has approached the idea and practices of media professionalism that are common in the West. The author provides a social, political, and economic context for the work of Iranian journalists who have received attention by the international media mostly as victims of repeated attacks on the press or detentions of media workers.

The study focuses on newspapers, the only segment of the Iranian media where independent journalism has had an opportunity to develop. Radio and television which have almost always been controlled by the state, and the much younger but fast growing online journalism, are discussed separately to provide a fuller picture of Iran's media environment. Separate chapters are dedicated to Iranian women's contribution to journalism; organization, education, and training of journalists; and the legal framework in which Iranian journalists have had to work since the country's first Press Law was introduced, following the 1906 Constitutional Revolution. Relying on critique of the Iranian media by journalists and academics writing in Iran, Hossein Shahidi argues that urgent and thorough reform of editorial policies and practices in Iran's major media organizations is vital to provide the public with the regular flow of high quality information that is needed for a healthy society.

Written to pay homage to Iranian journalists, without ignoring their shortcomings, this richly systemic evaluation of journalism in Iran will appeal to scholars and students of Iranian Studies, as well as anyone interested in Media Studies and Middle Eastern Studies.

Hossein Shahidi teaches Communication at the American University of Beirut. He was a journalist and journalist trainer for more than twenty years, mostly at the BBC World Service, and Gender and Media Specialist with the United Nations Development Fund for Women (UNIFEM) in Afghanistan (2003–04).

Iranian Studies

Edited by
Homa Katouzian
University of Oxford
Mohamad Tavakoli
University of Toronto

Since 1967 the International Society for Iranian Studies (ISIS) has been a leading learned society for the advancement of new approaches in the study of Iranian society, history, culture, and literature. The new ISIS Iranian Studies series published by Routledge will provide a venue for the publication of original and innovative scholarly works in all areas of Iranian and Persianate Studies.

Journalism in Iran
From mission to profession
Hossein Shahidi

To Roya, Farhad, and Farhang

Contents

Tables

Guide to transliteration

Persian character	Roman character	Persian word example	Transliteration	Notes and examples of exception because of common or personal usage
آ	a	آمد	amad	
ا	a	اکبر	Akbar	
ِا	e	انتظامی	Entezami	
ج	j	جوان	Javan	This is by far the most frequent use of the letter 'J'.
ژ	j	ژیلا نژاد ویژگی مژگان پژوهش	Jilla Nejad Vijegi Mojgan Pajouhesh	Due to the less frequent appearance of this Persian character, the letter 'J' has also been used in such cases.
Initial س	s	سلام	Salam	
Medial س	ss	حسن	Hassan	Islam, Eslam, Mohsen, Rastakhiz, *Resalat*
Initial ع	A E	علی عزت الله	Ali Ezatollah	
Medial ع	'	معمار	Me'mar	سعید =Saied
غ	gh	غلط	ghalat	
ق	q	فرقان	Forqan	قابل = Ghabel قائد = Ghaed
ّ	Double character	حجت الاسلام	Hojjatoleslam	
Long و	ou	روزنامه	rouznameh	
ءو	ow	نوروز	Nowrouz	
Short ی	e	رضا	Reza	Kurdistan
Long ی	i	تسخیر	Tasskhir	

Foreword

There were two full-scale revolutions in Iran in the twentieth century. The first one, begun at the turn of the twentieth century, was a revolt of the society against the state for the establishment of government based in law as opposed to arbitrary rule which had been the ancient form of government in the country. All the revolutionaries were united in this central objective while democracy and socio-economic modernization were the further aims of the more radical and modern elements in the revolution. Twentieth-century Iran did experience socio-economic development but its system of government still revolved around the age-old cycle of arbitrary rule-chaos-arbitrary rule.

The second revolution was also a revolt of the society against the state which no social class or organized political party would be prepared to defend. The principal objectives of this revolution were the overthrow of the arbitrary state and the rejection of its Westernist culture and politics, alike by religious traditionalists, Marxist–Leninists and – to a lesser extent – social and liberal democrats. But the anti-Westernist stance of the revolution – clear though it was – was itself a product of the fact that the arbitrary state had identified itself with the West, otherwise it would not have become a common goal of the entire society.

The media played an important role in both revolutions. A modern public sphere had begun to emerge alongside the constitutionalist movement of the earlier revolution. Whether or not a public sphere of sorts had existed in Iranian history, there can be little doubt that modern public sphere of the kind that had emerged in Europe from the late seventeenth century had had no precedent in Iran before the twentieth century. Modern newspapers, virtually all of which were pro-revolutionary, spread rapidly through the constitutionalist movement. But just as the government in law was soon replaced by social and political chaos, much of the press ignored all limits and bounds to freedom of expression, liberty giving way to licence whereby reckless journalism left little for the reputations of those who were targeted, be they the Shah, ministers, politicians, ulama, merchants, or other journalists.

The chaos that had been the unanticipated and illegitimate offspring of constitutionalism came to an end together with constitutionalism itself with the rise of the Pahlavi state in the mid-1920s. Within a few years little was left of freedom of the press and expression. In the previous period chaos had tuned liberty into licence and now liberty was lost with the application of order and arbitrary rule. In 1941 the intrusion of World War II into Iran once again let loose the chaotic forces embedded in Iranian society.

This was immediately manifested in the press, much of which was disorderly and licentious, although a part of it behaved with greater responsibility. This period came to an end with the coup d'etat of 1953 which ended the chaos and licence but left some room for freedom of the press and public expression. It was from the failure of the revolt of June 1963 that absolute censorship began to be applied, such that until 1977 critical public opinion virtually ceased to exist, the press being unable to disseminate news and opinion which was not officially approved.

Hossein Shahidi's rich and fascinating account covers the development of Iranian journalism since the revolution. He describes the missionary zeal of frustrated journalists turned freedom lovers overnight, who both reflected and enhanced the public belief that the millennium would be at hand simply by the abolition of the monarchy. There were differences of views among journalists as there were among the public, but there was virtually no doubt among them along with the entire society that the fall of the monarchy and with it the rejection of the hated Westernism would promise the dawn of a golden era. They were soon disappointed after the triumph of February 1979. 'The Spring of Freedom' did not last much longer than the season itself and by the end of the summer many newspapers were shut down.

The onset in 1980 of the long war between Iran and Iraq left little freedom to speak of any kind, including that of the press, except to some extent within the few technical and scientific journals. It was a reflection of the war without and the intense civil conflict within the society itself. Like the period before 1977, what was left of the public sphere was not much more than the limited space tolerated by the state. By then many if not most of the old hands in Iranian journalism had emigrated, moved to other activities or gone to prison.

The early 1990s saw an opening up with the emergence of newspapers and journals which, often in difficult circumstances, began to disseminate news and express opinions other than those strictly desired by the state. This was a small but promising opening which further spread as a result of the reform movement which began in the late 1990s. By the year 2000 however the conservative forces, with the judiciary as their main vehicle, began to apply sanctions against liberal journalism, although the move was not entirely retrospective and some of the achievements of the 1990s survived. Still Iran is a long way from a free as well as responsible press.

Shahidi's account and analysis is virtually compulsory reading not only for those interested in the development of Iranian journalism in the last 30 years, but for anyone with a serious interest in the history and politics of contemporary Iran. He has used many primary sources, both newspapers and interviews.

His narrative of revolutionary events is balanced, fair, and competent. His description of the evolution of Iranian journalism into a public profession is unique and original. And above all his analysis of almost three decades of social and political developments is acute and insightful. This is a book the study of which will benefit teacher, student, and lay reader alike for years to come.

Homa Katouzian
St Antony's College and the Oriental Institute
University of Oxford
August 2006

Preface

This book is the result of the author's experience in and study of Iranian journalism over some twenty-five years. The last decade of this period was spent seeking an answer to the question whether Iran, with a history of propagandistic official media and a highly politicized, mostly underground, anti-establishment press could see the development of professional journalism, with practitioners who would make their living out of reporting without promoting party political aims, and a state and a public who would acknowledge that such a feat was possible and, indeed, required for the smooth functioning of the country's affairs. The author's own understanding of journalism in Britain, much of it gained while working at the BBC World Service (1983–2001), helped shape the viewpoint through which the Iranian experience was observed.

The initial incentive for the research was provided in the mid-1980s by four specialist Iranian periodicals: *San'at-e Haml-o Naghl* (Transport Industry), *Film*, *Keshavarz* (The Farmer), and the literary magazine *Adineh* (Friday). All four were staffed by journalists not affiliated to the state, working under Iran's 'traditional' conditions of censorship that had been exacerbated by the bloody confrontation between the Islamic Republic and its domestic opponents on the one hand and the war with Iraq on the other. Surprisingly, all four, and several other similar publications, seemed capable of tackling a wide range of issues, some technical and some general, in a calm and factual language, much closer to that of the best of their contemporary newspapers in the West, rather than the angry and flowery one used by the campaigning Iranian opposition press abroad, or the 'symbolic' style of the pre-Revolution dissident press inside the country.

Visits to Iran and meetings with journalists on the four publications confirmed that accurate, fair, balanced, and comprehensive journalism was indeed the goal shared by them all, in spite of their widely differing political views. One of the most intriguing comments came from my friend and colleague, Mohammad Ghaed, who had worked on Iran's youngest daily newspaper before the Revolution, *Ayandegan* (Posterity), had remained with the paper until its closure soon after the establishment of the Islamic Republic, and later joined *San'at-e Haml-o Naghl*. While we were drinking tea on a pleasant Tehran autumn afternoon in the early 1990s, he said rather casually: 'Nowadays in Iran, one can make a living out of writing.' The search for the causes of this phenomenon gave a new dimension to the author's investigation of journalism in Iran, which was completed at St Antony's College, Oxford, in 2005.

Acknowledgements

The author has been inspired by the collective effort of hundreds of Iranian journalists over the past quarter century, has learned from many of them, and is grateful to them. Special thanks are due to Mr Mohammad Ghaed, who provided the author not only with a stronger motivation for this research, but also with invaluable information, insight and comments on the typescript. The author is also indebted to Mr Ali Zarghani, the founder of the monthly, *San'at-e Haml-o Naghl*, and Mr Mass'oud Mehrabi, the founder of the monthly, *Film*, for their friendship and professional support, and to Dr Hassan Namakdoost-Tehrani, who carefully read and commented on the final typescript. Mr Hossein Taghavi, of Matbou'ati-ye Pars (Pars Press Services) in Tehran, greatly facilitated the research by providing books on the Iranian press and collections of publications, some of them rare.

Dr Ali Mohammadi of Nottingham-Trent University helped the author with the first academic steps in his research, and Mr Bob Nelson at the BBC enabled the author to continue the research at St Antony's College. The author is grateful to Mr Mark Brayne, then at the BBC World Service, Professor Roger Griffin of Oxford Brookes University, and Dr Mohammad Nafissi of London Metropolitan University for having supported his application for research at St Antony's; to Dr John Gurney of Oxford University for his administrative help; to Dr Saiedeh Lotfian of Tehran University, Professor Mark Gasiorowski of Louisiana State University, and Professor Reza Sheikholeslami of Oxford University for their encouraging and enlightening comments during the author's preliminary examinations; and to the final examiners, Professor Sheikholeslami, and Professor Vanessa Martin of the Royal Holloway College, University of London. Homa Katouzian, as a friend and academic supervisor, has been a unique source of strength during the author's career at the BBC, throughout his research, and beyond.

Any errors or shortcomings are the author's responsibility alone. The author hopes that this first systematic examination of post-Revolution journalism in Iran will provide the starting point for much more thorough investigations of one of the most fascinating aspects of life in Iran in recent times.

Hossein Shahidi
London, August 2006

Introduction

Before the 1979 Revolution, most professional Iranian journalists, that is those who relied on journalism as their main or only source of income, worked in newspapers which were not independent of the state. On the other hand, many of those who wrote for the independent press relied either on personal wealth or on income from other activities, very often working for the government. The full-time journalists usually referred to their occupation as *khedmat* or service – rather similar to being enlisted in the armed forces.[1] Writing for the independent press was often considered not a career, but a *mission* to enlighten the public.

The battles for power that immediately followed the Revolution and were intensified by the Iran-Iraq war left little room for the emergence of independent, professional journalism, except for a small number of specialist monthlies. The gradual relaxation of political tensions and the country's economic recovery after the war led to a rise in the number of independent specialist journals and the appearance of a range of political newspapers representing various factions within the Islamic Republic. The independent press was increasingly staffed by journalists who did not have any other significant sources of income. At the same time, journalists working on the state-owned or state-controlled newspapers often complained of government officials who would refuse to provide them with information or would take action against journalists whose reports they disliked. Some journalists working in the state-owned media were also critical of the compulsory coverage of official functions irrespective of their news value.

The two groups of journalists found common cause in seeking recognition as professionals, similar to physicians and lawyers, entitled to regulate their affairs independently, an effort that has been the subject of the present research. Although 'journalism' usually refers both to the print and the electronic media, the study will focus on newspapers, the only segment of the Iranian media where independent journalism has had an opportunity to develop. Radio and television which have almost always been controlled by the state are discussed separately, as is the much younger but fast growing online journalism, in order to define Iran's media environment more clearly. The study is based on literature mostly in Persian, published in Iran, and interviews conducted in Iran and abroad.

Chapter 1 provides an overview of the build-up and eruption of the revolutionary movement during 1977–79, when Iran's tightly controlled press gradually came into confrontation with the state, journalists in major newspapers went on strike, and some of them were imprisoned. The circulation of newspapers rose rapidly following the overthrow of the monarchy. However, even before the Shah had left the country, journalists found themselves in conflict with the religious leaders of the Revolution who were to set up the Islamic Republic.

Chapters 2 and 3 cover the intensification of the clash between the new state and the secular press, especially the high-circulation dailies *Kayhan* and *Ayandegan*, and dozens of other newspapers, many of them left-wing, that had appeared during and shortly after the fall of the Shah's regime. As a result, dozens of newspapers were closed down and many professional journalists left the country, gave up journalism or began working in specialist monthlies that gradually appeared under the Islamic Republic.

Chapters 4, 5, and 6 cover the emergence of a range of newspapers reflecting the views of various tendencies within the Islamic Republic, followed by new conflicts between the state and the press, with more newspaper closures and imprisonment of more journalists, most of whom had been avid supporters of the new regime.

Chapter 7 examines women's contribution to journalism in Iran, from the appearance in 1910 of the first women's newspaper, *Danesh* (Knowledge), which lasted less than an year, to early twenty-first century when women made up nearly a quarter of the country's estimated 5,000 professional journalists.

Chapter 8 outlines the origins and operations of Iran's radio and television and the country's emerging online publications, as well as the rapidly proliferating 'weblogs' or online personal diaries that enabled a large number of people, most of them young, to express themselves in public at a fraction of the cost of publishing a newspaper. Online news agencies and news sites were also used by rival political factions within the Islamic Republic following a series of newspaper closures that began in April 2000. This, in turn, led to the closure of some of the sites operated by the reformist groups and the detention of journalists who had been working on them.

Chapter 9 examines the emergence of journalists' unions and centres for journalism training and education whose numbers increased along with the rise in the numbers of journalists in the country.

Chapter 10 discusses the legal framework in which Iranian journalists have had to work since the 1906 Constitutional Revolution, which introduced the first of Iran's six Press Laws. Journalists have argued that each version of the law has placed new restrictions on press freedom.

Chapter 11 concludes that while the quality of journalism in Iran has suffered by the repeated closure of newspapers and detention of journalists, the number of newspapers and of journalists and their trade organizations today is so large that the profession is more resilient than it was at the time of the 1979 Revolution which drove out many of those who had already been active in the press. However, this encouraging quantitative growth needs to be supported with a qualitative development that requires a stable and secure environment.

1 The Shah's last years (1977–79)

The 1978–79 Revolution found the Iranian press in a state of deep hibernation, with about 100 newspapers, 23 of them dailies,[1] compared to around 300, including 25 dailies, in 1952,[2] a year before Mohammad Mosaddeq's government was overthrown in the coup organized by the United States and Britain. The fall in the number of newspapers was all the more remarkable since over the same period Iran's population had doubled to 35 million – 50 per cent of them living in cities, a rise of around 70 per cent[3] – and the literacy rate had risen by five times, to just over 50 per cent.[4]

The sharp decline in the number of newspapers had been caused principally by three rounds of mass closures by the government, almost exactly at 10-year intervals. The first round, immediately after the 1953 coup, affected dozens of left-wing and nationalist newspapers that had emerged during the movement for the nationalization of Iranian oil.[5] In March 1963, when the number of newspapers had risen to 227, the government closed down 71 of them, using a cabinet resolution that banned the publication of Tehran-based newspapers with circulations below 3,000 copies and magazines with circulations below 5,000.[6] In August 1974, the government used the same resolution to close down 63 newspapers, even though some of these had very high circulations.[7] The satirical weekly *Towfiq*, one of the highest-selling papers in Iran, was closed down in the same year without any official explanation.[8] *Towfiq*'s publishers said the main reason behind the closure had been the desire by the then Prime Minister, Amir-Abbas Hoveyda, to turn the magazine into 'an obedient and sycophantic' paper, so the Shah who read it would not receive any unfavourable reports about the way the country was run, and Hoveyda's tenure would continue unperturbed.[9]

Of the 100 or so newspapers that remained in circulation by 1978, 64 were being published in Tehran, most of them specialist periodicals on health, sports, religion, and science.[10] There were also six national daily newspapers, including the country's oldest – the afternoon dailies, *Ettela'at* (Information), founded in 1925, and *Kayhan* (Universe), founded in 1942. Nicknamed 'The Twin Giants',[11] they were, and are, the flagship papers of firms with the same names. The other four dailies – all of which were to disappear soon – included two large circulation, young, morning dailies, *Rastakhiz* (Resurgence), launched in 1975 by the single party of the same name created by the Shah, and the 11-year old

Ayandegan (Posterity); the much smaller *Paygham-e Emrouz* (Today's Message), which adopted an increasingly crucial tone before the Revolution developed; and the business paper, *Bourse* (Stock Exchange).[12] While circulation figures have been among the most tightly guarded secrets of the Iranian press, *Kayhan* is reported to have sold 300,000 copies a day in 1977.[13] *Ettela'at* could be assumed to have had a similar circulation, with the other papers selling far fewer copies.

Ettela'at and *Kayhan*, firms of comparable sizes, with a wide range of publications in Persian, English, French, and Arabic, were among the country's major employers. In 1976, *Kayhan* had a staff of 1,500 in Tehran and 1,200 in the provinces.[14] By comparison, the average number of staff in Iran's large industrial firms in the same year was 60. The biggest employers were the car manufacturing companies, with an average staff size of 1,100, soft drink factories with about 600 and the textile industry with 378.[15] Most of the employees in both newspapers worked in the administrative, technical, and distribution areas, with the editorial staff accounting for about 100, or less than 10 per cent, in each firm. Financially, the two newspaper groups were highly profitable businesses with huge amounts of advertising, printing, and distribution revenues from the state and private sectors. Even during the 1978–79 Revolution, when Iran's economy had slowed down because of widespread strikes which closed down the newspapers themselves for more than two months, *Kayhan* made a profit, albeit a modest one, of about 0.4 per cent.[16]

Politically, both firms were parts of the Shah's establishment, *Ettela'at*'s founder and owner, Abbas Mass'oudi, and *Kayhan*'s Mostafa Mesbahzadeh having become members of the Senate. After an early period of intense rivalry, by the mid-1970s the two papers were hardly seen as different from each other. The heads of both firms were among the shareholders of several banks and large firms, owned major properties, and had family links with the owners of other big businesses.[17] Any new firm, organization or group would try to have one or both of the newspaper owners on its management board to ensure that its news would be carried by the papers. For the papers too, such membership was a means of gaining more influence.[18]

Multiple occupations, including holding official and editorial positions simultaneously, were also common amongst the staff of the two papers, without any apparent concerns for conflict of interests. Journalists could be found on the payroll at high levels of important ministries, or at lowly posts at Tehran Municipality 'on the same grade as street sweepers'.[19] As a member of staff of the Ministry of Finance, a business correspondent could benefit from advance knowledge of changes in the tax or customs regulations. Links with the municipality could lead to information about the latest urban development plans, enabling the journalist to buy land in the areas concerned and make a profit by selling it once the plans had been announced. Senior staff would also receive gifts in cash or kind from public or private bodies, the total value of which could amount to several times a journalist's monthly salary.[20] The very close relationship between the newspapers and the government not only made it easy for the government's views to be expressed by the papers, but it also made it unnecessary for the security services to have resident officers at newspapers. Senior editors had to have clearance from, and maintained regular contacts with, the Shah's intelligence organization, the SAVAK. Any open expression of dissent by the editorial rank and file would be suppressed, sometimes leading to a journalist being jailed or banned from writing.[21] Managers or senior editors would receive daily telephone calls from the Ministry of Information on what they should or should not write and would issue some of these instructions as circulars.[22]

'Silent giants'

Ettela'at and *Kayhan*, the only newspapers with their own networks of reporters, had come to rely heavily on the state-owned Pars News Agency and the competing news service run by the state-owned National Iranian Radio and Television, NIRT. In the not too distant past, the two papers had been the main sources for Iranian radio's evening news bulletin.[23] By 1974, limitations on the press had led *Ettela'at* itself to complain that 'the press is not able to investigate anything independently, to find out about the deep roots of the issues.' In the words of the historian of the modern Iranian press, Mass'oud Barzin, during the preceding decade,

> neither of the two papers had raised any major social issue which would matter to the millions of human beings. They only tackled marginal subjects or those of interest to small groups. They would pit painters against each other; act as emissaries in the battle between classical and modern poets; carry reports on crime and murder; and limit themselves to printing short foreign news items and mutilated translations of articles from non-Persian language publications. I will not say anything about the other newspapers, for their circulation figures are so low that even if they had meant to have an impact, they have had none.[24]

According to another chronicler of the Iranian newspapers, Mehdi Beheshtipour, press criticism of government officials was so rare that when an official was criticized in a newspaper, most readers would assume that the piece had been written after consultation with the SAVAK or the Royal Court, and that the 'shattering blow' at the official concerned had in fact been delivered by another official.[25] There was such deep distrust in the Iranian press in the last decade of the Shah's rule that it was often said the only truth in the papers was to be found in their death notices.

In the midst of this bleak picture, Iranian journalists of different backgrounds and political views refer to the creation of their trade union, *Sandika-ye Nevissandegan va Khabarnegaran-e Matbou'at* (The Syndicate of Newspaper Writers and Reporters), as one of the brightest chapters in the history of their profession. The Syndicate was formed in 1962 by 41 journalists, only a handful of whom could have been described as professionals relying on their work for the press as their main source of income. In 1977, the Syndicate had around 500 members, including radio and television journalists. By one account, more than

50 per cent of the members were 'one hundred per cent professionals', with the rest made up of part-time or freelance journalists. Among other activities, the Syndicate provided support for some 250 journalists who lost their jobs after the mass closure of newspapers in 1974; it set up an Arbitration Board to look into complaints against Syndicate members; and established a collective employment agreement, approved by the Ministry of Labour, and agreed upon by several publishing houses, including *Kayhan*, *Ettela'at*, and *Ayandegan*. Most importantly perhaps, in view of Iran's chronic housing shortage, the Syndicate built 122 affordable apartments for its members in a west Tehran suburb that became known as 'Kouy-e Nevissandegan' (Writers' Quarter)[26] where some journalists, or their survivors, still live.

One aim that the Syndicate could not achieve was the implementation of a 'Press Code' it had approved at the end of its first year of activity, in October 1963, which said:

1. Any journal that is published for the general public belongs to the public. The journalist should be aware that if he does anything other than serve the interests of the public, s/he[27] will have betrayed a trust.
2. No journalist should commit an act which would not be committed by an honourable individual.
3. Journalism must be firmly based on impartiality, the love of truth, accuracy and knowledge.
4. Publication must be based on public interests and aim to shed light on truth, not to please individuals and personal interests. At the same time, the journalist should stand by his/her promise to keep the names of his/her sources confidential or not to publish [what s/he has promised not to divulge].
5. When writing his/her piece, the journalist should be aware that its publication might inflict irreparable damage on an official or an ordinary member of the public, unless this is required by public and national interests.
6. It is unbecoming of a journalist to publish unsubstantiated material and should s/he make a mistake, s/he should admit the error openly and seek ways of correcting it.
7. When quoting other journals, it is necessary to mention the source or to seek permission. Journalists should not distort the material they adapt, or publish an interview without permission.
8. A journalist has the right, as does any other professional, to expect material and moral rewards from his/her occupation, but not at the cost of lying, covering up the truth, straying from the purity of the pen, or damaging public and national interests.[28]

Compared with these principles, by 1978–79, state control over the press had become so tight and the journalists' habit of self-censorship for self-preservation so deep-rooted,[29] that while the rising revolutionary movement was making international headlines, Iranians had to turn to foreign sources, chiefly foreign radio stations, to find out what was happening in their country. The expanding protests inside Iran and increasingly strong criticism of the Shah's regime by foreign governments as well as protests by Iranian students abroad and exiled political activists were reported by the official Pars News Agency's confidential 'Special Bulletin' but not by Iranian newspapers.

One chronological account of the Revolution[30] lists 480 events between 8 July 1977, when the Shah dismissed his longest-serving Prime Minister, Amir-Abbas Hoveyda, and 27 August 1978, when Hoveyda's successor, Jamshid Amouzegar, was replaced with Ja'far Sharif-Emami. Less than a quarter of these reports are attributed to public Iranian sources. The rest are based on confidential Iranian reports or international news agencies. The ratio falls to less than a fifth if one sets aside the last five weeks of Mr Amouzegar's premiership, when international news stories would break from Iran on a daily basis, including protests across the country with slogans against the Shah, the bombing of a restaurant in Tehran in which 10 Americans were wounded, and the Cinema Rex fire in the south-western city of Abadan, which killed several hundred people. When the domestic newspapers did report the protests, they would often speak of 'subversive elements shouting anti-patriotic slogans'.[31]

The weeping monarch

Jamshid Amouzegar, a former Minister of Finance who had been in charge of oil negotiations, had been appointed Prime Minister to deal with the economic crisis that had gripped Iran since 1976, following the fall in oil revenues which had risen by several times only a few years earlier.[32] The move also followed widespread Western criticism of Iran's human rights record, a subject which the US President Jimmy Carter had raised during his election campaign. Among the most serious comments were those from US Congressional committees which raised doubts about the stability of the Shah's regime, and argued that he should not be sold the sophisticated American weapons he had asked for.[33] Announcing his cabinet's plans on 18 July 1977, Mr Amouzegar said the Government would 'respect freedom of expression and pen and the consolidation and strengthening of constructive forces created by them, and in turn would expect that the press and the mass media, while reflecting the people's problems and views, will observe the people's privacy and dignity and the society's moral values.'[34]

Mr Amouzegar's cabinet included a former journalist and founder of *Ayandegan*, Daryoush Homayoun, as Minister of Information and Tourism and later as the Government's Spokesman. Mr Homayoun too announced that 'from now on, no one should fear criticism.'[35] Before appointing Mr Amouzegar, the Shah had already taken moves to ease political restrictions. Between February and August 1977, he had pardoned 357 political prisoners and allowed the International Committee of the Red Cross to visit many more; had allowed foreign lawyers to observe the trial of 11 dissidents accused of terrorism; and had ordered major reforms to the trial procedures in military courts, including the right of civilian defendants to choose civilian lawyers.

During the same period, a variety of Iranian organizations which saw in the Carter presidency a chance to push for reforms in Iran took increasingly daring actions in challenging the regime, denouncing its human rights record and calling for an end to censorship and to the violation of Iran's 1906 Constitution. These included groups of lawyers, nationalist politicians, writers, poets, and intellectuals who formed or revived professional organizations such as the Writers' Association and wrote open letters to Premier Hoveyda. The protests rose in the autumn of 1977, with the formation of more opposition and professional organizations, including the Iranian Committee for the Defence of Freedom and Human Rights and the National Organization of University Teachers. The Writers' Association issued another open letter to the government, saying that the SAVAK continued to censor the media. Theology students in Qom formed an Educational Society and demanded, among other things, Ayatollah Khomeini's return from exile in Iraq, and freedom of the press.

In mid-November, thousands of people attended 10 evenings of poetry reading at the German Cultural Centre, the Goethe Institute, and the Aryamehr University of Technology, organized by the Writers' Association. Police efforts to break up the last session led to a march out of the University campus onto the streets. A clash ensued in which one student was killed, many were injured and some one hundred were arrested. During the following weeks, there were more student protests and strikes at universities across the country.[36] The Shah's troubles were compounded when, during a visit to Washington in November, thousands of demonstrators encircled the White House where he was being welcomed by President Carter. Iranians watching live coverage of the visit on television could see the Shah and the President wiping tears off their eyes, after police had fired tear gas to stop a clash between the protestors and a smaller group of pro-Shah demonstrators. Iranians could also hear, for the first time ever, the slogan 'death to the Shah' being shouted outside the White House.

Ettela'at reported that 100 people had been wounded in the clash in Washington. The report, typical of journalism under censorship, described the pro-Shah group as 'Iranian women, men and children resident in the United States who had come to Washington to see the Shahanshah [King of Kings]'. The Shah's opponents had been 'a group of masked people who had covered their faces with masks [*sic*] or white or colourful cloths and were shouting English language slogans against Iran's interests. From the colour of the skin of the hands that were carrying long and thick sticks it was clear that some black people were taking part in the demonstration.' *Ettela'at* also reported that there had been further demonstrations in Washington on the same day, 'with some demonstrators reportedly carrying red flags with the hammer and sickle insignia and pictures of Karl Marx'.[37] Other Iranian press reports quoted President Carter as having called for a 'strong Iran under the Shah's leadership', and having said that 'agreement over oil, arms and the Iran–US military alliance was unshakeable', that 'Iran was supporting stable oil prices', and that 'the United States would meet Iran's military needs.'[38] In an effort to give the Shah further support in the face of rising opposition, President Carter visited Tehran a few weeks later, celebrated the 1978 New Year at the royal palace, and described Iran 'an island of stability in one of the most troubled areas of the world'.[39]

Shortly before President Carter's visit, Ayatollah Khomeini had issued an angry attack on the Shah, warning 'the Shah and his gang that even if he manages to renew his position as a servant [of the United States] and to consolidate his illegal office, the Iranian nation does not want him and will not give up the struggle until it has taken revenge for its blood-stained youths, and has saved Islam and its rules from this dynasty.' Referring to critical articles that were appearing in the Iranian press, mostly aimed at officials associated with Mr Hoveyda's term in office, Ayatollah Khomeini said such criticism was 'hypocritical' and the writers were 'opportunists' who had kept silent when 'all types of atrocities against the religion and against the people' were being committed by the Shah's regime, beginning specifically with 'the day of the massacres of 5 June [1963] and the ransacking of the seminaries and other places by agents of the foreigners'. These writers, said the Ayatollah, were now hoping 'to be rewarded either by the Shah for diverting the public's attention and attributing the atrocities to the government, or by the people in the likely event of a change of regime'.[40]

The Indian 'Seyyed'

A week later, on 7 January 1978, in its 'Opinions and Ideas' page, *Ettela'at* carried a piece that triggered the cycle of demonstrations by unarmed citizens, their shooting down by the police and the army, and memorial marches in honour of the victims, usually 40 days after they had been shot dead, that eventually brought down the Shah's regime on 11 February 1979. The article, under the pseudonym Ahmad Rashidi-Motlaq, was entitled 'Iran and Red and Black Colonialism', referring to the Soviet Union and Britain, respectively, and accused Ayatollah Khomeini of being their joint agent. 'These two well-known types of colonialism', said the article, 'rarely happen to cooperate with each other, except in certain cases, one of which is their close, sincere and honest cooperation against the Iranian Revolution [i.e. the Shah's "White Revolution"], especially the progressive programme of land reform in Iran'. This cooperation had culminated in 'the riots of 5–6 June 1963',[41] when the army suppressed big demonstrations across Iran, killing fewer than 90 people, according to government officials, or 5,000 to 6,000 according to unofficial figures.[42] The riots, said the *Ettela'at* article, had been instigated by Iran's pro-Soviet Tudeh Party, 'whose hopes for deceiving the peasants had been dashed by the land reform', and by 'big landowners who for long years had robbed millions of Iranian peasants'. Big landowners who had 'failed to get the senior clergymen' to declare that the land reform had been against Islamic laws, had tried

> to find an adventurous clergyman, lacking in convictions, subservient to colonialist centres, highly ambitious, and capable of meeting their objective, and they easily found such a man. A man with an unknown past, attached to the most dogmatic and most reactionary agents of colonialism, who had failed,

in spite of all the support [he had been given], to achieve a place amongst the country's high-ranking clergymen, and was looking for an opportunity to enter political adventures at any cost and gain himself name and fame. Rouhollah Khomeini was a suitable agent for this objective and the Red and Black reactions found him the most suitable person to confront Iran's Revolution, and he was the person known to have caused the shameful event of 5 June.

Saying that Ayatollah Khomeini had been known as 'the Indian Seyyed' – 'Seyyed' being an honorific title indicating direct descent from the Prophet Mohammad – the article implicitly questioned the Ayatollah's nationality and then proposed a number of theories for the provenance of such a title. One was that 'he had lived in India for a while and had had links with British colonialist centres'. Another was that he had 'written romantic poems in his youth using "Indian Seyyed" as a pen-name'. What was certain, said the article, was that Ayatollah Khomeini had earned

> his fame as the instigator of the 5 June chaos, the person who rose against the Iranian Revolution, with the intention of implementing the Red and Black reactions' plan and, through certain well-known agents, engaged in a battle against land distribution, women's freedom, nationalization of the forests, shed the blood of the innocent and showed that there were still those who were ready to make themselves sincerely available to conspirators and anti-patriotic elements.[43]

The article appeared on the Shah's mother's birthday, designated by the regime as the Iranian Women's Day. It is said to have been ordered by the Shah himself, and prepared at the office of the former Prime Minister and now Minister of Court, Amir-Abbas Hoveyda, who then instructed the Minister of Information and Tourism, Daryoush Homayoun, to arrange its publication by the press. The instruction is then said to have been confirmed by the Prime Minister, Amouzegar, and the article was carried on the same day by *Ettela'at*, in spite of its editors' expression of concern that the article would infuriate the religious circles.[44] *Kayhan* and *Ayandegan* carried the same piece the following day, but it was *Ettela'at* that was mainly blamed. As soon as the paper had reached Qom its copies were torn to pieces and set on fire by angry protestors.[45] The following two days saw the closure of seminaries and bazaars. An attack on the Qom headquarters of the Rastakhiz Party on 9 January resulted in clashes with the police in which, according to the government, two people were killed. The opposition said 70 had been killed and more than 500 wounded. There were angry statements by high-ranking religious leaders, as well as various opposition organizations, and Ayatollah Khomeini called for more demonstrations. The protests reached a peak on 19 February, the 40th day after the killings, when more demonstrators were shot dead, this time in Tabriz, the first in the 40-day cycle of mourning and commemoration services which were violently suppressed.[46]

The journalists' first protest

Against the background of widespread demonstrations and bloody clashes, the journalists engaged in their first open battle with the state, spurred on by Mr Amouzegar's speech to the Majlis on 3 March 1978, when he said his government had 'established absolute freedom for the newspapers, offering them only advice and guidance, so that editors and writers would write whatever they saw to be in the country's interest'.[47] The Prime Minister's claim was dismissed within two weeks in an open letter prepared by the journalists' Syndicate and signed by 90 journalists who said censorship had become more widespread under his government, in violation of the Iranian Constitution. Ninety-four more signatures were added to the letter just over a month later. The letter said that not only were the newspapers receiving direct instructions from the government about what to publish, but the editors themselves, 'having been given more responsibility without any authority', were 'more cautious than in the past, reinforcing the policy of censorship'. It also attacked the government's practice of forcing the newspapers to carry unsigned, official articles, 'misleading the readers into thinking that such reports and articles are based on research conducted by newspapers and journalists'. Warning that the public's lack of trust in newspapers was preventing the government from using them to mobilize public support for 'its correct actions', the letter asked for the 'full and immediate lifting of censorship as stated explicitly in the Constitution', and the 'prevention of the publication of fabricated news which is against the interests of the nation and the honourable social and national personalities, and which is now being imposed on the press'.

The government counteracted by preparing a letter, with about 60 signatures, 'expressing gratitude for the country's open political environment' and 'supporting the government's actions in combating the agents of street riots.' The letter had been part of a plan by the Information Minister, Homayoun, to 'purge the press of un-patriotic and deviant elements', and to punish the signatories of the open letter of protest 'gradually, with the least amount of hullabaloo.'[48] On 15 April 1978, Mr Homayoun reported confidentially to the Prime Minister that 'some of the signatories who had been contacted had expressed regret over their action'; one of 'the opposition ring-leaders' at *Ettela'at* had been removed from his job; 'several ring-leaders at *Kayhan*' had been ordered 'to write signed positive reports', in order to keep their jobs; and the only signatory at *Ayandegan* 'would soon lose his job'. Similar pressures were being exerted on dissident journalists at *Rastakhiz*.

In his methodical style, Mr Homayoun then laid out his future plan of action. Journalists who also worked for government organizations were to be forced to choose one of the two jobs, with more pressure being exerted on 'opposition journalists'. The journalists' Syndicate was to be 'purged from non-journalists who use their votes to keep a group of infamous individuals at sensitive positions in the Syndicate'. Newspaper managers were to be 'subjected to financial pressures, especially by pegging the newspapers' approach to their tax payments', so they would control their staff. Managers were also expected to ensure the 'gradual removal' of journalists 'unwilling to change their approach or to express regret'.[49] There was not enough time for these measures to be put in place, since the Amouzegar cabinet fell on 26 August, following continuous protests, especially after the shock of the fire at Cinema Rex. The new Prime Minister, Ja'far Sharif-Emami, said he was committed to 'trying to establish a system which would allow for the free exchange of news and information [. . .] adopting an approach which would allow the press to enjoy the freedoms delineated by law'.[50]

On 5 September, Mr Homayoun was being sued by the journalists' Syndicate on charges which included imposing censorship on the press and depriving the journalists of their freedom, banning a group of journalists from writing, forcing the press to publish articles against national and religious figures respected by the public, obstructing the activities of the Syndicate of Newspaper Writers and Reporters, and preparing and collecting forced signatures for the purpose of mis-representing the truth about the lack of press freedom.[51] Mr Homayoun was arrested on 6 November, after Mr Sharif-Emami's government had been replaced with General Azhari's military cabinet, which had an even bigger confrontation with the press. General Azhari also arrested a number of other former senior figures, including the former head of the SAVAK, General Nassiri, in an effort to calm down the protests against the regime. Most of the detainees were kept in prison until after the Revolution and were executed by the Islamic Republic. Mr Homayoun and several others escaped from the military barracks where they were kept after it had been stormed by armed youths on 11 February 1979.[52]

The Shah had hoped that Mr Sharif-Emami, who came from a clerical family and had maintained contacts with a number of leading clergymen, would be able to negotiate with the moderate clergy.[53] However, having served as minister, prime minister, the leader of the Senate, and the head of the royal financial institution, the Pahlavi Foundation, he was in the public mind very much associated with the Shah's regime.[54] Not only were there more protests, but also more strikes, among others, by 1,000 employees at the Central Bank.[55] Daily street clashes took place in Tehran, Qom, Mashhad, and other cities, and there were several massive demonstrations in Tehran, with the protestors eventually calling 'Death to the Pahlavis', '[Imam] Hossein is our Master, Khomeini is our Leader', and for the first time on the streets of the capital, 'We want an Islamic Republic.'[56] While such slogans would not be reported by the papers, the press did carry news of the protests and the strikes. More importantly, not only was Ayatollah Khomeini's name being mentioned in the Iranian press, but his picture also appeared on the front pages.[57]

'Black Friday' and the 'awakening of the press'

Martial law that had been imposed on Isfahan during Mr Amouzegar's term was extended to 12 other cities, including Tehran, under Mr Sharif-Emami. Friday, 8 September, the day on which martial law was imposed in Tehran and in other cities, saw the worst bloodshed since the movement against the Shah had erupted and became known as 'Black Friday'. In east-central Tehran's Jaleh Square, protestors who had gathered, presumably unaware of the early morning announcement of martial law, came under fire from soldiers who had been unable to persuade them to disperse. In southern Tehran, helicopters were used to dislodge demonstrators who had set up barricades and were throwing petrol bombs at army trucks. The government said 87 were killed and 205 wounded. The opposition said more than 4,000 had been killed, 500 of them in Jaleh Square alone.[58] The killings produced a temporary mixture of fear and anger, driving people out of the streets, but also away from their workplaces, most importantly in the oil industry. Tehran refinery workers went on strike on 9 September, demanding higher wages and protesting against the imposition of martial law. They were joined within days by oil workers in Isfahan, Shiraz, Tabriz, and Abadan, and cement workers in Tehran. On 18 September, Central Bank employees published a list of 177 prominent individuals, claiming they had recently transferred a total of more than $2bn out of the country.[59]

Very little of this was being reported in the Iranian press, partly because heavy censorship had been re-imposed following Black Friday[60] and several journalists had been arrested,[61] partly because many journalists refused to work under the new conditions.[62] An account of the events at *Kayhan* is given in a book, *Tasskhir-e Kayhan* (The Seizure of *Kayhan*), which chronicles the fate of the paper from just before the Revolution up to its takeover by the Islamic Republic and the dismissal of many of its editorial staff several months later:

> Almost all of *Kayhan*'s editorial staff stopped work the day after Friday, 8 September, in response to the massacre of the people of Tehran. For journalists, the experience of 8 September was a unique and awakening one. For the first time, not just the odd reporter or photographer, but almost all the journalists were becoming closely familiar with the immensity of what was happening on the country's streets.
>
> Since several days previously, many journalists had taken part in street demonstrations on the pretext of gathering news. On Friday, 8 September, many of them were out on the streets, not out of a sense of professional duty, but only to take part in the demonstration [...] A reporter who would voluntarily go to the office the morning after the massacre to report what he had seen was a newly awakened journalist, taking along to the newspaper office a new experience, that of direct involvement in events, not merely watching them professionally. Several reporters broke into tears on that day and suffered shocks.[63]

An earthquake that hit Tabas in eastern Iran on 16 September, killing 25,000 people, ended the 'undeclared strike' at *Kayhan*, as journalists returned to work 'to expose the government's shortcomings'. They were also concerned that a paper produced by the managers, using official reports and martial law communiqués would 'in the long term give the impression that the country was safe and secure and under the armed forces' control'. Another reason for the journalists' return to work was their eagerness to cover the heated debates that had recently started in the Majlis, although these were dismissed by some as 'a noisy game' aimed at 'diverting the people's attention form the expanding battle scenes' on the streets.[64]

A declared strike, the first in the history of the Iranian press, came on 11 October, after a deepening wave of strikes with economic as well as political demands had already closed down the National Bank, the steel industry, copper mines, many factories, shops, universities and high-schools, and most of the oil industry. The strikes had gained in strength after 6 October, when Ayatollah Khomeini was forced out of Iraq and went to France, and they became even more powerful after 16 October, 40 days after Black Friday, when there was more bloodshed in major cities.[65]

The newspaper strike resulted from conflicting policies being followed by the Prime Minister, Sharif-Emami, and the Martial Law Administrator, General Oveissi. On 11 October, Mr Sharif-Emami and two of his ministers met a delegation of the journalists' Syndicate leaders and reached an agreement with them on a range of issues, including the preparation of a draft press law by the Syndicate. The journalists returned to their papers only to learn that General Oveissi had sent two officers to *Ettela'at* and *Kayhan* to censor them. The officers were withdrawn quickly following protests by journalists and the technical and administrative staff at the two papers, a total of 4,000 people, and their colleagues at *Ayandegan*. The strike also stopped the publication of *Rastakhiz*, which was printed by *Kayhan*. A Strike Committee representing *Ettela'at*, *Kayhan* and *Ayandegan* demanded the complete abolition of censorship and guarantees for the journalists' professional security and protection under the Constitution, and for these guarantees to be announced officially through the papers at the end of their strike, and also on radio and television. The demands were met after four days of negotiations with the Sharif-Emami government.[66]

The journalists' *Ayandegan*

Following this victory, the *Ayandegan* staff went on a three-day strike of their own, 30 October–1 November, 'in protest against internal censorship', and demanded curbs on the powers of the paper's Managing Director and former Information Minister, Daryoush Homayoun, as well as its editor, Houshang Vaziri. The strike resulted in the establishment of the first 'Editorial Council', instead of an individual editor, on Iranian newspapers.[67] The move, described by the *Ayandegan* journalists themselves as 'the first example of democracy in our country's press',[68] led to a much bolder style of journalism, which was to bring the paper into conflict with the Islamic Republic much sooner than the other major news-papers. More immediately, *Ayandegan*, *Kayhan* and *Ettela'at* came into their second confrontation with the Shah's regime on 6 November, after two weeks of reporting the increasing strikes, renewed big demonstrations, and attacks on government officials, and statements by opposition leaders, including ayatollahs Mahmoud Taleqani and Hossein-Ali Montazeri, who had just been released 'after years in prison', in the words of *Ettela'at*, 'thanks to the nation's unstinting efforts.'[69] By contrast, the Shah had lost his prominent position in the newspapers, which were now referring to him simply as 'the Shah',[70] rather than using his official title of Shahanshah Aryamehr, that is, the King of Kings and the Light of the Aryans.

On 4 November, soldiers fired at protestors in several cities, including students demonstrating near Tehran University, killing and wounding many. The violence prompted the closure of the Tehran bazaar the following day and a verbal attack on Mr Sharif-Emami by the Mayor of Tehran. The oil industry strike had disrupted fuel distribution in Tehran and the operation was now in the army's hands.[71] For some time there had been rumours that the Shah would like the National Front leader, Karim Sanjabi, to be involved in a government to succeed Sharif-Emami's. On 6 November, however, *Ayandegan* reported on its front page that Mr Sanjabi, now in Paris for talks with Ayatollah Khomeini, had announced the formation of 'The National Islamic Movement of Iran.' The very big headline of the report read, 'Ayatollah Khomeini and the National Front Unite Against the Regime.' Another report, with an even bigger headline reading 'The Capital Was out of Control Yesterday,' said that on 5 November, the British Embassy had been set on fire, as had many cinemas and liquor stores, and that protestors had handed flowers and sweets to soldiers on the streets. There were also pictures of troops attacking the demonstrators. All copies of that edition of *Ayandegan* were seized by troops sent in by the newly appointed Prime Minister, General Azhari. The troops also arrested five senior journalists from *Ayandegan*, *Kayhan* and *Ettela'at*, and occupied the offices of the newspapers with the intention of publishing them under government control. Staff at *Kayhan* and *Ayandegan* immediately went on strike, as did most of their colleagues at *Ettela'at*, where a small group helped prepare an edition of the paper in line with the wishes of the military. As soon as a few copies had been printed, a member of the technical staff removed a crucial piece of the printing machinery and brought the operation to a halt.

The journalists' long strike

Thus began Iran's second newspaper strike, this time lasting for two months, ending on 6 January 1979, the day the Shah's last prime minister, Shapour Bakhtiar, presented his cabinet to the Majlis, having promised to remove press censorship. The journalists' Syndicate announced that the strike had ended successfully. In a message from Paris, Ayatollah Khomeini called on the journalists to return to work 'until the people had decided the fate of the [new] illegal government'. He called on 'other respectable strikers to continue with their strikes, as it is hoped that victory should be close.'[72] Ten days later, the Shah was to leave Iran forever, with *Kayhan* and *Ettela'at* running identical main headlines, in huge fonts which in the case of *Ettela'at* filled a quarter of the front page, reading 'Shah Raft' (Shah Went).[73]

During this period, Iranian newspapers reached circulation figures that have not been repeated since. *Kayhan* and *Ettela'at* printed more than a million copies each, and *Ayandegan* 350,000.[74] Writing in *Ettela'at* the day after the end of the strike, the journalists' Syndicate's Secretary, Mohammad-Ali Safari, said: 'From now on, the press must speak for a nation that has risen for the sake of freedom, a nation that has proved its political maturity to the whole world, and has demonstrated to other nations the immensity and grandeur of its struggle.'[75] Although Ayatollah Khomeini had supported the strike and the strikers had received some financial backing from Islamic circles,[76] the journalists were by and large from secular backgrounds, many of them members or supporters of various left-wing or nationalist groups.[77] This led to a confrontation with the Islamic leaders even before the Shah's overthrow, with the religious leaders demanding more prominent coverage of their activities, and less attention being paid to secular forces, especially the left.[78] At the same time, dozens of left-wing newspapers had begun to appear on the streets. The scene was set for a new battle over freedom of press in Iran.

2 The 'Spring of Freedom' (1979)

As the Shah's regime disintegrated, the SAVAK softened its approach to the press. Unlike the past, when its agents would call the newspapers to tell them what to print and what not to print, the SAVAK would now write to the press, asking for correction of reports it considered to have been untrue or distorted. On 8 January 1979, for instance, *Kayhan* ran the SAVAK's denials of three of the paper's reports from the previous day. One had been about 'the discovery of a secret SAVAK torture chamber' on one of Tehran's central streets. Another had been about 'the cutting off of welfare facilities at Evin prison', and the third had said that SAVAK officers in the southern town of Firouzabad had surrendered to the public who had attacked their offices and freed the prisoners held there. There were similar denials in the days to come, with the effect that 'the SAVAK was being seen by journalists as just another, normal government organization [...] such as the General Department of Sugar and Cube Sugar, or the Ministry of Water and Electricity,'[1] which would be routinely covered by newspapers.

Between Mr Bakhtiar's formal assumption of office as Prime Minister on 6 January 1979 and the Shah's departure from Iran 10 days later, the head of the SAVAK, General Nasser Moqaddam, held two meetings with journalists at his headquarters in north Tehran.[2] The first was with the journalists' Syndicate's Secretary, Mohammad-Ali Safari, and the second with him and a group of other senior journalists from the three main dailies. At the first meeting, Mr Safari recalls, General Moqaddam said the press had been highly exaggerating the scale and intensity of the street clashes with the security forces, 'rapidly dragging the country to the edge of the precipice.' Mr Safari quotes the General as saying that the SAVAK did not want 'to preserve the current regime', but 'to prevent the country from collapsing and losing its independence', to which end the SAVAK and the press had 'to join hands.'[3] At the second meeting, General Moqaddam announced that the Shah would soon be leaving the country and warned that this could lead to the public attacking the security forces and the military. Repeating his criticism of 'sensational headlines and photographs', he asked the journalists to help calm down the public in order to prevent 'pointless bloodshed.' While making it clear that they could not be seen to be co-operating with the SAVAK, the journalists agreed to give due coverage to any action by the security forces and the military to maintain calm once the Shah had left the country.[4] They also said they would be 'reflecting the views and decisions of the society's leaders', meaning the opposition leadership, and that 'it was they who should be asked to call on the public to remain calm.'[5]

The same evening, six members of the journalists' delegation held another meeting, this time with senior clergymen representing Ayatollah Khomeini. The meeting, the first between secular journalists and the clerical leaders of the anti-Shah movement, was held at the house of Hossein Mahdiyan, an iron merchant with close ties to the clergy, who also had contacts with the press and whose office was located next to the *Ettela'at* headquarters in Tehran's commercial district. The clerics included Ayatollahs Mohammad-Hossein Beheshti and Morteza Motahhari, and Hojjatoleslam Mohammad Mofatteh, all three of whom were assassinated after the revolution by Islamic groups opposed to Ayatollah Khomeini's rule. The journalists included the Syndicate's Secretary, Mohammad-Ali Safari; the *Ettela'at* editor, Gholam-Hossein Salehyar; the *Kayhan* editor, Rahman Hatefi, who was executed after the Revolution by the Islamic Republic for his membership of the Tudeh Party, a fact which was not known at the time of the meeting and for a long time afterwards; a *Kayhan* deputy editor, Ali-Reza Farahmand; *Kayhan*'s economics editor and the chairman of the board of directors of the journalists' Syndicate, Mohammad-Ali Khansari; and *Ayandegan's* Editorial Council member, Firouz Gouran.[6]

While generally complimenting the press,[7] the clerics complained that newspaper coverage of the Revolution had given too much credit to secular opposition groups, 'placing them at the same level as the clergy' as leaders of the movement. They also announced that in future each newspaper would have to declare its ideological stand openly. Responding to the former point, the journalists argued that their reports were influenced by independent editorial decisions about the course of events and only the future could tell who had had a bigger share in the movement. As for the future of the press, the journalists said the clerics' approach appeared to indicate a return to conditions from which they thought they would be freed by the Revolution, especially since they had gone on strike twice in protest against censorship. One journalist said later that he and his colleagues 'had left a meeting with the SAVAK only to attend one with the SAVAKH,'[8] a pun using the letters K and H at the beginning of Ayatollah Khomeini's name.

'The Imam' – a lexical compromise

The two sides did reach agreement on two editorial issues. One concerned the clerics' complaint that the newspapers had not been running Ayatollah Khomeini's statements in full. The journalists replied that they could not carry the Ayatollah's direct attacks on the Shah while he was still in the country and 'the military governor's bayonet is hanging over our heads.' The compromise agreement was for the papers to use 'dots' in place of direct attacks on the Shah, to keep the journalists 'safe from the regime' and also give a hint to the readers that the statement had been edited. The other agreement was for the newspapers to refer to Ayatollah Khomeini as the 'Imam', rather than 'His Eminence the Grand Ayatollah', in order 'to save space, especially in big, front page headlines.'[9]

Newspaper coverage during the Shah's last days in Iran indicates that the discussions with the SAVAK about helping maintain calm had been effective. On 9 January, *Kayhan*'s top headline quoted the National Front leader, Karim Sanjabi, as saying that 'the repeat of the August 1953 coup would hurt everybody', and calling on the public not to 'insult the army or be disrespectful to it.' A front page picture showed several hundred demonstrators facing a row of soldiers, with the caption saying 'calmly facing each other'.[10] The accompanying story said the soldiers had used military vehicles to block a demonstration by the protesters who had then staged a sit-in on the street. However, the mildly worded, long-winded style of writing suggested an effort to underplay the confrontation. *Kayhan*'s headlines over the next few days were similarly no-confrontational. The paper also carried pictures of members of the public throwing flowers at military vehicles, and soldiers with carnations in the barrels of their guns. The flowers, said the caption to the latter picture, conveyed the message of 'friendship and brotherhood between the people and the army: organs of the same body, only wearing clothes of different colours.' One photograph, on 15 January 1979, showed a soldier in a military truck holding a big picture of Ayatollah Khomeini.[11]

Kayhan's 16 January front page, printed just after the Shah's plane had taken off from Tehran airport, summarized what had gone on until then, and signalled what was to come. A big picture underneath the massive headline, 'Shah Raft' (Shah Went), shows a group of soldiers on top of an army truck, one of them holding Ayatollah Khomeini's poster, and a group of civilians, including a black-turbaned clergyman, shouting slogans, having crowded around the truck. The caption reads, 'The people and the army link-up.' The front page is completely free from the clutter of ads that even today fill up its lower half. A prominent headline at the centre of the page quotes 'Imam Khomeini' as saying 'Marxists are free to express [their] opinion, provided they do not conspire,' and it goes on to say that 'Iran considers itself at war with Israel.' Another headline is 'Imam Khomeini's warning to members of the Majlis and the Regency Council,' which had been appointed by the Shah to take over the monarch's duties in his absence. A small headline at the top of the page says 'the Shah cancelled the press conference at the last moment'. An even smaller Shah-related headline reports that he would not be staying in Beverly Hills, California, where his sister Ashraf had been living.[12]

There are headlines on the mid-air explosion of an airplane carrying the Mashhad military governor; the killing of American military officers in Tehran and Kerman; demonstrations in various parts of the country; and a complaint from the central city of Kashan about inadequate press coverage of the protests held in the city. One front page story covers Tehran's 'first Islamic co-operative clothing shop', offering free clothes to the poor, produced by workers who had 'agreed to work at one-fifth their normal salary'; and another report covers protests by the inhabitants of a village close to the Dizin ski resort, near Tehran, against what they describe as the Ministry of Information and Tourism's 'medieval, discriminatory' decision to prevent ski instructors from the village from working at Dizin.[13]

At the bottom of the page, there is a statement from Tehran University students protesting against attacks on their meetings and demonstrations by 'suspicious elements' shouting 'Party only Hezbollah [party of Allah], Leader only Rouhollah [Khomeini]', and 'Death to Communism'. The statement calls on the 'Militant leader, His Eminence the Grand Ayatollah Khomeini, to clarify the democratic spirit of the people's movement' and to prevent such 'divisive actions' which are 'clearly against the spirit of Islam, and also in violation of democratic principles and the Universal Declaration of Human Rights'. The same theme is taken up in a front page editorial, with the title 'I must say, you must not say'. Alluding to Ayatollah Khomeini's call for *vahdat-e kalameh* (unity of word) which was some-times used as the justification for attacks on non-conformist views, the *Kayhan* editorial described 'diversity as the embodiment of real unity,' and 'the essence of life and truth' that had to be respected.[14]

Bakhtiar 'frees' the press

On 5 January 1979, the day before he took office as Prime Minister, Shapour Bakhtiar invited representatives from *Kayhan, Ettela'at* and several other news-papers to his house to tell them that 'they would be completely free to write as they wished'. He would not send censors to the newspapers 'out of a sense of patriotism,' but the journalists had to be 'mindful of the problems facing the country.' On 11 January, when his cabinet received the Majlis' vote of confidence, Mr Bakhtiar recalled the meeting with the journalists, saying 'the gentlemen went away free, are free, and will be free as long as I am here'.[15] To radio and television, though, he said he 'neither would, nor could, give as much freedom', since 'even the BBC, of which a lot is being said, is under the British Government's very strong and thorough control.' Governments in France and other European countries too, said Mr Bakhtiar, 'had to exercise some control' over radio and television sta-tions run with public money. He then attacked the Iranian radio and television staff who had been on strike for more than two months, accusing them of having been SAVAK agents. He said he would not name 'these gentlemen, because every Iranian's honour has to be protected', but warned that they would be identified 'by any free government that may come to power, whether Ayatollah Khomeini or a social democratic party.' It was, therefore, 'in their interest not to make much more hue and cry.'[16]

Leaders of the journalists' Syndicate, who had attended the 5 January meeting at Mr Bakhtiar's house, said later that they had seen his promises of press freedom as a 'ruse aimed at winning over the major newspapers.' According to the Syndicate, 'a few journalists were deceived' by Mr Bakhtiar, but they 'were driven out of the press after the victory of the Revolution'. The majority, however, heeded Ayatollah Khomeini's 'instructions issued in Paris and, while forcing Bakhtiar to comply with freedom of press, they never sided with Bakhtiar and his freedom-loving posturing, and continued to work as the fully-fledged organs of the Revolution and the revolutionary people.'[17] While Mr Bakhtiar was trying to establish his authority, newspapers were running regular front page lead stories on the latest decisions by Ayatollah Khomeini, including the formation of a Revolutionary Council, and reports of continued demonstrations and clashes with the military and security forces across the country.[18]

Journalists would receive groups of the public who would visit the newspaper offices to celebrate the lifting of the censorship, and would themselves go to government offices and other organizations to speak at meetings held in support of the Revolution.[19] Prime Minister Bakhtiar, for his part, on more than one occasion attacked the journalists, saying they had been 'mercenaries of corrupt governments for 25 years', but were now 'abusing the freedom' he had given them, 'poisoning the public opinion by publishing lies and arousing sensations in order to raise their circulations'. Mr Bakhtiar said he would treat anything written about him with 'contempt and indifference', but 'continued insults or accusations against the army or other people would not remain unanswered'.[20] He also implied that the opposition movement led by Ayatollah Khomeini was imposing a new dictatorship on the press.[21]

In a mid-day prayer sermon at his residence near Paris on 21 January, Ayatollah Khomeini described Mr Bakhtiar's government as traitorous and called on the people to overthrow it. He also said he would return to Iran as soon as Tehran airport, where Iran Air staff had been on strike for 10 days, had been reopened. A subsequent announcement said Ayatollah Khomeini would return to Tehran on a special Iran Air flight on Friday, 26 January. Striking radio and television staff, who had already sued the Prime Minister for accusing them of having been SAVAK agents, said they would go back to work to provide live coverage of Ayatollah Khomeini's return.[22] The Prime Minister said Iran Air staff would have to end their strike and resume domestic flights before they could be allowed to fly Ayatollah Khomeini back to Iran. Tehran airport, towards which people from across Iran were travelling to witness the Ayatollah's return, was taken over by the military, leading Ayatollah Khomeini to announce that he had postponed his flight by two days.[23]

On 25 January, agents from the Tehran martial law administrator's office arrested five journalists, two each from *Ettela'at* and *Ayandegan*, and one from Kayhan, on unspecified 'security charges'. The arrests were followed by widespread protests in Iran and abroad, but there were no newspaper strikes, in keeping with a request by the detainees themselves who believed that the military had arrested them in order to provoke a press shut down. Four days later, the detainees' protest note, slipped out of the barracks where they were being held, appeared in *Ayandegan*. Within hours, they were freed by the Bakhtiar government.[24] Back at work, they received a hero's welcome, being carried on the shoulders of their colleagues, with flower garlands round their necks and sheep slaughtered in front of them in celebration.[25] 'The offices and pages of the newspapers', recalled one of the five, 'were awash with passionate slogans that spoke of a decisive struggle for the consolidation and sustainability of freedom of the pen, backed by the precious experience of two dictatorship-breaking press strikes. The revolutionary people also visited our newspapers in droves to ask for the expansion and elevation of that struggle until the complete victory of the Revolution. Thanks to the joint efforts of the press and the people, victory of the pen over the sword had been proved once again. It was not long before the dictatorial, ungodly state was thrown into the dustbin of history.'[26]

When Ayatollah Khomeini returned to Iran on a chartered Air France flight on 2 February, *Kayhan* and *Ettela'at* once again used massive headlines to report the event. *Ettela'at*, repeating the style of its headline on the Shah's departure, spread the two words 'Imam Amad' (Imam Came) across the top of its front page. *Kayhan's* headline consisted of a phrase from Ayatollah Khomeini's speech at Tehran's main cemetery, saying he would strike Mr Bakhtiar's 'government in the mouth'.[27] Ayatollah Khomeini had been driven from the airport to Tehran's main cemetery, Behesht-e Zahra, through streets packed with people many of whom might not have left their homes had television's live coverage of his arrival not been cut off by the military. However, a recording of the event was made and preserved by the radio and television staff. On 11 February, a group of *homafar* air force technicians watching the tape in their east Tehran barracks were attacked by armoured units of the Shah's Immortal Guard. The Immortal Guards were beaten back by the public and armed members of guerrilla organizations. A second day of armed clashes led to the downfall of the imperial regime and Shapour Bakhtiar's replacement by Mehdi Bazargan, the Prime Minister of the Provisional Islamic Revolutionary Government.

During Mr Bakhtiar's 38 days in office, and for a few weeks afterwards, Iranian journalism enjoyed its greatest degree of freedom since the 1953 coup. Apart from the strength of the revolutionary movement, best manifested in regular massive marches in cities and towns across the country, three other factors allowed the journalists great freedom of action, particularly against the government. These included the disintegration of the Ministry of Information, whose premises had been set on fire on the so-called Tehran Burning Day, 5 November 1978, the last day of Mr Sharif-Emami's government;[28] the dissolution of the SAVAK, one of the first decisions announced by Mr Bakhtiar on taking office; and the departure of owners and senior editors of the major newspapers from their offices or the country.[29]

Qotbzadeh takes on the press

The first open confrontation between the Islamic authorities and the Iranian media came soon after the change of regime and the takeover of national radio and television by its staff and the general public on 22 February. Renamed *Seda va Sima-ye Enqelab-e Iran* (Voice and Vision of the Iranian Revolution), radio and television went on air in the evening, with television showing its logo of two Persepolis-style lions standing back to back, but holding flowers, rather than spears, in their hands. For several hours, radio and television broadcast revolutionary songs, calls on the public to protect the station against attacks by 'counter-revolutionaries', and messages from religious leaders as well as secular personalities and left-wing organizations congratulating the Iranians on the victory of the Revolution.[30] All this came to an end within hours, when one of Ayatollah Khomeini's companions in France, Sadeq Qotbzadeh, took over as the head of radio and television, now renamed as 'The Voice and Vision of Iran's Islamic Revolution'. The next morning, Ayatollah Khomeini's office announced that 'programmes broadcast on radio and television since last night had been produced by its striking staff. Today, this situation will be taken care of and a delegation from the Prime Minister's office will be despatched to take control of these two departments'.[31]

Mr Qotbzadeh, who soon became notorious as an aggressive, sharp-tongued politician, rapidly purged the organization not only of known and reputed SAVAK agents, but also of many of its directors and heads of departments. The output was 'Islamicized', with religious programmes making up much of the content. News bulletins did not report meetings and demonstrations by left-wing groups. Nor did they give much coverage to the first public celebration, since the 1953 coup, of the International Women's Day, on 8 March 1979. Few women presenters appeared on television, many having preferred to resign rather than appear on-screen with the Islamic headgear, the hijab. The ban on the screening of women without hijab also meant that very few movies or TV series could be shown. All music, except military marches and revolutionary songs, was banned from the airwaves.[32] While still in France, Mr Qotbzadeh had declared that after the victory of the Revolution cinemas would be re-opened, newspapers could publish whatever they wanted, and all parties, including Marxist ones, could publicize their views.[33] As the head of the national radio and television, however, Mr Qotbzadeh frequently attacked the press in broadcast speeches which, in turn, were followed by press attacks on him. Barely a week after his appointment, an *Ettela'at* article described him as a 'newcomer' whose past was 'not clearly known to millions of Iranians', and whose 'knowledge of the press and radio and television's mission in guiding the people is question-able.' The article, by the journalists' Syndicate's Secretary, Mr Safari, recalled a saying common among Iranian journalists, '*ba ahl-e qalam harkeh dar oftad, var oftad*' (He who takes on the people of the pen, shall end up in oblivion).[34]

The next morning, a crowd gathered outside the *Ettela'at* headquarters to protest against the article, copies of which the protesters had torn to pieces and hung from tree branches. Among their chants was a call for the execution of the writer. The protest ended after the crowd had entered the newspaper's offices and shouted more slogans. Over the following days, *Ettela'at* was to receive threatening letters and phone calls. Some of the strongest attacks came in a printed leaflet which described the journalists as 'the Shah's and Hoveyda's tools', who were now attacking Mr Qotbzadeh for 'not allowing radio and television to carry out the mission, similar to that of the press, of distorting the Islamic aspect of this Revolution'.[35] Similar protests were held regularly outside the offices of all the main newspapers until July 1979, when dozens of newspapers were closed down, bringing to an end what had become known 'The Spring of Freedom'. The well-documented case of *Kayhan* demonstrates that these pressures had started well before the victory of the Revolution, with newspapers coming under concerted pressure by groups of people demanding an 'Islamic press'.[36]

On 17 January, the day after the Shah's departure, several thousand people describing themselves as 'West Tehran residents' assembled outside the offices of

Kayhan, in the capital's commercial centre, not far from *Ettela'at*, to call for the expulsion of 'international news agencies which are dependent on the CIA and imperialism', and demanding the establishment of 'a revolutionary Islamic news agency'. *Kayhan* journalists found this a 'legitimate request', and the protesters left after a journalist had joined them to express agreement. The protest was led by a man who later turned out to be a close associate of Abol-Hassan Bani-Sadr, another one of Ayatollah Khomeini's companions in France,[37] who was to become the Islamic Republic's first president in January 1980, before being dismissed by the Majlis and Ayatollah Khomeini in June 1981 and later returning to exile in France. The same person made several other visits to *Kayhan* after Ayatollah Khomeini and his companions had returned to Iran, sometimes as the head of a group, to protest against the paper's 'hypocritical line'. After Mr Bani-Sadr had set out to launch a newspaper, the protesters outside *Kayhan* would often shout 'Kayhan and Ayandegan must be destroyed; Bani-Sadr's newspaper must be deployed', raising the suspicion that Mr Bani-Sadr was trying to take control of *Kayhan*. The protests ended after Mr Bani-Sadr decided to start his own newspaper, *Enqelab-e Eslami* (Islamic Revolution).

'The 1 per cent minority'

Kayhan was then targeted by protesters associated with other factions within the new regime, including the business community in the Tehran bazaar and the clerical establishment in Qom. Some protests would be over inaccurate reports, others over material which the Islamic regime considered provocative. One of the biggest such protests followed *Kayhan*'s report of a speech by Ayatollah Khomeini on 6 March, in which he had attacked Mr Bazargan's government, saying members of the cabinet had taken up residence in palaces and the ministries were full of 'naked women', and decreeing that female civil servants should wear the Islamic hijab at work. The speech led to demonstrations against compulsory hijab, which were attacked by gangs who became known as 'hezbollahi' (Party of God activists) or 'club wielders', leaving several people injured. Ayatollah Khomeini's supporters, in turn, would demonstrate outside *Kayhan*'s offices, accusing the paper of having caused what became known as the '*chador* crisis'. Another 'provocative' *Kayhan* headline announced the appointment of Taher Ahmadzadeh as the Governor General of the eastern Khorassan province. Two of Mr Ahmadzadeh's sons had been members of the Marxist–Leninist guerrilla group, the Fadaiyan-e Khalq, and had been killed fighting the Shah's regime. The headline had therefore been seen by the protesters as yet another sign that *Kayhan* was being run by leftists and 'hypocrites'. Claiming that the leftists made up 'only 1 per cent' of Iran's population, the protesters argued that the left should receive only 1 per cent of the newspaper's coverage.[38]

Kayhan was a particular cause of anger both because of its high circulation and influence, and also because it was considered to be under the influence of the Tudeh Party. It was the only newspaper to have spoken of the Tudeh Party's 'armed members' having taken part in the February uprising. It often reported the activities of the small, Tudeh Party-affiliated 'Syndicate of Needlework Weavers', and frequently carried the views of the prominent pro-Tudeh translator, Mahmoud E'temadzadeh, better known by his pen-name, Behazin. Compared to other left-wing groups, the Tudeh party may have had fewer supporters among the *Kayhan* journalists, but two of its members did have senior positions.[39] One was the editor, Rahman Hatefi, who had been a co-publisher of the party's underground newsletter, *Navid* (Harbinger) since 1975.[40] The other was his deputy, Houshang Assadi, who after the Revolution was first 'exposed' as a SAVAK agent, but was then said by the Tudeh Party to have been instructed to infiltrate the intelligence organization.[41]

Although the three main dailies would proclaim that they were not following any party lines, the new Islamic state was confronted with dozens of other publications which either did not hide their political hostility towards it, or were publishing material which it considered immoral. According to one research, 105 new publications were launched in Iran during the last months of the Shah's rule, and at least 253 came into existence between the Shah's departure on 16 January 1979, and Iraq's invasion of Iran on 22 September 1980. Of the total of 358, more than 60 per cent belonged to political organizations very few of whom supported the Islamic Republic. During the new regime's first six months, no new publication had obtained the licence to print which had been required under the Iranian Press Law.[42]

Most publications launched prior to the Shah's departure were reincarnations of papers that had been closed down by his regime and were allowed to appear under Sharif-Emami and Azhari in order to defeat the strike by major newspapers. These were denounced by the opposition as the 'organs of the thieving, plundering generals, the mouthpieces of butchers and murderers'.[43] After the victory of the Revolution, some of these publications specialized in running exposés of the Pahlavi regime, with pictures of female members of the former Royal Court which 'bordered on pornography'. One magazine, for instance, published a picture of the Shah's twin sister, Ashraf, in a very revealing dress, with the caption asking, 'Which one is better: the Islamic hijab or this poisonous figure?'[44]

As far as the Islamic authorities were concerned, the proliferation of leftist and other secular publications was the result of an American effort 'to diminish the Revolution's Islamic colour and content'. It was for this purpose, the authorities argued, that towards the end of the Shah's regime some publications began 'to reflect some of the realities, but along American lines, and by promoting the nationalists, leftist forces and supporters of a democratic government'. The newspaper strikes, of which the journalists had been so proud, were also seen by the authorities as an inevitable outcome of 'the realities of the Islamic revolution'. The most important achievement of the press during the strike, the authorities said, had been 'superficial purges at the editorial level with the purpose of saving face and carrying on along their impure path during the Revolution', at which stage 'because of their performance, the public turned against them.' [45]

The nationalists, the leftists, and the satirists

Following the overthrow of the imperial regime, as the revolutionary period's unity continued to break down and protests over economic, political, social, and ethnic differences spread across the country, newspapers came under heavier attacks by the Islamic authorities, including the Bazargan cabinet, who accused them of aiding and abetting the opposition. During the 49 days between the victory of the Revolution and the 1 April referendum that formally established the Islamic Republic, the press was said to have been involved in 'promoting the nationalist, leftist and eclectic groups', the last label referring to the Islamic guerrillas, the Mojahedin-e Khalq; 'creating personalities in Kurdistan', especially through the coverage of the activities of the Sunni Kurdish religious leader, Ezzeddin Hosseini, who was a vocal critic of the new regime; 'desecrating the Leader's standing', by referring to other religious leaders alongside Ayatollah Khomeini; 'weakening and breaking down the army', by reporting the demand by many political groups that the armed forces built up by the Shah should be dismantled; and 'weakening the revolutionary institutions', by reporting the public's complaints against the *komitehs* (revolutionary committees) that had taken over many functions of the police.[46]

Some papers would come under attack for accusing Mr Bazargan's Provisional Government of being under American influence. While only some extreme opposition groups would accuse Ayatollah Khomeini himself of being in line with the United States policies, the highly successful satirical weekly, *Ahangar* (Blacksmith), specialized in making such attacks against three of the Ayatollah's companions, Abol-Hassan Bani-Sadr, Ebrahim Yazdi, and Sadeq Qotbzadeh.[47] A very angry demonstration against *Kayhan* followed its publication of a few pieces by the well-known satirist, Hadi Khorsandi, who had been living abroad for sometime and had returned to the country after the victory of the Revolution. By the time Mr Khorsandi arrived back in Iran, a poem he had written attacking the Shah and praising Ayatollah Khomeini had already spread across the country. But the *Kayhan* pieces which were critical of the post-revolutionary conditions led to protests, with calls for his execution. Mr Khorsandi was forced into exile, where his life continued to be under threat by the Islamic Republic government.[48]

As far as news coverage was concerned, some of the charges of bias levelled against the newspapers resulted from the interpretation laid on particular news items, rather than the journalists' animosity towards the Islamic Republic. Among these were items such as 'the National Front has declared tomorrow as a national day of mourning';[49] 'the role of the bazaar and bazaar merchants in the great national movement';[50] 'armed groups declare their support for the Imam';[51] and 'Bani-Sadr to become the Republic's Minister of the Economy.'[52] However, there were reports, among them the coverage of demonstrations by women, ethnic minorities, and workers which may have indicated sympathy for the protesters. Such items reflected the diversity of political views among the staff, and the newspapers' inability to develop a clear editorial stand in the rapidly changing post-revolutionary circumstances. There were also inevitable factual inaccuracies, all the more so considering the Iranian journalists' lack of the high level of skills required for covering such complex events accurately.[53]

'Self-censorship' at *Kayhan*

Criticisms of the press were not confined to those made by supporters of the new regime. There were also those who accused the newspapers, especially *Kayhan*, of self-censorship in the interest of the Provisional Government. The image of journalists as mouthpieces of the government, developed by the press's 'almost unquestioning obedience' to the state during the last years of the Pahlavi regime,[54] had not been completely dispelled. Journalists, who until a few months ago had never had to answer a question from their readers, now had to

> weigh and measure every line and every word and be answerable about them. As the crisis over the newspapers heightened, every sentence could be used as an excuse by pressure groups to mount agonizing demonstrations outside the newspaper offices. Such pressures would consume the energy that the editorial staff could have used to review and correct the paper's direction, and would instead place the paper in a defensive position, limiting its activities to crisis management. This, in turn, would lead to new mistakes and oversights which would bring about a new wave of pressure.[55]

The attackers also targeted the newspapers' representatives and newspaper kiosks across the country. Several representative offices, especially those of *Ayandegan*, were destroyed. Attacks on the Tehran offices of the small, left-wing daily, *Paygham-e Emrouz* (Today's Message) reached the stage where the staff had to leave and its editor, Reza Marzban, went into hiding, before going into exile. Clergymen in a number of provincial cities forbade the reading of certain newspapers. Elsewhere, rumours of such moves were so widespread that they had to be denied repeatedly by senior state and religious figures.[56] In addition to the external pressures and political divisions in their own ranks, ranging from leftists to nationalists, supporters of the new regime and monarchists, the journalists also suffered from two other problems: financial difficulties which sometimes made it impossible for salaries to be paid, and the administrative disruption that had followed the flight of the newspaper owners.[57] Advertising revenues had virtually disappeared because of the economic slowdown caused by industrial action, capital flight, and transfer of ownership, especially the expropriation of big businesses by the new regime.[58] In the first few months after the Revolution, *Kayhan* would sometimes appear in 8 pages, without any ads, whereas under the previous regime it would have run 12 or more pages of ads every day. With little revenue from advertising, the papers had to rely on sales as their only source of income, but the lack of advertising, especially classified ads, would also reduce circulation, creating a vicious circle. The financial commitments were now the responsibility of journalist-managers.[59]

During the Revolution, the three main dailies saw their circulations rise rapidly, with *Kayhan* and *Ettela'at* on several occasions printing more than one million copies each. On 28 August 1978, *Kayhan*, which until then had been selling an average of 250,000 copies a day,[60] sold more than one million copies with a large front page picture of Ayatollah Khomeini and a very big headline on 'negotiations for the return of His Eminence the Grand Ayatollah Khomeini', a report which was immediately denied by the Shah's government.[61] When the newspaper strike ended on 6 January 1979, *Kayhan* and *Ettela'at* printed more than one million copies each, and *Ayandegan* 350,000.[62] Circulations remained high throughout Mr Bakhtiar's 38 days in office, except for the last few days when armed clashes disrupted newspaper distribution. Following the victory of the Revolution, *Kayhan*'s circulation began to decline. By the end of April 1979 it had dropped to around 500,000 copies per day.[63]

Pressure groups outside *Kayhan*, and supporters of the new regime inside it, mostly among the administrative and technical staff, would point to the fall in circulation as evidence that the journalists had alienated the 'Moslem public'.[64] The influence that the administrative and technical staff had gained over editorial issues was a result of the two-month strike that had brought them into regular contact with each other and with the journalists. During the first few weeks of the strike, the three groups, with the journalists making up about 10 per cent of the total numbers, would hold meetings in the newspaper offices to discuss the situation, organize protests, and produce their strike bulletins. After the military had closed down the newspaper offices on 14 December 1978,[65] contacts continued through the strike committees on which all three groups were represented.[66]

After the strike, *Ettela'at* and *Kayhan* followed the example of *Ayandegan* where the staff had set up a council to run the paper, but their success was much more limited. At *Ettela'at*, a 21-member 'High Council', representing the editorial, administrative and technical staff, held its inaugural meeting the day after the fall of the Shah's regime, 13 February. The council was meant to 'fully examine and review the occupations and positions of those in charge of the institute, eliminate past discriminations, restore the just rights of the staff, ensure collective participation in decision making, carry out thorough supervision of financial and technical matters and, finally, protect and safeguard freedom of the pen, expression and thought in all of the institute's publications and prevent the influence of any personal views.' Paying the staff before the Iranian New Year, 21 March, and electing an editorial council were among the most urgent issues.[67]

However, the High Council was soon paralysed by political differences among the workforce, especially the journalists, which led to an attempted strike in protest against the new management and the journalists' Syndicate, ostensibly in support of the country's new religious leadership. Continued disputes led to the intervention by the local Islamic Revolutionary Committee, who arranged for Hojjatoleslam Mofatteh, a member of Ayatollah Khomeini's delegation to the press during the Revolution, to attend a meeting of *Ettela'at*'s High Council as an arbitrator. After the meeting, Farhad Mass'oudi, a member of the family who owned *Ettela'at*, was invited back to Iran to deal with the paper's financial matters. He returned two days before the end of the year, and 'the financial problems were resolved to some extent.' An 'Editorial Council' comprising the editor and four elected journalists was set up on 8 May, once again after another intervention by Mr Mofatteh.[68]

The *Kayhan* staff elected a five-man 'Editorial Council' on 25 February and later set up a 15-man High Council with 5 representatives from each of the three groups of journalists, administrative staff, and the technical workers. In effect, though, the management of the paper was left to the journalists on the Editorial Council.[69] Under the new style of management, journalists' by-lines appeared in the paper, editorial issues were discussed openly with all the journalists taking part, and there were also some pay rises. But the reforms were seen by many journalists as 'minor, without any impact on the general structure of the organization.' The critics were particularly unhappy with the fact that the Editorial Council included three members of the paper's old management, including the editor, Mr Hatefi, and his two deputies. However, the critics themselves acknowledged that the 'general internal and external environment' in which they were working did not allow any greater changes.[70]

Kayhan changes colour

Externally, *Kayhan* continued to come under attack by groups who wanted it to act as the 'organ of the revolutionary, Moslem people'. The paper gave in. Editorials on 18, 19, and 20 March, before the week-long Iranian New Year holiday, described the paper as an 'organ of the Islamic Revolution', and a supporter of 'Islam, Iran's independence and general freedoms.' *Kayhan*'s readership, however, had been largely made up of the urban middle class, with a wide range of secular political views, among whom the left were the biggest single group. By now, *Kayhan* had 'demonstrated such vacillation in its political stance that no large group of its readers would rise up in its defence. Instead, they simply stopped buying the paper after the appearance of the pro-Islamic editorials, cutting its circulation by about 200,000.'[71]

The loss of readership provided further ammunition for the journalist-managers' opponents at the paper who had already set up the 'Islamic Association of *Kayhan* Staff', one of the first such pro-government staff organizations to be formed after the Revolution, with the aim of expelling 'opportunists and pseudo-revolutionary, pen-pushing mercenaries.' Most of the Association's founding members were from amongst the administrative staff. Of the rest, several were highly paid technical supervisors, and one had been a close associate of the paper's owner, Senator Mesbahzadeh, who was now in exile. The only journalist member of the Association, whose father was a clergyman based at a nearby mosque, was soon revealed to have written an article in praise of the Shah's longest serving prime minister, Amir-Abbas Hoveyda.[72] By mid-May, when it took over the paper, the Association put the number of its members at 750.[73]

At their first meeting with the journalists,[74] the Association asked them to 'ally themselves with the Moslem nation's demands, to learn a lesson from the fall in the paper's circulation', and to prevent the collapse of the paper that was 'providing thousands of people with their daily bread'. Later meetings were seen by the journalists as tribunals with predetermined sentences, during which they would be interrogated about their beliefs and lifestyles, often with the aim of proving that they were communists. Some questions would date back to months before, indicating that the collection of information had preceded the Islamic Association's formal establishment. Some journalists would be openly asked to leave their jobs. The names of some senior journalists would be given to the protesters outside the paper, who would then demand that they 'should be executed'.

At some meetings, representatives of the protesters would sit side by side with the Islamic Association members.[75] The Association also had the support of the representatives of the paper's owner, Mr Mesbahzadeh, who were still in senior managerial positions. They opposed the High Council, especially its journalist members who had said they would look into the paper's books to find ways of dealing with its financial crisis.[76] Such measures included cutting off payments to many who had never worked for the paper but had been on its payroll, giving *Kayhan* a reputation for overstaffing and extravagance.[77] Only much later did the journalists learn that the Islamic Association had also been backed by the Islamic Republic's first and soon to become most powerful political organization, the Islamic Republic Party, whose formation had been announced on 20 February.[78]

Soon after the Association had been formally set up, *Kayhan*'s print-workers began a series of short strikes. At the beginning, the strikes would be held in protest against certain items in the paper or specific actions by journalists, but eventually they targeted the paper's general editorial line, with the aim of removing senior journalists. During the strikes, protesting workers would be joined by administrative workers and leaders of the Islamic Association.[79] Some of the Islamic Association's most active members were from the paper's advertising department, accused of being 'one of the most corrupt parts of the organization, not least because of the commissions paid to its staff by advertisers.'[80] By the end of April 1979, the Islamic Association was demanding that the Editorial Council be dissolved and the paper be placed under the control of Rahman Hatefi. The campaign did succeed soon, but this was due to a dispute related to *Ayandegan*.

3 The battle for *Kayhan* and the demise of *Ayandegan*

Iranian journalists were aware of the tainted image of newspapers that had been established under the former regime and, therefore, their vulnerability in the post-revolutionary environment. Writing in the first issue of its newsletter, *Payam-e Ma* (Our Message), the *Ettela'at* staff's High Council said that under the previous regime, the firm's 'various publications, especially its daily newspaper', had been 'the mouth-pieces of the dictatorial regime and its colonialist masters, singing the praises of the corrupt, money-grabbing Pahlavi family, and their appointed government officials and mercenaries'. All this, said the newsletter, had taken place 'against the wishes and interests of the majority of the technical, administrative and editorial staff'. At *Ettela'at*, as well as at the other newspapers, 'there had been very little room for freedom of thought, pen and expression, and those in possession of such human gifts had often been ensnared by censorship and repression.'[1]

The councils set up at the major newspapers, in line with the general move towards workers' control in Iranian industries,[2] were partly aimed at 'purifying' the newspapers from 'the corrupt agents of the past'. Several employees were expelled from *Kayhan* and *Ettela'at* because of 'cooperation with the former regime.' The journalists' Syndicate too expelled members who had 'continued to cooperate with the former regime's agents, even during the strike'. The Syndicate would also liaise with the Ministry of Information and Publicity, the Islamic regime's successor to the Ministry of Information and Tourism, to seek its assistance with the 'purification of the press', to discuss the drawing up of a new draft press law, and to advise the Ministry on granting newspaper publication licenses.[3] Nonetheless, the papers continued to come under attack by protesters, especially after a statement by Ayatollah Khomeini on 28 March which said 'there would be freedom of expression, pen and views for all, but the people will not tolerate conspiracies.' Ayatollah Khomeini also said he had 'repeatedly been called upon to take action' about 'newspapers that after the Islamic Revolution had presented themselves as being at the service of the Revolution and in line with the nation', but had published material that was 'against the course of the Revolution and had caused the people dissatisfaction and dismay'. He said the press should 'avoid being influenced by the right, the left, the east or the west', and called on 'the youth and the class that is causing discord at this sensitive time [...] to return to the bosom of Islam'.[4]

Shortly after the referendum on the Islamic Republic, the journalists' Syndicate wrote to Ayatollah Khomeini, Prime Minister Bazargan and the Minister of Information and Publicity, Nasser Minachi, asking for their assistance in identifying those who had to be purged from the press. The Syndicate's planned action was aimed, among others, at 'those in the press community who had taken part, directly or indirectly, in the former Shah's and his regime's atrocities'; those who had received financial and other benefits from state organizations, or from firms linked to the Royal Court; those who had been agents of the secret police, 'sending militant and honourable' journalists 'to the regime's dungeons'; and those with such records who 'had changed colours under the Islamic Republic and were carrying on with their destructive activities through cooperation with the corrupt remnants of the [former] regime inside or outside the country, by running anti-people publications or groups'.[5]

At a meeting with the Syndicate leaders, Mr Minachi said 'purification had to begin at the journalists' Syndicate itself, by the Syndicate's 400 members', not by the Government naming names and 'confronting the public.' Once the Syndicate had been 'purified', its action could 'spread to the newspapers'. The Minister also questioned the appropriateness of the current state of the press, for instance the fact that the regulations for granting publication licences did not include anything about the applicant's 'character'. He said newspapers would be required to 'clarify their approach and intellectual orientation one hundred per cent at the time of seeking a licence to publish'. He also called on the Syndicate 'to determine if, in view of the unlimited freedom in which we believe and according to which we act, there should not be certain limits, otherwise, the licence holder could even be a traitor, or allied with foreign policies'.[6] Such concerns were to permeate the Islamic Republic's first press law, passed by the Islamic Revolutionary Council on 11 August 1979.

The religious establishment, as well as Prime Minister Bazargan and his Iran Freedom Movement, had been traditionally suspicious of the leftists, considering them agents of foreign powers, especially the Soviet Union. As the Revolution developed, Ayatollah Khomeini issued repeated warnings against its being taken over by the left. The Islamic revolutionary committees had it as one of their main functions to limit the activities of the left, and the Mojahedin-e Khalq, especially during and after the two days of armed clashes in February, when the public raided arsenals across the country. In spite of their ideological and political differences, the Mojahedin, the biggest left-wing organization, the Fadaiyan-e Khalq Guerrillas, the Tudeh Party, and several other smaller groups had declared their support for Ayatollah Khomeini's leadership of the Revolution. However, not only did several small but vocal communist groups continue to campaign against the new regime, but the Mojahedin and the Fadaiyan were soon to find themselves in serious conflict with the Islamic Republic over a range of issues, from the name of the new state to the rights of women and ethnic minorities, and the ownership of factories, farms, and other commercial enterprises, many of which had been abandoned by owners who had fled the country.

Matters came to a head in the run-up to the referendum which asked for a 'yes' or 'no' answer to the question whether the monarchy should be replaced with an

Islamic Republic. Some secular groups and personalities boycotted the referendum, arguing that with the monarchy already overthrown, the voters were not in fact being given a choice. Having won the referendum with an official result of 99 per cent, the Islamic authorities were then faced with a demand for their new, draft constitution to be debated by a constituent assembly, rather than the referendum being seen as its ratification. The campaign for a constituent assembly was championed strongly by *Ayandegan*,[7] which was already moving to the top of the list of newspapers regarded by the new regime as the most offensive.[8]

Ayandegan had been established in 1967, in the words of its founding editor, Daryoush Homayoun, as a 'liberal newspaper with the aim of elevating political discourse' in Iran. Homayoun had left *Ettela'at* a few years earlier because of his involvement in setting up the journalists' Syndicate,[9] and had later gone to the United States on a Harvard University fellowship.[10] *Ayandegan* did sometimes carry sharp criticisms of government policy, in Mr Homayoun's words, 'testing the limits of censorship more bravely than the other major newspapers'.[11] Such bravery was no doubt partly due to the fact that the paper had been founded with the approval of the Prime Minister, Amir-Abbas Hoveyda, and the chief of SAVAK, General Ne'matollah Nassiri, and had the government as its major shareholder. Nonetheless, *Ayandegan* did at times anger the Shah, on one occasion leading to Mr Homayoun's brief expulsion from the paper. Among the public, the paper's reputation suffered after it defended the United States' role in the Vietnam War, and when it became known that the government had been closely involved in its establishment.[12] Added to this was the widespread belief that the purchase of its print-works had been financed by Israel.[13]

Secular press, religious divide

When it was launched, *Ayandegan* was Iran's first national newspaper for nearly a quarter of a century, and innovative in being a morning daily, unlike the afternoon newspapers, *Kayhan* and *Ettela'at*. Furthermore, it was distinguished from them by its fresh-looking typeface and layout, and a younger, better educated and more energetic staff, 'writing for better educated people.' Because of the paper's own relative youth and small size, with an editorial team of about 20 compared to *Kayhan*'s 100, journalists could move up the hierarchy on the basis of professional merit more rapidly. Having made their mark before the Revolution, particularly with their social and cultural coverage, *Ayandegan*'s staff found more room to operate after the fall of the Shah's regime, when the paper was being edited by a council of five senior journalists, themselves relatively young by the other papers' standards. Although undeniably secular, with a left-of-centre stance, the journalists avoided siding with any political organization. The approach was neither popular with some leftist groups, especially the Tudeh Party, nor with the government, particularly with Prime Minister Bazargan who, ironically, accused the paper of being under the Tudeh Party's influence.[14]

Ayandegan came into sharp confrontation with the Islamic Republic after it published a detailed, analytical report on the assassination, on 2 May 1979, of one of Ayatollah Khomeini's closest aides, Ayatollah Morteza Motahhari, by a hitherto unknown armed Islamic group called *Forqan*, an Arabic word that means 'the divider of truth from falsehood' and is used to describe the Qoran. The group, which declared itself in favour of Islam without the clergy, had already said it had assassinated the Islamic Republic's first chief of staff of the armed forces, General Valiollah Qarani. By the time of his assassination, General Qarani had resigned from his post because of the Provisional Government's disagreement with his request to take a harsher line towards Kurdish groups seeking autonomy in western Iran. Because of the increasingly intense disputes between the new regime and the armed leftist groups, especially over the issue of Kurdistan, there were suspicions that the assassinations had in fact been carried out by the leftists, hiding behind an Islamic name unfamiliar to most people.

At a memorial service for Mr Motahhari, two days after he had been killed, another of Ayatollah Khomeini's close aides, Hojjatoleslam Rafsanjani, accused the left of the assassination, after having 'brazenly boycotted our elections and referendum' and having 'taken up arms and occupied government centres'. Mr Rafsanjani described those opposed to the Islamic Republic as 'desperate' people standing up to '99 per cent' of the population who had voted for the new regime. He dismissed accusations of media censorship in the Islamic Republic as an effort by 'agents of reaction and Red and Black imperialism', in order to deceive the youths. What had been censored, he said, had been the 'views of 99 per cent of the people' that had not been broadcast on national radio and television. Among these had been slogans against 'eastern imperialism' shouted during Mr Motahhari's funeral which had 'not been heard clearly from television'.[15] Mr Rafsanjani's remarks were all the more significant as they were delivered in the presence of Ayatollah Khomeini, clearly having his approval.

Upon hearing the news of Ayatollah Motahhari's assassination, while they were preparing the next morning's edition, *Ayandegan* journalists realized that 'not only did they not know who the Forqan group were, but that they did not have any information about Ayatollah Motahhari either.' The staff were able to find Ayatollah Motahhari's books at Tehran bookshops, but literature on Forqan became available only after the paper had asked its readers for information about the group. Within days, the journalists received a call informing them that a bundle containing all of Forqan's publications had been placed under a vehicle parked near the *Ayandegan* offices in central Tehran.[16] On Thursday, 10 May, *Ayandegan*'s front page was dominated by a big headline quoting Ayatollah Khomeini as having said in an interview with the French daily, *Le Monde*, that 'the left had nothing to do with these atrocities.' One sub-headline quoted Ayatollah Khomeini as having said that General Qarani's and Ayatollah Motahhari's assassinations had been the work of 'American agents who have hidden themselves behind the false religious organization, Forqan'. Inside, there was a full-page report on Forqan, saying the group was in favour of Islam without the clergy, and its publications had often referred to the Shi'ite clergy by the pejorative terms 'akhound' and 'mullah', describing them as 'supporters of landlords and capitalists', and accusing them of 'dictatorship' and 'reaction'. The group, said the *Ayandegan* report, was in favour of armed struggle and revolutionary violence and belittled political activities such as holding meetings or staging sit-ins.[17]

The article also said that although Forqan had claimed responsibility for General Qarani's assassination because of 'his cooperation with America and the former regime and his attempts at suppressing the people of Kurdistan', there was evidence to suggest that a religious motive had also been at work. Quoting Forqan's literature, *Ayandegan* described the group as a strong supporter of Dr Ali Shariati, the Islamic thinker and critic of the Shah's regime who gathered a huge following among the youth by preaching a radical version of Islam which many considered to have a lot in common with socialism. Shariati, who died in exile in England shortly before the Revolution, had also criticized some senior Shi'ite clerics, who in turn had denounced him as heretic. Among these was the Mashhad-based Ayatollah Milani, described by Shariati as a religious authority 'all of whose decrees have been aimed at splitting the Moslem people and suppressing any movement among the Moslems'. General Qarani, who himself had served a prison term under the Shah for a coup attempt in 1958,[18] had said that, in his 'efforts to overthrow the regime', he had 'been in touch with Ayatollah Milani, and had benefited from his moral and financial support'. *Ayandegan*'s report suggested that Marxists would regard Forqan's strict concept of Islam as 'even more dogmatic than classical Shi'ism', and wondered why Mr Bazargan and Mr Rafsanjani would link the group to Marxists.[19]

In the introduction to the report, *Ayandegan* journalists made clear their opposition to the assassination, saying such action could not be backed by any of Dr Shariati's writings, adding that the paper had been informed of speeches by Ayatollah Motahhari and Dr Shariati in which they had praised each other. Other reports on the same page of *Ayandegan* gave a picture of the deepening turmoil across the country. During commemorations for Mr Motahhari in the province of Fars, there had been demonstrations with anti-communist slogans. In Isfahan and Azarbaijan provinces Islamic Revolutionary Guards had seized weapons, including automatic rifles, from members of the public. In the northern province of Guilan, journalists were calling on the government to punish those responsible for the recent killing of a reporter in the south-western city of Abadan; to protect news-paper offices and journalists against attacks by 'club-wielders'; and to 'safeguard individual and social freedoms on the basis of the Universal Declaration of Human Rights'.[20]

The Imam stops reading *Ayandegan*

In the early hours of the morning on Thursday 10 May, before *Ayandegan* had reached many of the news-stands even in the capital, Tehran, the news bulletin on Iranian radio said that Ayatollah Khomeini had 'been disturbed by the manner in which the interview [with *Le Monde*] had appeared in *Ayandegan*', which he would 'never read again'. The news item was broadcast frequently on radio and television throughout Thursday and Friday, sometimes followed by stronglyworded commentaries. Although Ayatollah Khomeini was said to have been offended by

Ayandegan's coverage of the *Le Monde* interview, it was not specified what exactly had caused the offence. A later statement from the Ayatollah's office said the announcement that he had stopped reading *Ayandegan* 'had not been because of this single news item, but had followed a series of news items and several cases'.[21] Outside the regime, there was little doubt that the real cause of his anger had been the report on Forqan, with its suggestion of deadly splits within the Islamic movement, and the airing of the group's slogans for 'Islam without the clerics'.[22] Given Mr Rafsanjani's attack on radio and television a few days earlier, the unusual step of broadcasting such a news item so frequently seemed to some to have been an attempt by the head of the organization, Sadeq Qotbzadeh, to deflect criticism from himself. The broadcasts were followed by a rise in attacks on *Ayandegan* offices across the country.

At an emergency meeting the same Thursday, normally a day off for *Ayandegan* that did not appear on Fridays, the paper's senior staff reviewed the situation. Concluding that continued publication of the paper would merely invite further attacks, they decided to limit their next issue to a four page edition carrying only an editorial under the title 'Should *Ayandegan* continue publishing?' The paper was then to be suspended until it was deemed safe for it to reappear.[23] The special edition, which became known as *Ayandegan-e Sefid* (*The Blank Ayandegan*), reached the unprecedented circulation of 500,000.[24]

The editorial began by distancing *Ayandegan* from Daryoush Homayoun, who had not been 'in charge of the paper for two years', and went on to give an account of the staff's participation in the strikes during the Revolution, including one aimed at 'overthrowing internal censorship'. Their 'most strong revolutionary and freedom-seeking line' during Shapour Bakhtiar's term had led to the imprisonment of two senior editors and the names of three being placed on a 'hit list'. After the Revolution, commitment to publishing a free, independent newspaper 'struggling against reaction, imperialism, oppression and repression', had so enraged those 'with narrow-minded personal interests' that they had resorted to attacks, including assassination threats, and had stopped 'the paper's distribution in parts of Tehran and certain cities, including Qom'. There had also been attempts to take over the paper. The 'organized, comprehensive' campaign against *Ayandegan*, said the editorial, had intensified after the announcement that Ayatollah Khomeini had stopped reading the paper, with attacks on its offices across the country.

Armed men had taken over the office in Shiraz, and the office in Bushehr had been set on fire. In Ahvaz the names of those buying *Ayandegan* were being taken down. Those behind the campaign had been demanding that the paper 'clarify its stand', but *Ayandegan* was not 'a political party to issue instructions'. The paper merely saw it as its 'duty and responsibility, in line with revolutionary Islam, through which such a movement has manifested', to reflect what was happening in the country 'without any cover-up, sycophancy, or censorship'. Whether 'what had taken place, said or written' was liked or disliked was a matter for the readers themselves to decide. Turning to what was said to have offended Ayatollah Khomeini, the editorial said if the report had indeed been incorrect, the *Le Monde* interview should have been denied, rather than *Ayandegan* that had merely carried the news of the interview. [25]

Kayhan **covers** Ayandegan

News of the publication of the 'Blank *Ayandegan*' and the paper's decision to suspend publication was covered prominently in the afternoon by *Kayhan*, which reproduced the full text of the *Ayandegan* editorial, in spite of strong opposition from the Islamic Association's print-workers.[26] In the same issue, *Kayhan* also had a front page editorial critical of the radio and television's attacks on the press ver the previous two days. The campaign, said the editorial, gave the impression that radio and television had been 'waiting for an opportunity to put [...] all the newspapers on trial', with 'pre-determined sentences'. On its front page, *Kayhan* also announced that it was carrying an interview with Mr Qotbzadeh conducted before the broadcast campaign against the press had begun. The appearance of the interview, the paper said, did not imply that *Kayhan* was in agreement with his attacks on the press, but indicated it did not 'mix personal issues with national interests'. In the interview, Mr Qotbzadeh said some critics of his did not know 'the difference between editing and censorship', while others belonged to minorities who expected to be given as much air time 'as the 99 per cent' majority.'[27]

The next morning, 13 May, Kayhan's Islamic Association members began a strike and a sit-in to protest against the paper's publication of the *Ayandegan* editorial. The protesters described the journalists' action as a 'divisive' move in support of a 'counter-revolutionary' paper and, above all, an insult against Ayatollah Khomeini, who had said he would no longer read *Ayandegan*, but was now being forced to read it again, through *Kayhan*. The strike ended after the journalists had agreed to run the protesters' statement in full on the front page. The statement explained that the paper's publication had been held back by the strike, and apologized to 'the Moslem people and the esteemed Leader of the Revolution' for the delay. The strikers had also given the editorial board 'one last chance' to remove the 'hypocrites' and 'counter-revolutionary' journalists from the paper.[28]

About one half of *Kayhan*'s front page the following day was taken up by news and statements about *Ayandegan* and the conditions of the Iranian press in general. These included statements against *Ayandegan* by the Islamic Republic Party and the 'Tehran Clergy Association', and expressions of support for it, and for freedom of press, by other groups, including the National Democratic Front, an umbrella organization for several secular groups. A statement from the Ministry of Information said *Ayandegan* had not been banned and could resume publication, while a report from Bandar Abbas, on the Persian Gulf coast, said *Ayandegan*'s local office had been attacked by 'about thirty students, shouting slogans' against the paper.[29]

The journalists lose *Kayhan*

What *Kayhan* did not report was a second strike and sit-in at the paper the same morning, 14 May, which had ended with the naming of six journalists, including two members of the Editorial Council, who had to be expelled. By the following morning, the number of 'undesirable' journalists had increased to twenty. These were prevented by the paper's security guards from entering the building, each being given a note saying that their employment had been terminated 'following a decision by the *Kayhan* staff'. Most of the expelled journalists, who became known as the 'Group of Twenty', had been strong opponents of the Tudeh Party and none had been well known outside the editorial offices. Hence, there were strong suspicions that their names had been provided by Tudeh Party members at the paper, especially the two members of the Editorial Council, who had already been suspected of cooperating with the Islamic Association.[30]

Not only did an immediate sympathy strike by about 100 other *Kayhan* journalists and the intervention of government officials fail to secure the return of the 'Group of Twenty', but the Islamic Association took over the paper completely and, aided by a few journalists,[31] produced that afternoon's edition of *Kayhan*. The paper's top story, under the headline, 'Workers and Administrative Staff Publish Today's *Kayhan*, following lack of cooperation by some members of the editorial staff,' expressed regret that 'some of our colleagues among the editorial staff' had ignored Ayatollah Khomeini's advice two months previously that 'newspapers should purify themselves.' The sit-in at *Kayhan*, said the report, had been an ultimatum to those journalists who had not yet 'moved out of their short-sighted, self-glorifying ideological shell'. The protesters had been determined 'to break the unholy alliance of pseudo-leftists, counter-revolutionaries, and agents of the past, decadent regime', to make sure that *Kayhan* would not be 'a loudspeaker for the worn-out statements and views of hypocrites and dividers and sworn agents of the former, blood-sucking regime who may have put on revolutionary cloaks'.[32]

The Imam praises the new *Kayhan*

Having taken over publication of the paper, the Islamic Association members travelled to Qom for an audience with Ayatollah Khomeini. The timing of the visit was significant because meetings with Ayatollah Khomeini would have had to be scheduled well in advance. The fact that the *Kayhan* Islamic Association members were received by him on the same day that they had expelled the 'Group of Twenty' has been interpreted as a sign that they had either planned their action long before, or that they had very close access to the Ayatollah.[33] But there can be little doubt that Ayatollah Khomeini himself would have been keen to hold such a meeting to express his views on the press, and the media in general. He had been known as 'a voracious consumer of the media', following them in detail. Besides listening to Tehran radio and foreign radio stations, he watched television,[34] received daily reviews of the Iranian press, and often read the newspapers himself.[35]

On 16 May, reports of the Qom meeting and of 'the public's congratulating and welcoming the people's *Kayhan*' covered nearly two-thirds of *Kayhan*'s front page, with the top headline quoting Ayatollah Khomeini as saying 'newspapers must be in line with the people's views.' Addressing the *Kayhan* staff, Ayatollah Khomeini had said that, after all the blood that the Iranians had given for the Revolution, and after the establishment of the Islamic Republic with a 'near unanimous majority', an attempt by the press to support 'the murderers and traitors' would itself amount to treason. The people, he had said, did not want the press to publish 'essays and stories', but wanted it to carry 'what is in line with the nation's path.' Some newspapers that had been publishing the writings of 'agents of foreigners, who want to ruin the country once again', would 'either distort or ignore articles or material about Islam'. Some were 'abusing freedom to take away the people's freedom, open the plunderers' hands and create oppression among the people'. This was not 'freedom, but treason'. Such newspapers had been 'tolerated so far', but the 'press and all the publicity media [had] to correct themselves', and the Ayatollah hoped the 'newspaper owners themselves would correct the newspapers.' Newspapers that would not meet with the people's approval would not be bought, and would have to close down.[36]

At the beginning of their meeting with Ayatollah Khomeini, the *Kayhan* visitors had described their edition of the paper as 'the first newspaper of the mostaz'afin [deprived]', produced by 'the workers and the administrative staff', and had apologized to 'the nation's Leader and the heroic Iranian people' for any shortcomings. Ayatollah Khomeini had said that *Kayhan* was 'now in line with the nation's liking' and had thanked the visitors for having produced the paper even though they had first been on strike. He had also called on them to remove those journalists who 'could not be corrected, are agents of foreigners and want to open the foreigners' hands' in the country's affairs. 'There are many writers around,' the Ayatollah had said.

The visitors had been concerned about their own editorial limitations and the impact of the strike by journalists following the expulsion of the 'Group of Twenty'. The same edition of *Kayhan* carried a poorly written front page appeal from the paper's 'toiling workers and administrative staff' for 'patriotic, honourable and committed' journalists to help with its publication. Such journalists were being asked 'not to tie their fate with that of a small group who, heedless of the ideals of the Revolution, had placed the pages of the newspaper in the hands of inflexible ideological fanaticism, [turning it into] a means of ostentation and false glorification by dogmatic, minority groups'.[37]

The appeal was not taken up by the striking journalists who refused to return to work without the 'Group of Twenty'. They tried for several weeks to win the support of government and religious leaders, but failed. Discussions with Ministers of Labour and Islamic Guidance were fruitless. A promised meeting with Ayatollah Mahmoud Taleqani, widely regarded as the most liberal senior clergyman, did not take place. A scheduled meeting with Ayatollah Khomeini on 2 June was postponed by a week after all his meetings for the week were cancelled. When the journalists did go to Qom, they only managed to meet a relative of Ayatollah Hossein-Ali Montazeri, who informed them that Ayatollah Montazeri was too ill to receive them.[38]

The iron merchant–publisher

The journalists' campaign ended after an intervention in the dispute by the iron merchant, Hossein Mahdiyan, who had been Ayatollah Khomeini's contact with the press during the Revolution, especially during the two month strike by the journalists.[39] A religious businessman, Mr Mahdiyan had been involved in Islamic publishing well before the Revolution as a trustee of Daftar-e Nashr-e Farhang-e Eslami (The Islamic Cultural Publishing House) set up in 1974, 'as a cover for political activity'. The trustees had also included four clergymen – Seyyed-Mohammad-Hossein Beheshti, Morteza Motahhari, Mohammad-Javad Bahonar, and Ali-Akbar Hashemi Rafsanjani, who emerged among the leaders of the Islamic Republic – and another lay person, the then school teacher, Mohammad-Ali Rajaie,[40] who was to become the Islamic Republic's second President in August 1981, before being assassinated a few weeks later.

Mr Mahdiyan's ties with the secular press dated back to the 1960s, when he had arranged for the publication of articles by Qom clergymen in *Ettela'at*, whose headquarters was next door to his own office in Tehran's commercial centre. In 1965, he arranged for the publication in *Kayhan*'s weekly women's magazine, *Zan-e Rouz* (Woman of the Day), of a series of articles on women's rights in Islam by the then Hojjatoleslam Motahhari, in response to *Zan-e Rouz* articles in support of the moves by the Shah's regime to revise women's rights in the Iranian legal system,[41] because of which the weekly was facing the threat of a boycott by the clergy. Not only did Hojjatoleslam Motahhari's articles remove the threat,[42] but they also helped boost the magazine's circulation.[43]

At the time of the *Kayhan* journalists' strike in 1979, Mr Mahdiyan was reported to have bought the paper 'as a bankrupt concern, for a price equal to its debts'.[44] The deal was highly controversial, with claims that the paper had been undervalued;[45] that its fugitive owner, the former Senate member, Mostafa Mesbahzadeh, had agreed to the sale in order to save his other assets in Iran; and that he had received money from *Kayhan* in the first few days after Mr Mahdiyan had taken over the firm.[46] Mr Mahdiyan himself denied having paid any money to Mr Mesbahzadeh; having had any contacts with him after he had left the country; or indeed having bought the firm in the first place. Buying *Kayhan*, Mr Mahdiyan argued, would have been impossible, given the fact that its assets had been placed with several banks as collateral for its debts. All he had done had been 'to pay the firm's debts to the suppliers of paper, ink and other printing material who had obtained court orders to seize the goods in warehouses, giving rise to the threat of stoppage at *Kayhan*, with its 1,300 staff'. Having saved the firm from collapse through what he regarded as a 'personal sacrifice', Mr Mahdiyan had become *Kayhan*'s 'supervisor, not its owner', and had 'gradually collected his own debts from *Kayhan*'.[47]

The confrontation over *Kayhan* had its roots in the wide gap between the paper's secular, broadly left-wing, middle class editorial staff, and the Islamic revolutionary movement that had taken over Iran, with particular following among the urban poor, the peasantry, and the manual workers. Just as the striking journalists saw the moves by the Islamic Association as part of a detailed conspiracy to take over *Kayhan*, the Islamists saw the paper in the grips of communists who would not spare any efforts to overthrow the new Islamic regime. The Islamist view is exemplified by Mr Mahdiyan's own assertion that 'in order to take over the paper, the leftists had even played an obedient role to the Shah before the Revolution, referring to him as "His Imperial Majesty." ' During the Revolution, their articles had been against the [Shah's] regime, but without having any religious or Islamic aim'. The prominence given to Ayatollah Khomeini had been due to the fact that leftists 'did not have any leaders to promote as a rival to the Imam, the only person who had had the courage to shout at the Shah'. They therefore saw Ayatollah Khomeini 'as the only person who could help them win their secular aims'.[48]

Kayhan is 'purified'

After taking control of *Kayhan*, Mr Mahdiyan set about 'purifying' it, with the help of Haj Mehdi Araqi,[49] a veteran of the Islamist movement whose 14 years in prison under the former regime for his part in the 1965 assassination of the Prime Minister, Hassan-Ali Mansour,[50] had given him close knowledge of the leftist fellow-inmates. The striking journalists were invited to return to work under the Islamic Association's 'supervision' or to accept redundancy. A small group agreed to go back to work. A much larger group, including the paper's senior editors and veteran journalists, accepted Mr Mahdiyan's offer of 'substantial redundancy payments in cash', and left *Kayhan*, 'and in some cases journalism altogether'. The rest, comprising most of the 'Group of Twenty' rejected both options and set off to publish their own, short-lived newspaper, *Kayhan-e Azad* (Free Kayhan), backed by some twenty other *Kayhan* journalists, using *Ayandegan*'s printing facilities.[51]

The veterans' mass departure from *Kayhan* made it possible for their less experienced colleagues who had stayed on to move to positions of higher responsibility. Some joined the Editorial Council, where they would 'shiver and develop fever' through anxiety when 'writing headlines that were going to be read by a million people'. A movie reporter and critic was appointed as the paper's Political Editor, since he had been the only remaining journalist with a contact among the senior clergy. The Culture and Arts Editor had to cover radio, television and education and also later took over the Foreign Service, employing 'three ladies from the advertising department' of the daily's English language sibling, *Kayhan International*, and a freelance translator. All had to work under a 'head prefect', an agent sent in by the Islamic authorities, and to accommodate 'major interventions', such as those by a 'type-setter from the Islamic Association' who would tell the editors what headline they should be running.[52]

The end nears for the independent press

With its network of reporters and their contacts across the country in disarray, *Kayhan* would often run rehashed versions of stories carried by *Ayandegan*,[53] which had ended its self-declared suspension. On 7 August, however, *Ayandegan* was closed down when its offices were raided by Revolutionary Guards. Eleven *Ayandegan* employees, including three members of the Editorial Council, several senior journalists and several administrative and clerical staff members, were arrested. Most were released soon, but the members of the Editorial Council were imprisoned for three months, without any of them ever being charged with any offence.[54] Two days after the raid, the Government spokesman announced that *Ayandegan*'s assets had belonged to the public and should have been taken over by the government when it nationalized the country's industries.[55]

The day before the Revolutionary Guards stormed the offices of *Ayandegan*, Mr Mahdiyan had handed *Kayhan* over to Bonyad-e Mostaz'afan (The Foundation for the Deprived), the successor to the Shah's regime's Pahlavi Foundation, which was now incorporating assets belonging to the former regime and its associates, and had also taken over *Ettela'at*.[56] Several months later, Mr Mahdiyan wrote to Ayatollah Khomeini, asking him to appoint a new supervisor for *Kayhan*, someone 'with religious qualification and political piety'. On 28 April 1980, the post was given to Dr Ebrahim Yazdi,[57] the Foreign Minister in Mr Bazargan's cabinet that had resigned in the dispute over the seizure of the American Embassy the previous November. Running the paper had been a stressful experience, Mr Mahdiyan recalled more than twenty years later, because while 'God may forgive one for gambling, drinking wine or adultery,' He would not forgive 'even one line of deviation or intellectual poisoning or the tarnishing of a Moslem's reputation' in a newspaper that was reaching people everywhere.[58] In May 1980, Ayatollah Khomeini's former ambassador to Baghdad, Hojjatoleslam Mahmoud Do'ai, was appointed as *Ettela'at*'s supervisor,[59] and was still there at the time of this writing, the longest serving media manager in Iran after the Revolution.

Sixty-three other newspapers were also closed in August 1979 under the new press law which imposed strict limits on those who would be licensed to publish newspapers.[60] The banned newspapers included the organs of several left-wing organizations – who nonetheless continued to publish their papers for a long time afterwards – the recently founded *Kayhan-e Azad*,[61] the left-wing daily *Paygham-e Emrouz*, the satirical weekly, *Ahangar*, several other satirical papers, and a number of Azarbaijani Turkish language publications.[62] A demonstration called by the National Democratic Front to protest against the closure of *Ayandegan* and other papers was broken up by the Hezbollahis.[63]

The Islamic state began life without a systematic approach or its own administrative tools to exert effective control over the press. The Ministry of Information and Tourism, first renamed the Ministry of Information and Publicity, and then the Ministry of Culture and Islamic and Guidance, was from the very beginning accused by factions within the new regime of being too accommodating to 'the counter-revolutionary' press. At the same time, the Ministry would be attacked by journalists for having introduced a new draft press law, 'without any consultation with experts', and 'in spite of widespread protests by journalists and intellectuals'.[64] The last attempt to change Iran's 1956 press law had been made under the Shah's last two civilian prime ministers, Amouzegar and Sharif-Emami. Neither government lasted long enough to enact the draft laws that had been described by journalists as being against freedom of press and in contravention of Iran's 1906 Constitution.[65]

A new press law

The Islamic Republic's first press law, passed before the new state had a constitution, was drawn up in response to what the authorities saw as the country's 'chaotic press scene, and as a means of supervising the printing and distribution of the various publications that had appeared across the country without any clear criteria'. The new Press Law provided the basis for the banning of most of the 175 publications that were closed down in the first three years of the Islamic Republic. Some publications were banned under an article that took away the right to publish from 'the former regime's prime ministers, ministers and close associates who held office between 6 June 1963 [the day the uprising against the Shah's regime was suppressed] and 11 February 1979 [the day the Shah's regime was overthrown], and those who during this period provided publicity services to the former regime through the press, radio or television or by making public speeches.' Others were stopped according to another article which said 'any publication in which the Leader of the Islamic Revolution is insulted will be banned from one month to six months',[66] but did not appear again.

The law was criticized for introducing 'general, vague and imprecise concepts that would be open to abuse'. Among these was the requirement that those applying for a publication licence should be 'in possession of political piety and moral competence'. The concept of providing 'publicity services to the former regime' was also seen by the critics as not having a clear definition. However, the new law was praised for banning, for the first time in Iran, any pressure on or censorship of the press by government officials, stipulating that anyone committing such an offence would be liable to disqualification from government service and imprisonment from six months to two years (Article 29). The law was also praised for stipulating that 'offences committed by the press shall be dealt with at a criminal court in the presence of a jury' (Articles 30–39), using a language that was 'almost identical' to the Press Law introduced by Dr Mosaddeq's government in 1952.[67] The new law also allowed journalists to form trade unions,[68] although the old journalists' Syndicate was never allowed to hold a meeting and organize its activities,[69] and it would be years before a new union could be formed.

An intensifying struggle for power within the Islamic regime and clashes between the regime and its various opponents across the country formed the political background to the closures and takeovers of newspapers. The reflection of these conflicts, and the coverage of the country's social and economic problems in the press, even in those run by officials appointed by the Islamic Republic, continued to be seen as signs of a conspiracy against the Islamic Republic. *Kayhan* and, to a lesser extent, *Ettela'at*, were criticized not only for covering the activities of the still legal opposition groups, but also when they reported that prices and rents had risen.[70] After the closure of *Ayandegan* and *Paygham-e Emrouz*, some of the sharpest criticisms were directed against President Bani-Sadr's daily, *Enqelab-e Eslami* (The Islamic Revolution, 1979–81) and the Iran Freedom Movement's *Mizan* (Scale, 1980–81).[71] The independent daily *Bamdad* (Morning) that had been given a publication licence by the Islamic Republic in the summer of 1979, soon came to be seen as such a threat that its office was bombed, its editor was detained, and it was closed down in the spring of 1980.[72]

In his March 1980 Iranian New Year's message, Ayatollah Khomeini once again called on the 'press across Iran to join hands and write freely, but not to conspire'.

Although he had said 'repeatedly that the press should be free and independent,' he had nevertheless continued to see that 'unfortunately and most surprisingly, some of them are still implementing the evil intentions of the right and the left in Iran'. On 7 June 1981, in a message marking the Revolutionary Guards' Day, Ayatollah Khomeini issued another warning about the press. 'Enemies of Islam', he said, 'are lying in ambush; poisonous pens have been unsheathed from every direction to drive the Islamic Republic out of the scene, and to submit to anything but the Islamic Republic'.[73]

The fall of Bani-Sadr

During the 15 months separating the two messages, the conflict between the Islamic Republic and the Mojahedin-e Khalq and that between President Bani-Sadr and his clerical opponents within the Islamic regime had escalated sharply. 20 June 1981 saw the climax of the battle, with street clashes between the Revolutionary Guards and pro-Mojahedin demonstrators in which dozens were killed. There then followed the arrests of thousands and summary executions of hundreds of Mojahedin and other political activists, and the flight abroad of Mr Bani-Sadr and the Mojahedin leader, Mass'oud Rajavi.[74] The 1981 summer of bloodshed ended the period of open, mass political activity that had started with the anti-Shah marches almost exactly three years earlier. As far as journalism was concerned, the country's 'newspapers took on a calm and uniform appearance which continued to prevail until months after the end of the imposed war [with Iraq]'[75] in July 1988.

In the years to come, of the three main pre-Revolution dailies, *Ettela'at* continued its traditional position as a 'newspaper of record'. *Kayhan* too maintained its controversial pre-revolutionary character. One of its early supervisors, Mohammad Khatami (1981–90), was to promote considerable cultural and political openness in the Islamic Republic, first as the Minister of Culture and Islamic Guidance (1982–92), and then as President (elected twice, 1997 and 2001). Under another supervisor from the mid-1990s, Hossein Shariatmadari, *Kayhan* was seen as the organ of the Islamic Republic's conservative factions, with close links to intelligence organizations, and specialized in attacks on critics within and outside the regime. *Ayandegan*, in spite of its closure, continued to influence the development of journalism in Iran, with several of its former staff members becoming the founders of or contributors to the specialist, technical, or trade journals that were to appear in the country during the war years.

4 War, reconstruction, and the revival of journalism (1980–96)

Given Iran's 50 per cent rate of literacy in 1979, scarce resources of paper, machinery and skilled workforce, and the chronic newspaper distribution problems, it is highly likely that market forces alone would have put an end to the heady post-revolutionary growth of the country's press. In the event, escalating internal political conflicts and the Iraqi invasion in 1980 resulted in a much more rapid collapse of the sector. The number of new publications that emerged during the 8 year war (685) was smaller than those that had appeared in the two years before the war (720). None of the wartime papers represented any opposition to, or indeed any social or political ideas different from, those held by the state.[1] Official political views were expressed initially by the two old, afternoon dailies, *Ettela'at* and *Kayhan*, now safely in the hands of the Islamic Republic authorities, and two morning dailies, *Sobh-e Azadegan* (Morning of the Free), that had inherited *Ayandegan*'s facilities, and *Jomhouri-ye Eslami* (Islamic Republic), established in 1979 by the then Hojjatoleslam Seyyed-Ali Khamenei, who was to become Iran's third president in 1981, and Supreme Leader in 1989. The four papers were later joined by *Kar-o-Kargar* (Work and Worker), licensed in 1984, and *Resalat* (Mission), licensed in 1985, the latter the organ of conservative Islamic politics, with close links to Iran's traditional commercial interests based in the bazaars.

Publications that appeared between 1983 and the end of the war in 1988 included a small number of monthlies with crossword puzzles or children's stories, specialist journals published by universities and government organizations and a growing number of private sector specialist monthlies staffed by a mix of scientific and technical experts and professional journalists who could no longer work on daily or weekly newspapers. The specialist papers followed the example of earlier journals such as *Keshavarz* (Farmer) and *Danestaniha* (General Knowledge),[2] licensed in December 1980, and *San'at-e Haml-o Naghl* (Transport Industry) and *Film*, founded by former *Ayandegan* journalists,[3] both of which first appeared in February 1981, but were given their licences in 1990.[4] In the meantime, the publishers of both papers had to present each monthly issue to the Ministry of Culture and Islamic Guidance, where officials would check every page before allowing publication.[5]

In spite of tight wartime controls, both *San'at-e Haml-o Naghl* and *Film* were able to increase their readership among the public while influencing government policy by offering accurate and comprehensive information and analysis. After the war, they were able to expand the boundaries of the permissible. *San'at-e Haml-o Naghl* carried not only authoritative news, reports, analysis and commentary on transport, energy and communications, but also enlightening articles and essays on a whole range of other issues. One article, part of a major report on the electronic media in 1990, correctly predicted that in spite of efforts to ban the use of satellite television receivers, the equipment would soon find its way into Iranian homes, introducing the public to new lifestyles, raising their economic, social and political expectations and reducing their interest in domestic television programmes.[6] Another article in 1990 considered the question of more than a million Iranians living in diaspora and argued that in spite of the commonly held belief, or hope, in Iran that the émigrés and exiles would return to their homeland, history had shown such population movements to be irreversible.[7] And in 1993, in what many would consider a daring commentary even today, the paper criticized the design and construction of Ayatollah Khomeini's mausoleum in south Tehran, near the city's main Behesht-e-Zahra Cemetery, saying it reflected neither the status of the founder of the Islamic Republic, nor Iran's long tradition of creating architectural masterpieces.[8]

Well before post-revolutionary Iranian cinema won international acclaim, and at a time when many Iranian cities lacked functioning movie theatres, the *Film* monthly introduced its readers to the world of cinema in great detail and depth. The monthly's letters pages were full of accounts from youngsters across the country who would describe how the paper had changed their lives and how anxiously they awaited the arrival of each issue in their town or village. The paper influenced Iran's cinema industry and the government's policy makers and became the training ground for a generation of cinema journalists some of whom later founded their own publications, often close replicas of the *Film* monthly. By the mid-1980s, the concept of specialist journalism had become so well-established[9] that it could also be applied to two literary magazines, *Adineh* (Friday) and *Donya-ye Sokhan* (The World of Letters), members of one of the longest running strands of journalism in Iran.

The war years witnessed the deaths of at least 39 reporters on the battle fronts; the inauguration of news and report writing courses for members of the Revolutionary Guards Corps; journalism training courses at *Kayhan* and at the national news agency, Pars, now renamed the Islamic Republic News Agency (IRNA); and the use of satellites for nationwide broadcast of Iranian radio and television programmes.[10] Other notable events included the start in 1984 of the first, albeit mild, satirical column after the 1980 newspaper closures that had put an end to humour in Iranian journalism. The column, 'Do Kalameh Harf-e Hessab' (A Couple of Sensible Words), appeared in the daily *Ettela'at*, written by Kioumars Saberi, one of the few remaining writers of the pre-revolutionary satirical paper, *Towfiq*. Having declared allegiance to the Islamic Republic and total devotion to its founder, Ayatollah Khomeini, Mr Saberi used the column to criticize official actions that he believed were detrimental to the Islamic regime.[11] In 1986, the Islamic Republic's second press law was approved by the Majlis.[12]

Following the end of the war in 1988 and Ayatollah Khomeini's death a year later, Hojjatoleslam Ali-Akbar Hashemi-Rafsanjani took over as President and the then President, Hojjatoleslam Ali Khamenei, was promoted to Supreme Leadership. Now that economic resources did not have to be spent on the war, President Rafsanjani called on those who had been fighting at the battle fronts to turn to the creation of wealth and embark on what called a 'luxury parade'. The economic policy of investments in infrastructure as well as imports of consumer goods[13] was accompanied with a relaxation of the tight controls over culture and arts, implemented by Mr Rafsanjani's Minister of Culture and Islamic Guidance, Hojjatoleslam Seyyed-Mohammad Khatami, who inaugurated the first 'Seminar to Study the Problems of the Iranian Press' in February 1991.

Addressing the Seminar, the Deputy Minister for Press and Publicity, Mr Mohsen Aminzadeh, said that since its establishment in 1989, his department had tried to bring about diversity in the press; make it possible for the young generation to enter journalism; promote professionalism rather than politicization in the press; expand journalism education and training; and enhance the quality of the press by 'using modern and more complex publicity techniques', while advancing 'the principles of the Islamic Revolution and national unity'. Mr Aminzadeh said that while the number of publications had risen by about 2 per cent in the year preceding the creation of his department, the rise in the following year had been 49 per cent, with a total of 274 papers being published across the country. The number of daily newspapers had risen from 10 in 1988 to 19 in 1990, and there had been a 150 per cent rise in the number of scientific and specialist publications.[14]

Salam

The less stringent licensing regime had not only freed *San'at-e Ham-o Naghl* and *Film* from pre-publication censorship, but it had also led to the appearance of the literary monthly *Gardoun* (Universe, 1990) and the monthly *Kian* (Existence, 1991) that specialized in Islamic thought, both of which came into conflict with the state later on. The most important newspaper licence of the early 1990s went to the daily *Salam* [Peace]. The paper appeared in 1991, backed by a group of senior clergymen, members of *Majma'e-e Rouhaniyoun-e Mobarez* (the League of Combatant Clergy), who had been disqualified as candidates for election to the Assembly of Experts, the body in charge of appointing and supervising the Islamic Republic's Supreme Leader, and could not get any newspaper to publish their letter of protest.[15] *Salam* soon turned into one of the most widely read newspapers, not least for its 'Alo, Salam' (Hello, *Salam*) column, with questions or comments from the readers, some of which in effect were news reports provided to the paper by the public, rather than by its own editorial staff. *Salam* was among the Islamic Republic's first newspapers to carry out investigative journalism, leading to the exposure of a number of financial scandals. Before the Revolution, such journalism could only be found in newspapers published by Iranians in exile. In one of its early issues, *Salam* warned against 'some 40 confidential, private bulletins' produced by various state organizations that were shaping the minds of the 'elite', while undermining the confidence of the public in the press.[16] The same bulletins were used by *Salam* briefly as the source of stories about violence and sexual crimes, in a column called 'Grey News' that was discontinued because of strong protest from government officials.[17] Later on, *Salam*'s coverage led to several court appearances for its publisher, Hojjatoleslam Seyyed-Mohammad Mousavi-Khoeiniha, and the detention of its editor, Abbas Abdi.[18]

Technically, the major innovation in this period was the emergence in 1992 of Tehran Municipality's daily, *Hamshahri* (Fellow City-dweller) with a cheerful multicolour appearance and plenty of features, in sharp contrast with the grim looks of all the other daily newspapers. Backed by the then Tehran Mayor, Gholam-Hossein Karbaschi, the paper was set up by Ahmad Sattari, a former *Ettela'at* journalist, described by some of his colleagues as 'the father of Iran's modern journalism' after the Revolution.[19] Within three years, *Hamshahri* became Iran's best-selling newspaper, with a circulation of 400,000, twice as big as *Kayhan* and *Ettela'at*'s.[20]

'No' to the sound of music

Under Mr Khatami, the Ministry of Culture and Islamic Guidance also issued permissions for the publication of new works of fiction such as Shahrnoush Parsipour's *Zanan Bedoun-e Mardan* (Women without Men) which included the description of the life of a prostitute. There was also a rise in the production of music, which Ayatollah Khomeini had sanctioned shortly before his death, along with other *fatwas* lifting the religious bans on playing chess and eating sturgeon. Criticized by conservatives, who regarded such developments as increasing permissiveness, Mr Khatami resigned as Minister of Culture and Islamic Guidance in May 1992 and was appointed director of Iran's National Library. In his letter of resignation to President Rafsanjani, Mr Khatami warned that although opposition to Ayatollah Khomeini's views had started with the rejection of his view on music, it could lead to 'the disappointment and insecurity of wholesome thinkers and artists, even those who believe in and are infatuated with Islam and the Revolution'.[21] Following Mr Khatami's resignation, a group of his aides and assistants at organizations affiliated to the Ministry of Culture and Islamic Guidance and the *Kayhan* group were also replaced with officials close to or sympathetic with the military and intelligence organizations.[22]

Mr Khatami was succeeded as Minister by Ali Larijani, who had spent the war years as the Deputy Chief of Staff and Acting Chief of Staff of the Revolutionary Guards Corps.[23] Two years later, in 1994, Mr Larijani was appointed Director of radio and television, the Islamic Republic of Iran Broadcasting (IRIB), taking over from President Rafsanjani's brother, Mohammad Hashemi. The new conservative Minister of Culture and Islamic Guidance, Mostafa Mir-Salim, lifted the ban on video clubs and facilitated the imports of video recorders and cameras,[24] but critics maintained that this was merely a façade, covering the new officials' 'real aim of imposing subtle restrictions on the press, book publishing and cinema'.[25]

Not quite 'one hundred flowers'

Under Mr Rafsanjani's presidency, the Iranian press went through a series of contradictory experiences which, on balance, led to a quantitative growth, without allowing for sufficient qualitative development of journalistic skills. On the one hand, there were training courses for cartoonists and exhibitions of their works. On the other hand, the publication of a cartoon vaguely similar to the figure of Ayatollah Khomeini led to the closure of the monthly general knowledge magazine, *Farad* (the unit of capacitance, named after Michael Faraday)[26] A demand by newspaper publishers that press offences be tried in the presence of a jury, as stipulated by the Constitution, was accepted, with the first jury appointed in July 1995 (Table 4.1).[27] However, the make-up of the jury was such that its verdicts more often than not pleased the prosecutor rather than the defence. Several papers were banned, including the daily *Jahan-e Eslam* (World of Islam), Is published by Seyyed-Hadi Khamenei, Ayatollah Khamenei's brother, which was charged with having insulted the Islamic Republic's leaders; the weekly *Havadess* (Events) that had gained a huge audience by covering crime stories; and the secular literary monthly *Takapou* (Endeavour), that published the works of dissident writers and poets. There were also new papers, including the full colour daily, *Iran*, published by the Islamic Republic News Agency (IRNA); several other dailies representing a range of views, mostly in support of President Rafsanjani's administration; and the political weekly, *Yassarat-al-Hossein* (Oh for Hossein's Blood),[28] strongly critical of the secular thinkers outside the Islamic regime, as well as anyone within the Islamic regime who could be described as liberal or reformist.

By 1992, Iranian journalism was marked with a high degree of diversity both in titles and in the range of subjects and by the rise in the numbers of professional journalists, working on newspapers and periodicals to make a living, rather than using them to promote a political agenda. A survey of 2,145 journalists found that 52 per cent of them were full-time or part-time staff members (27 per cent and 25 per cent, respectively), and the rest worked as casuals and freelancers. More than 50 per cent of those surveyed were working for publications owned by or affiliated to the state. More than two-thirds had university education, most of them in fields other than journalism or communication; only 12 per cent had received any training since taking up journalism. Their average experience was 4.14 years, with only 25 per cent of

Table 4.1 Members of the first press jury appointed in 1995

Main members	Substitute members
Ali-Akbar Ash'ari	Rouhollah Hosseinian
Seyyed-Reza Taqavi	Hadi Marvi
Mohammad-Ali Nezamzadeh	Seyyed-Ja'far Shobeiri
Ali Jannati	Ahmad Alizadeh
Habibollah Asgar-oladi	Ahmad Pournejati
Mohsen Chiniforoushan	Gholam-Hossein Elham
Seyyed-Abdol-Hassan Navab	Abbas-Ali Amid-Zanjani

them having been in the profession during its heyday, immediately after the Revolution. The journalists' average age was 38.1 for men and 32.8 for women, who made up 278, or about 13 per cent, of the total number of journalists.[29]

However, a comparison of the number of journalists in 1992 with those registered in the only comprehensive directory of Iranian journalists, published in 1973,[30] revealed a very fragile workforce. Even though the country's population had grown by about two-thirds during the two decades, the number of full-time journalists had increased from 536 to 579, a rise of 8 per cent. In contrast, the number of part-time journalists had increased by more than 10 folds, from 154 to 1,566. The oil boom of the 1970s had been replaced by the economic disruption following the Revolution and the devastation of the country's infrastructure during the war, leaving a large pool of casual labour – more highly educated than the full-timers, with an 85 per cent rate of university graduation – at the disposal of the newspaper industry, with consequences such as low wages, lack of job security, and little opportunity to gain experience. Journalism was the main source of income for 32.6 per cent of all the journalists covered by the 1992 survey, but for slightly more than 10 per cent of the part-timers, with the rest having to supplement their income by taking on other occupations, many of them (42.9 per cent) not related to communication. The average monthly pay for full-time journalists was 124,290 rials ($77.7), and for part-timers 78,663 rials ($49). The licence-holders were earning on average 1,778,871 rials ($1,112)[31] a month – more than 14 times greater than the full-time journalists and 22 times greater than the part-timers.[32]

Not enough readers

Newspaper circulation figures arrived at in the survey were another cause for concern, estimating Iran's annual per capita newsprint consumption in 1990 at 0.6 kilos, compared to 0.4 kilos in Pakistan, 1.8 in Iraq, 2.4 in Turkey, 9.8 in Kuwait, 23.5 in Germany, and 51.6 in the United States. Noting that daily newspapers made up 65 per cent of the country's total newsprint consumption, the researchers concluded that the quality of the dailies must have an impact on the low sales figures. This, in turn, was related, on the one hand, to structural factors such as ownership, technology and equipment and, on the other, to human resources and their levels of skill and income. Low circulations made it difficult to raise advertising revenue, which in turn would prevent the publishers from employing a skilled workforce. Repeated suspensions in publication and even 'early deaths' of newspapers could well ensue.

The situation was even worse in the case of scientific and specialist journals, which in 1992 made up 49 per cent of the total number of titles, and whose rising numbers had a great role in the recent improvement in the image of Iran's newspaper industry. These had small circulations, a part-time workforce and weak financial support. The history of the Iranian press had shown that such journals had an average lifespan of six years. Since the scientific and specialist journals had been less vulnerable to political pressures than other newspapers, the researchers argued, their 'early deaths' could only have resulted from internal, structural factors and the society's newspaper consumption pattern. Most of Iran's new publications, the researchers concluded, were 'mere saplings that may not be able to stand up to even a slight breeze'. Such newspapers needed to be provided with substantial support before they were able to grow roots and overcome the Iranian press's 150-year old problem of premature death.[33]

The 'internal, structural' features were highlighted in a 1994 investigation into the economics of Iran's newspaper industry, with its 'highly negative real rates of return on capital'. Seventy per cent of the start-up capital was found to be tied up in premises and the running costs of the first two to three issues. Paper and printing material, mostly imported, highly susceptible to the fluctuations in the rates of exchange, and out of management control, accounted for 75 to 88 per cent of the productions costs. Private sector papers were under pressure from the heavily subsidized state-owned publications, who could afford to charge lower cover prices and offer more attractive rates to advertisers. Private sector publishers could try to keep their costs down by cutting staff salaries and payments to contributors, at the cost of losing editorial quality; raise revenues by selling the subsidized paper provided by the government on the free market; or they could do both. The study argued that the state would soon find it impossible to continue subsidizing the press, but argued that the subsidies should be maintained until such time that the real rate of return in the newspaper industry had improved. It also called on newspaper publishers to combine their resources, for instance by setting up shared printing facilities, in order to lower their costs,[34] a move that was followed up by the Press Cooperative that had recently been established by a group of newspaper publishers.[35]

Low self-esteem

The socio-political and structural pressures exerted on the press had led to a very low opinion of journalism and journalists, among the practitioners themselves, as revealed in a 1994 survey of the views of 315 journalists, 12 per cent of them women. The respondents had an average experience of 8.1 years and came from a wide range of publications, most of them based in Tehran. Seventy-five per cent of their criticisms concerned the top 10 subjects: (1) censorship and self-censorship; clichéd and unimaginative content; (2) shortage of specialist journalists; (3) politicization of the media; (4) lack of awareness of readers' views; (5) ignorance of journalistic principles; (6) commercialization of the press; (7) lack of attention to the real social issues; (8) lack of job security; (9) laziness; and (10) reliance on news agency reports. Some respondents described the newspapers where they were working as: illegitimate; trading house; vulgar; materialistic; deaf; dumb; blind; paralysed; and opportunistic. The respondents had an even lower opinion of the journalists, that is, themselves – or perhaps their colleagues – displayed in adjectives such as: lacking identity; careless; suppressed; rent-a-pen; dishonest; coward; semi-literate; irresponsible; superficial; unaware of Iranian culture; lacking any belief in the people; puppet; and parrot.[36]

The most visible products of the industry were daily newspapers with 'long-winded front page headlines' on subjects that did 'not interest the public', who did 'not have much trust in the press'. Without skilled news staff of their own, the five morning newspapers – all of them launched after the Revolution – mostly carried reports filed by news agencies, chiefly the official agency, IRNA. Many of the reports were not attributed to any source at all.[37] The country's oldest newspapers, the afternoon dailies *Ettela'at* and *Kayhan*, used photographs scarcely and badly and had very little front page coverage of sports, cultural and arts news, subjects that interested the youths, who made up one-third of the country's population, and could therefore 'be attracted by foreign cultural manifestations'.[38]

By the mid-1990s, the most novel, and perhaps the most successful, phenomenon in Iranian journalism were the weekly tabloids with a fondness for huge headlines, often in red, and front pages mostly packed with pictures of football players. On the inside pages there was more sports news, stories about Iranian and foreign cinema and television celebrities, and occasional articles criticizing the state of traffic, education or food prices. Some tabloids also serialized tales of morality and romance by relatively unknown writers, a genre that was also extremely successful in book form, much to the dismay of some of the country's more established literary figures.

President Rafsanjani's second term, 1993–97, was marked by three major developments related to the press. The first was the inauguration of the annual press festivals in May 1994.[39] There then was the 1995 withdrawal of a bill presented to the Majlis by the government to amend the 1986 Press Law,[40] one of the rare cases of a government-sponsored bill not going through parliament. The withdrawal of the bill came after almost all newspaper publishers – many of them leading figures in the Islamic Republic and several of them clergymen – had described it as too restrictive.[41] The third development, also in 1995, was the appearance of signs of concern within the state about the multiplication of critical newspapers and their popularity.

The 'progressives', the 'neutrals', and the 'sleepers'

Addressing a meeting during the Second Press Festival, in April 1995, a senior official from the Ministry of Culture and Islamic Guidance divided Iran's newspapers into four categories: (1) 'progressive and goal-oriented' papers, that had a 'correct understanding of society and raised the sensitive social issues'; (2) 'neutral' ones whose presence 'did not make a difference'; (3) 'superficial' publications, such as the commercial sports newspapers; and (4) 'sleepers', affiliated to the country's intellectuals who had 'always been sick' and whose papers would 'write about the most banal issues in the most remote corners of the world' but would 'not make a reference to the Holy Defence', the official expression used to refer to the war with Iraq.[42]

Three-hundred publications were on display at the Third Press Festival in April 1996 which included the first exhibition of children and young people's press. Speaking at the Festival, the Minister of Culture and Islamic Guidance, Mostafa Mir-Salim, said there were now 750 licences for publication of newspapers and periodicals, and the newspapers 'could operate freely, as long as their reflection of critical and social aspects does not disrupt the foundations of people's beliefs'.[43] There were 63 award winners at the Festival, including eight women.[44] More than 70 per cent of the Festival's visitors said the quantity and quality of the newspapers had improved in recent years. Tehran Municipality's colourful daily, *Hamshahri*, the student union's weekly, *Payam-e Daneshjou* (University Student's Message), that reported allegations of financial corruption, and the *Film* monthly were the visitors' most popular papers. More than 50 per cent said they trusted the press more than the authorities – a proportion that increased with the respondents' level of education.[45]

However, speaking to the managers and staff members of the newspapers represented at the Festival, Ayatollah Khamenei expressed dissatisfaction with the Iranian press whose quality, he said, was 'not worthy of its history.' Ayatollah Khamenei said 'intellectualism in Iran [had been] born sick' and had never turned into 'a current that could merge with the Iranian people, learn from them and teach them.' But the Iranian press, he said, had not been 'born sick', and some of what had been published 90 years before, at the time of Constitutional Revolution, with 'mature satire, mature writing and lofty literature', was 'not too out of date even today.'

'Cheerleaders, bystanders, enemies'

Ayatollah Khamenei divided Iran's newspapers into three categories: (1) a wide range that accepted the Islamic Republic, though they might be critical of this or that ministry or organization; (2) those who were indifferent towards the state, such as the scientific, purely cultural or specialist magazines; and (3) those he described as *mo'aned*, or hostile, who would strike blows at the Islamic Republic whenever the opportunity arose. He said newspapers that supported the Islamic Republic had to avoid weakening it by presenting the public with a 'dark and foggy horizon' and 'killing their hopes in their hearts'. They had to remind the public that although the United States and Israel were challenging Iran, their threat was not important, and while the prices of some consumer items might have gone up, they would also come down at some stage. Such concerns, said Ayatollah Khamenei, should not allow the principles of the Revolution to be questioned by 'dilettante writing' by a newspaper's own staff, or by the publication of what others might 'cleverly plant in the paper'. The pro-Islamic Republic papers were warned that they too had to try to improve their quality. 'Sometimes', said Ayatollah Khamenei, 'one would take a look at a poetry page, without feeling the urge to read any further. One would look at the editorial, to find that it lacked any attraction.' There was no sign of 'the elegance of the Persian language or the art of tasteful writing'. The papers had to use new and beautiful words and expressions, artistic skills, cartoons and photographs.

The politically indifferent newspapers also had to be supported by the government, if they were strengthening the country's culture, promoting literacy and Persian language and literature. But the Islamic Republic would not expect anything from such papers and anyone saying the state was putting pressure on them would be lying.

Those writing for the third, 'hostile', group of newspapers, Ayatollah Khamenei said, included many 'unreliable elements': 'hard-line Marxists' who had 'worked at the office of the [former] Queen' Farah; writers who had 'cooperated with and praised the Shah's regime, in spite of its black oppression', but were now presenting themselves as freedom-lovers; and those who preferred 'Christmas, which comes at the beginning of winter with its ice and snow and cold', to the Iranian Nowrouz, at the beginning of spring. They would repeat any accusation levelled against the Islamic Republic by its enemies abroad – about women, human rights, terrorism, and the government's 'incompetence' and about the 'Islamic system being ossified and mediaeval'. Even though the Islamic Republic had been the only regime in Iran that had prevented the country's disintegration and had stood up to the alliance of the East and the West and NATO for eight years after Iran had been invaded by Iraq, such people would mention the war only to 'ridicule those who had fought in it, because they wore beards', or because the *baseej* (mobilization) militia members were religious. Having stressed that no one would be allowed to cross the 'red line' by questioning the Revolution or the Islamic Republic, Ayatollah Khamenei said 'the third group' of newspapers would continue to be tolerated, but they had to 'correct themselves.'[46]

Following Ayatollah Khamenei's speech, there were calls by media officials for better training of journalists to make sure they would 'make their mistakes while still at school'.[47] A seminar was held on 'the need to polish the media language', where one linguist said 'semi-literate' translations appearing in the media were causing 'chaos in the Persian language', while another described such 'chaos as an inevitable side-effect of the evolution of language'.[48] There were discussions, 'unprecedented in the 160 year history of journalism' in Iran, about ethical standards that were needed to ensure 'immunity against the damages that could arise from the use of the pen, such as lying, libel, and depriving individuals of their dignity'.[49] The strong emphasis on ethical standards was not shared by all the journalists commenting on the subject. The editor of *Salam*, Abbas Abdi, said one could only speak of ethics in a society where the rule of law had already been established. He said individuals who 'would ignore the most basic laws' and 'some of the most abusive people' were now talking of ethics, using it 'to cover their ugly, anti-law faces'.[50]

A woman journalist, Minou Badii, said ethical standards were being violated by those

> accepting bribes to publish news and reports; blurring the boundaries of advertising and news; accusing individuals without producing any evidence; using abusive language; bowing down to [...] organizations in order to obtain material and moral privileges; accepting money from individuals to publish their articles; and sometimes working for public relations offices.

In order to promote ethical standards among journalists, Ms Badii suggested, there had to be improvements in their living conditions and professional standards governing their practical work. Grounds for the application of ethical standards in the press could be prepared by a journalists' union,[51] an institution that was urgently called for by almost all newspaper managers and editors.[52]

Floral patterns, Kantian thought, active carbons

At the Fourth Press Festival, in April 1997, the last to be held during Mr Rafsanjani's presidency, many of the 41 awards went to reports and articles with religious, scientific or cultural themes, such as 'A Review of Floral Patterns in Islamic Arts',[53] 'Kant's Influence on Religious Thought in the West',[54] 'Raising the Efficiency of Active Carbon for Chemical Defence',[55] 'The Battle of Water and Stone'[56] and 'The Nutritional Value and Standards of Iran's Mushrooms'.[57] One prize winning article, 'A Historical Review of the Question of Islamic Jurisprudence and Time',[58] had sought 'to briefly set out the problems of Islamic jurisprudence in recent years; report the theories that have been presented in an effort to solve them; and to define areas for studies aimed at "coordinating jurisprudence with time."' Another winner, 'A Jurisprudential and Economic Analysis of Guaranteed Profit in the Usury-free Banking System', argued that 'twelve years after the approval of the law on usury-free banking operations', Iran's banking system had 'still not been freed from the ill effects of domination by usury'.[59]

The few exceptions to this rule included a series of reports in *Kayhan* on allegations of financial irregularities in government-owned companies;[60] a challenging interview in *Salam* with Mohsen Rafiqdoust, the controversial head of the major state-owned commercial-industrial conglomerate, Bonyad-e Mostaz'afan va Janbazan (The Foundation for the Deprived and the Selfless [those disabled in the war]), whose brother, Morteza, had recently been given a life sentence in the biggest case of financial corruption reported in the Islamic Republic;[61] and a powerful report, by one of the four women award winners, on the Tehran Coroner's office, with its daily routine of medical examinations to establish age, maturity, insanity, drunkenness, paternity, virginity, rape, and sexual deviations, not to mention autopsies to establish the cause of death.[62] Another notable winner was a satirical piece with subtle references to officials in the Islamic Republic alleged to have used their positions to acquire personal wealth, including real estate in the West.[63]

The organizers of the Festival said that while Iran was witnessing one of its 'most prosperous press periods', with 750 publications available in the country, the 160-year history of the press had also raised expectations among the observers and the jury who had selected the prize-winners.[64] The make-up of the jury itself, six men, only two of them working journalists,[65] was criticized by working journalists who said they themselves should have chosen the award-winners. They also said that in order to be able to work 'independently and courageously', they needed to have a trade organization committed to defending their rights.[66]

On 18 May 1997, less than a week before the Presidential election that was won by Mr Khatami, the Press Court ordered the closure of the children's newspaper, *Aftabgardan* (Sunflower), published by President Rafsanjani's close aide and Mayor of Tehran, Gholam-Hossein Karbaschi. The paper had been found guilty of having twice published a satirical piece about the national radio and television – the second occasion coinciding with an address by the Supreme Leader, Ayatollah Khamenei, to the officials in charge of radio and television. Less than two months before the paper's closure, two of its contributors had won best journalism awards for children and adolescents.[67]

5 The second 'Spring of Freedom' (1997–2000)

During President Khatami's first year in office the number of publications rose to more than 850, with the total circulation exceeding two million copies a day;[1] the Association of Iranian Journalists was established (September 1997);[2] and there were changes in the make-up of the press jury (Table 5.1)[3] that resulted in more decisions in favour of journalists, in trials some of which were shown on television, very late at night, but with big audiences.[4] The new Minister of Culture and Islamic Guidance, Ataollah Mohajerani, made a point of personally attending the meetings of the Press Supervisory Board, the body dealing with applications for new papers.[5] Early into its operation, the new Board awarded licences to two dailies, *Jameah* (Society) and *Zan* (Woman),[6] both of which were innovations in post-revolutionary Iranian journalism and early participants in what was going to be a long and escalating confrontation between the Iranian judiciary and the press.

At a news conference on 27 December 1997, the head of the Judiciary, Ayatollah Mohammad Yazdi, dismissed a question from the correspondent of the official news agency, IRNA, about the reported arrest of an opposition political leader, Dr Ebrahim Yazdi, saying it was 'none of [the reporter's] business'. Two months later, the Ayatollah was angered by a question from a *Salam* reporter, Ozra Farahani, who asked if a group of local mayors in Tehran arrested on corruption charges had been treated 'in violation of the judicial proceedings', an allusion to the detainees' allegations that they had been tortured. Ayatollah Yazdi accused the reporter of slandering the Judiciary and threatened to have her arrested unless she produced evidence to prove the allegation. The threat was dropped after protests by the journalists' union and media officials,[7] including a statement signed by 194 journalists putting the same question to Ayatollah Yazdi, challenging him to arrest all of them.[8]

The Fifth Press Festival, in May 1998, was significantly different from its predecessors. The jury had been selected by the journalists' Association. There were 72 awards, compared with 40 the previous year, going to submissions from 47 publications, up from 17 the year before. The winners included nine women, 12.5 per cent of the total, up from the previous year's 7.5 per cent. While the main dailies, *Kayhan*, *Ettela'at*, *Salam*, and *Hamshahri* collected up to three awards each, entries from *Khaneh* (House), the very young weekly newspaper of the Centre for Young Journalists, received four awards. Six prizes went to journalists working on three newspapers recently launched by the state news agency IRNA – the daily

Table 5.1 Members of the first press jury appointed after President Khatami's election in 1997

Main members	Substitute members
Rouhollah Hosseinian	Seyyed-Mohammad Asghari
Sayed Ja'far Shobeiri	Ali Jannati
Habibollah Asgar-oladi	Kambiz Nowrouzi
Mohammad-Reza Takhshid	Morteza Lotfi
Mehdi Hojjat	Mohammad Agha-Nasseri
Ali Khoshrou	Fatemeh Ramezanzadeh [Ms]
Hadi Khaniki	A'zam Nouri [Ms]

Iran, the sports daily, *Iran-e Varzeshi* (Iran Sport), and the youth weekly, *Iran-e Javan* (Young Iran) – and six to the children's and young people's weeklies of the national radio and television's publishing arm, *Soroush* (Divine Voice of Conscience). There were also winners from the independent monthly, *Film*, and from other specialist periodicals covering photography, management, standard-ization of consumer goods, and forestry and pastures. The top prize went to an editorial in *Hamshahri* by Ahmad Zeidabadi, who had suggested that 'national interests' may not necessarily have to include 'territorial integrity', citing the examples of Lenin and Saddam Hussein ceding territory in order to safeguard the states over which they were presiding. National interests, the editorial went on to say, did not have to be seen as 'tangible and immutable', nor did they have to be 'identical to the wishes of governments, whether healthy or corrupt'. National interests, argued the writer, were in fact 'the resultant of the people's views', articulated by 'a responsible and answerable government'.[9]

The Festival was followed in June 1998 by 'The Second Seminar to Study the Problems of the Iranian Press', with papers, among other subjects, on freedom of press and the need for its legal protection, and the links between civil society, political development and the press. In his opening remarks, the Seminar's Academic Secretary, Dr Kazem Mo'tamednejad, spoke of 'the expansion of press freedom' and 'conditions unprecedented in the history of the [Iranian] press... with 32 national daily newspapers published in Tehran and 10 or 12 dailies in the provinces.' The rise in the number of newspapers, he said, had come at a time when 'even in advanced countries, including the United States', the numbers and circulations of newspapers had been falling for 15 years. These were 'exceptional conditions,' Dr Mo'tamednejad said, 'which we must appreciate and use in such a way that in future we can develop the press continuously in different directions'.[10] Dr Mo'tamednejad defended direct state support for the press, 'without damaging the independence of the press and other media'. He said the state had been giving indirect aid to the press, which in recent years had also been provided with newsprint, printing equipment, and material and even facilities such as motorcycles, automobiles, and minibuses. Direct state support, he argued, would help improve the quality of the press and 'confront the unprincipled publication of advertisements in daily newspapers and magazines and prevent the undesirable consequences of the spread of opportunistic and self-promoting advertisements, and those that promote the undesirable values of consumerist, capitalist societies'.[11]

There were less jubilant comments from other speakers, including a journalist with more than 30 years of experience who said the Iranian press could not develop as long as the government maintained a monopoly over printing resources and had near total control of the advertising market. Not only were state-owned papers putting pressure on the advertising revenues of the independent press, but the whole newspaper industry had to compete with the much lower advertising rates charged by national television. Three state-owned dailies, *Kayhan*, *Ettela'at*, and *Jomhouri-ye Eslami* were consuming 60 per cent of the foreign currency allocated to the press. High start up costs, unpredictable quality, uncertain advertising revenues, and the low prices of state-owned newspapers had made the press unattractive for the private sector. The state-run newspapers were staffed by civil servants, not by professional journalists, who could only work on weekly and monthly newspapers where they would not be heard. The unprecedented proliferation of the press, said the speaker, had created 'an ocean one millimetre deep', with newspapers that lacked solid foundations and could be blown away by the slightest breeze.[12] Other speakers described an industry with poor technical resources,[13] operating in a historical environment of mistrust between the state and the press.[14] A journalist with more than 40 years of experience likened reporting in Iran to walking through a minefield, especially difficult 'in the early days of a civil society, when the location of the mines is not clear.' Good news reporting, said the speaker, required the ability to collect reliable data, a task that was particularly difficult in Iran where even ordinary people would censor themselves in everyday conversation, let alone organizations that, for instance, might be reluctant to provide a journalist with official photographs to illustrate a report.[15]

Photojournalism, without cameras

Papers on journalists' education and training revealed a very disturbing picture. Ninety per cent of the country's working journalists had had no training or education related to journalism.[16] While huge numbers of high-school graduates were keen to study medicine or engineering, or even to enter the police and military academies – 'thanks to the permanent presence of police series on Iranian television' – very few were eager to study journalism. No journalism college had a serious student newspaper, and some even lacked the resources for the production of photocopied student papers. Very few of the 150 journalism graduates leaving colleges and training centres every year entered the profession. There were no journalism students working as trainees on any of the large number of daily newspapers in Tehran.[17] Fifty per cent of a sample of final year journalism students had never been to the editorial offices of any newspaper.[18] And there were students who had finished photojournalism courses without ever having taken a photograph.[19]

Another speaker said that while newspapers were legally allowed to publish the views of 'the public and the authorities, constructive criticism, suggestions and explanations',[20] there was no accepted definition of constructive criticism, nor was there any definition of criticism accepted both by the Iranian statesmen and by the country's journalists. Although 27,000 lines of texts on journalism had been produced in the country during the preceding 40 years, only about 0.5 per cent of it had dealt with writing critique – and, at that, mostly in arts or sports.[21] In a highly polarized political environment, some newspapers opposed to the reform movement had adopted a style that one speaker described as 'lumpenist', with a vocabulary that included not only innuendos and ridicule, but also open personal insults.[22]

Jameath, Tous, Neshat – musical newspaper licences

All these issues came into play in the first few months in the life of the independent daily, *Jameah* (Society) that described itself as 'the first newspaper of the civil society in Iran'. The paper was founded in February 1998 by Hamid-Reza Jalaiepour, who had been a local governor in Kurdistan from the early days of the Islamic Republic until the end of the war with Iraq in 1988. Later, he had gone to Britain on a scholarship and received a PhD in political sociology from the University of London. Upon returning to Iran in April 1997, Mr Jalaiepour had first sought to set up a private university teaching humanities, but had been informed by officials that such a move would be against the Islamic Republic's Constitution. He had then thought of setting up 'a cultural institution, from primary to high school', but had not found any partners, and had also realized that it would not be easy for him to obtain the necessary permit for such an enterprise. At this point, he had 'thought of establishing a private, independent newspaper', for which he was able to obtain a licence from President Khatami's administration. Mr Jalaiepour was joined by Mohammad-Mohsen Sazegara, who had been one of the founders of the Islamic Revolutionary Guards Corps, a Deputy Minister of Industries, and a founder of the Press Cooperative. Mr Sazegara became the Managing Director of the newspaper publishing company, Jameah Rouz. Mashaallah Shamsolva'ezin, a former editor of *Kayhan* daily and *Kayhan-e Farhangi* (Cultural Kayhan) monthly, who had been editing the Islamic intellectual monthly *Kian*, took over as the new paper's editor.[23]

In a 10-point declaration in *Jameah*'s first issue, Mr Shamsolva'ezin declared the newspaper's commitment to professional 'dissemination of information, within the framework of the Press Law, without any judgement or prejudice'; the paper's respect for 'all institutions, parties, organizations and social groups, be they modern or traditional'; and its intention to help the government by 'careful scrutiny of the operations of all official institutions'. The paper was also going to publish all its articles, reports and pictures with the 'real names and identities' of their producers, as 'a mark of respect' for them and 'in order to train a responsible and courageous staff'.[24]

On 24 May 1988, before *Jameah* had reached its 100th issue, Mr Jalaiepour appeared for the first of two court hearings, in front of a jury, on six charges. One had come from a woman publisher who had accused the paper of libel for having said that her firm had recently published mostly calendars and diaries, rather than books. The Revolutionary Guards Corps had filed two complaints, accusing the paper of discrediting the Corps and libelling its Commander, General Rahim Safavi, by publishing reports and comments about a speech in which he had said some newspapers were undermining national security; that 'the roots of counter-revolution will be cut off'; and that 'there are those whom we must behead and those whose tongues we shall cut off.' Some of the commentators quoted by *Jameah* had likened General Safavi to Pol Pot and Saddam Hussein.

The Prosecutor General had accused *Jameah* of disturbing the public's mind, publishing anti-Islamic material, libelling the Judiciary, and promoting indecency by publishing material that included cartoons about limits on the freedom of expression, a photograph of a group of men clapping as one of them danced, passages from a novel in which the contours of an attractive girl's face and shoulders had been described, and an article by a clergyman saying that the rule of the Taliban in Afghanistan and that of the clerical establishment in Iran were based on identical theological foundations. There was also a complaint from Bonyad-e Mostaz'afan va Janbazan that accused the paper of discrediting it by linking it to the financial corruption case for which Morteza Rafiqdoust, the brother of the Foundation's Director, Mohsen Rafiqdoust, had been imprisoned, and for suggesting, in a satirical column, that Mr Rafiqdoust should receive the title of 'The Driving Commander', for having driven the vehicle that took Ayatollah Khomeini from Tehran airport to the Behesht-e Zahra cemetery after his return to Iran in 1979. The prison authorities had accused *Jameah* of having discredited them by falsely reporting that Morteza Rafiqdoust had been allowed to travel abroad, while serving a prison term.[25]

The 'old flames' and the forgotten image

Between the two hearings, the publication of a front page photograph of an ageing couple sitting against a wall covered with the faint image of the former President Bani-Sadr, now in exile as a prominent opponent of the Islamic Republic, was added to *Jameah*'s indictment. The picture, with a romantic caption about sweet old times, was also attacked by Mr Mohajerani, the Minister of Culture and Islamic Guidance. Writing in his own column in the daily *Ettela'at*, Mr Mohajerani said there would have to be 'serious doubts about the competence' of the paper's manager and editor, if they had not noticed the Bani-Sadr image. If the picture had been printed deliberately, in full knowledge of the image concerned, said the Minister, then the manager and the editor had in effect 'committed an act of aggression against the Revolution and the people.' In his reply, *Jameah*'s editor, Mr Shamsolva'ezin, said the publication of the picture had been a mistake, and that no one on the paper's editorial staff had noticed the barely visible image in the background. He also said that if every institution in the country were operating to the same standards of quality that were expected of the press, then 'all of the country's problems would have been resolved'. Mr Mohajerani himself came under attack by *Jomhouri-e Eslami* for having adopted 'tolerance and moderation' as his Ministry's motto and for having declared his support for *Jameah* by visiting the paper's offices soon after its launch.[26] The trial ended on 22 July 1998 with the Court of Appeal confirming the withdrawal of the paper's licence, a cash fine imposed on Mr Jalaiepour, and banning him from newspaper publishing for two months.[27]

Immediately after the Appeal Court's decision, *Jameah* was replaced on the news-stands by another daily, *Tous*, identical to the banned paper in every respect other than name, with the same editorial staff. Speaking at the following Friday Prayers, the head of the Judiciary, Ayatollah Yazdi, pointed out that in the late 1940s and early 1950s, the pro-Soviet Tudeh Party had engaged in the practice of using a stock of publishing licenses to launch a new paper as soon as one of its publications had been banned. Without naming *Tous*, Ayatollah Yazdi called on the Tehran Justice Office to act according to an article in the press law that prohibited the publication of a newspaper so similar to another paper that the two could be mistaken for each other. The following day, the offices of *Tous* were broken into by a group who also beat up Mr Shamsolva'ezin, saying the paper's publication had been illegal, because it had been identical to *Jameah*.

The next day, the Press Court issued a statement saying *Tous* was 'in no way a new newspaper' and was now being 'banned until further notice'. The statement said *Tous* had also committed other offences including 'the publication of the picture of an uncovered sportswoman', questioning the powers of the Guardian Council in vetting the candidates for parliamentary elections, publishing a commentary in which a fate similar to that of Chile's Salvador Allende and Iran's Dr Mohammad Mosaddeq had been implied for President Khatami, and insulting the Head of the Expediency Council, former President Rafsanjani, by describing him as 'dastard'. However, following an intervention by the Ministry of Culture and Islamic Guidance, and protests by students at Tehran University, a deal was reached, with the sentence to be commuted to a cash fine. *Tous* was allowed to resume publication on 4 August 1998, with a front page that was noticeably different from that of *Jameah*. The one-day gap had been filled by another daily, *Aftab-e Emrouz* (Today's Sunshine).[28]

'The cultural offensive'

During the summer of 1998, there were repeated attacks by senior figures against Iran's new press. In addition to Ayatollah Yazdi, a member of the Council of Guardians, Ayatollah Jannati, and former President Rafsanjani's Foreign Minister, Dr Ali-Akbar Velayati, said the 'mushrooming' newspapers were insulting the great religious leaders, including the late Ayatollah Khomeini, and 'promoting corruption, disregard for the Islamic hijab and free relationship between women and men.' The Minister of Culture and Islamic Guidance, Mr Mohajerani, was asked 'to take action so that there would be no need for others to do so'. A conservative member of the Majlis's presiding board, Mohammad-Reza Bahonar, said the Minister could be questioned about the conditions of the press.[29]

Ayatollah Khamenei himself repeatedly warned against a 'cultural offensive by the West' with its 'old technique of "divide and rule" ', sometimes using 'negligent, careless elements' within the Islamic Republic. At a meeting with the Revolutionary Guards Corps' commanders and officers on 16 September 1998, Ayatollah Khamenei said there were those who wanted the nation to forget the memories of the war, 'in which they were not present', and called for measures to do 'the exact opposite and maintain the glorious memory of the great days of the Holy Defence.' He also said the Islamic Republic believed in 'freedom of expression and freedom of social activities', but these freedoms were limited by Islam. There was no 'freedom to commit treason' or to 'conspire'. He said he was giving 'the officials an ultimatum' to 'take action, to see which newspaper is stepping beyond the limits of freedom'.[30]

The French Connection

The following day, the publisher of *Tous* once again received a judicial notice, informing him that the paper had carried 'material contrary to the country's security and public interest' and that its publication was being stopped until a full investigation had been carried out. The only specific reason given for the paper's closure was that it had insulted Ayatollah Khomeini by quoting the former French President, Valéry Giscard d'Estaing, as having said that Ayatollah Khomeini had applied for asylum after arriving in France from his exile in Iraq in 1978. Mr d'Estaing's statement was denied by several authorities, including the organization in charge of publishing Ayatollah Khomeini's works, which said that although the interview had been factually incorrect, it did not constitute an insult against the Ayatollah.[31] Nonetheless, at a meeting 12 days after the closure of *Tous*, the Press Supervisory Board, on which the Ministry of Culture and Islamic Guidance was represented, revoked the paper's licence.[32]

On the day *Tous* was closed, Revolutionary Court bailiffs were stationed at the paper's offices with arrest warrants for the publisher, Mohammad-Sadeq Javadi-Hessar, the editor, Mashaallah Shamsolva'ezin, Chairman of the publishing company, Jameah Rouz, Hamid-Reza Jalaiepour, the company's Managing Director, Mohammad-Mohsen Sazegara, and the paper's satirist, Seyyed-Ebrahim Nabavi. Judiciary officials had already visited *Tous*'s print-works and stopped its distribution. Messrs Javadi-Hessar, Shamsolva'ezin, and Jalaiepour were arrested on the same day;[33] Mr Nabavi, who had been away from Tehran at the time, turned himself in three days later.[34] Mr Sazegara, who was on a visit abroad, returned to Iran but was hospitalized because of a heart condition and remained under medical care until his four colleagues were released on bail,[35] at different intervals, by 20 October, two days before elections to the Assembly of Experts.[36]

Mr Mohajerani supported the closure of *Tous*, which happened while he was on a visit to Lebanon and 80 members of the conservative majority in the Majlis had signed a letter calling for him to attend a parliamentary hearing. Speaking to the Lebanese daily, *Assafir* (Messenger), Mr Mohajerani said those in charge of *Tous* had believed that the right wing of the Islamic Republic had been defeated in the Presidential elections and that they could replace President Khatami, just as Boris Yeltsin had succeeded President Gorbachev in the former Soviet Union. Mr Mohajerani also said *Tous* had pretended to support President Khatami, but had in fact been speaking for *Nehzat-e Azadi-ye Iran* (Iran Freedom Movement). The Iran Freedom Movement's leader, Dr Ebrahim Yazdi, denied any affiliation with the paper, saying that Mr Mohajerani was merely defending himself against the right wing of the Islamic Republic.[37] The Mojahedin of the Islamic Revolution, a political organization that had supported President Khatami, described Mr Mohajerani's stand as 'completely passive and opportunistic', while a conservative politician, Ahmad Tavakoli, who had been Mr Khatami's rival during the June 1997 Presidential elections, said the Minister should have stopped *Tous* as soon as it was launched.[38] During his successful defence against a motion of censure by conservative Majlis deputies on 1 May 1999, Mr Mohajerani questioned the validity of the charges against the five *Tous* defendants, including the capital offence of 'having waged war against God' and of having been paid by foreign powers, pointing out that the five had been released without any of the accusations being followed up.[39]

Mr Nabavi was jailed again the following year and both he and Mr Sazegara later went abroad where they became active against the Islamic Republic. Mr Nabavi continued to write satire and performed comedy programmes and Mr Sazegara became a founding member of wide-ranging alliance calling for a referendum to change Iran's constitution. Mr Javadi-Hessar was unable to continue working as a newspaper publisher, but Messrs Shamsolva'ezin and Jalaiepour resumed their work, using the licence for a daily newspaper called *Neshat* (Joy), held by a former member of the Islamic Majlis, Latif Safari.[40] *Neshat* appeared first on 19 February 1999 and was closed down by the Press Court Judge Saied Mortazavi on 3 September 1999 after it had published an article against the death penalty written by an exiled Iranian political activist, Hossein Bagherzadeh; an article on the Islamic punishment of *qesas* (retribution) by a contributor to several pro-reform newspapers, Emadeddin Baqi; and a critical open letter to the Supreme Leader, Ayatollah Khamenei, by Ezatollah Sahabi, who had been a minister and a member of parliament in the early months of the Revolution.[41] Messrs Shamsolva'ezin, Baqi, and Safari were imprisoned.

Prizes for banned papers

The Sixth Press Festival that had been due to start on 1 May 1999 was opened a day earlier to avoid a clash with Mr Mohajerani's censure. By now, the number of newspapers in the country had reached 930,[42] with a total circulation of 2.7 million copies.[43] The 7-member Press Festival jury, once again selected by the journalists themselves, included its first woman member (Laila Rastegar).[44] The Jury said submissions in descriptive reporting, graphic arts, children's stories, and satire had shown an improvement over the past years, but there had been a 'lack of quality' in other categories including Islamic studies and cultural articles. Submissions in the coverage of news and humanities had been so poor that no prizes could be awarded.[45] Thirteen of the top awards went to the banned daily *Jameah* and three to *Salam*, while several conservative papers including the dailies, *Kayhan*, *Resalat*, *Abrar* (The Free), and *Qods* (Jerusalem) had refused to attend the Festival.[46] Eight out of forty-six of the award winners (17.4 per cent) were women,[47] including a designer of bilingual, Persian–English crossword puzzles (*Shahla Keshavarznejad*).[48] Many of the awards had gone to strongly critical pieces. An article by the managing editor of the daily *Kar-o Kargar* (Work and Worker), Ali Rabi'i, written just after the November 1997 killing of nationalist political activists, Daryoush and Parvaneh Forouhar, said their cases and the suspected murders of other 'harmless' dissidents had to be investigated thoroughly, otherwise the 'defenders of the Revolution' were going to be the 'only losers'.[49] Other articles commemorated two writers, Mohammad Mokhtari and Mohammad-Ja'far Pouyandeh, who had been killed a few days after the Forouhars, in what became commonly known as the 'serial murders'. A cartoon in the daily *Zan*, banned shortly before the Festival, showed a writer shot in the head, with blood flowing out of the wound, but still writing, using the smoking barrel of a gun as his pen.[50] An award winning photograph in the independent political monthly *Payam-e Emrouz* (Today's Message) showed a scene from Mr Pouyandeh's funeral, with passages from his recently published translation of the Universal Declaration of Human Rights being carried by the mourners as banners.[51] The country's legal system, especially its treatment of journalists and that of the former Tehran Mayor, Mr Karbaschi, who had been jailed on charges of embezzlement, was sharply criticized in articles carried by *Jameah*,[52] and the monthly *Hoqouq va Ejtema'* (Law and Society).[53] A series of reports in the weekly *Iran-e Javan* (Young Iran), published by the national news agency, IRNA, gave graphic accounts of AIDS patients at a Tehran hospital; drugs use and drugs dealing in a park in the centre of the city; poor people offering their kidneys for sale; municipality officials demolishing a house in a poor south Tehran neighbourhood, saying it had been built without a permit; drug addicts in a vacant lot nearby, where the ground was littered with used hypodermic needles; and youngsters in rich north Tehran having fun by daring each other into shoplifting, knowing that if caught, they would be bailed out by their families.[54]

Criticizing the leader

A survey of the Iranian press for the years 1994–99 found that in that period, the amount of 'sensitive' criticism, dealing directly with the authorities, rather than with 'the state of traffic and potholes on the streets', had increased by 10 times. The reformist papers had carried much more sensitive criticism than the conservative ones and had directed their comments at the Judiciary, the Legislature, radio and television and 'anonymous political forces, including pressure groups'. Criticism in the 'right wing' press had been 'less concerned with public interest', 'more despairing' and 'more abusive', and directed mostly at the Ministry of Culture and Islamic Guidance and the other faction's newspapers and journalists. The survey found that in this period, for the first time since the Revolution, the press had 'entered very sensitive areas', not only by criticizing the President frequently, but also with its unprecedented criticisms of the Supreme Leader.[55]

Seen through the eyes of the conservative faction, the reformist papers – especially the sequence of *Jameah*, *Tous*, and *Neshat*, which the conservatives labelled as the 'serial papers' – had attacked religious faith by suggesting that differences in religions were rooted in geographical and environmental conditions and that all interpretations of religion were equally valid. They had attacked Shi'ite jurisprudence by saying that it was providing a pretext for those intent on promoting violence and had undermined Shi'ite mourning rituals by suggesting that they promoted sorrow or celebrated violence. They had promoted licentiousness by publishing pictures of pre-Revolution women singers and movie stars and encouraged relationships between boys and girls and, especially in the case of the official news agency's monthly, *Iran-e Javan*, had attracted 'customers by provocative reports and stories' and 'making use of sexual liberalism' by publishing 'provocative colour pictures and images'. The papers were also accused of having attacked the principle of *Velayat-e Faqih*, the rule of the Moslem jurisconsult, by describing it as dictatorial, and having attacked the Constitution by saying its Islamic jurisprudential outlook had led to contradictions and shortcomings. The 'serial papers' were also accused of having been a source of material for and supported by the opponents of the Islamic Republic abroad, 'demonstrating that the two were acting in tandem'.[56]

Iran's Sixth Press Law

In the autumn of 1998 and the first half of 1999, Ayatollah Khamenei issued more warnings against the 'cultural offensive' and called for countermeasures. He said the seminaries had to provide accurate answers to doubts about religious principles that were being raised, among others, by 'foreign radio stations'. 'Lovers of the system, Islam and Revolution' had to be 'vigilant and appreciate the value of the country's young population'. Those in charge of higher education had to try and instil religious faith in young university students and 'appropriately confront' any obstacles to this process. Although the press was 'a pillar' of people's freedom and their rights, 'not everything' that was going on 'in the press and the field of journalism' could be accepted, at the cost of ignoring 'the obvious, constantly rising, cultural dangers against the people's mind, religion and faith.' Artistic works 'with destructive moral effects' were not 'at all answerable' and had 'to be stopped in earnest', without the officials and publishers losing sight of this 'target in the hue and cry against censorship'. The Majlis had made the right decision to ban the use of satellite TV images, and 'parallel measures' had to be taken to 'immunize the youths' minds and thoughts.' [57]

On 30 May 1999, the Majlis began its first reading of a bill to amend the 1986 press law. The introduction of the bill led to strong criticism from the reformist press who argued that it would, firstly, diminish the influence of the Ministry of Culture and Islamic Guidance on the press by adding two clergymen to the Press Supervisory Board, which was in charge of examining newspaper licence applications and also allocated subsidies to newspapers. Secondly, said the critics, the bill would make it possible for the Press Court Jury to be appointed by Judiciary officials alone, rather than by representatives of the three powers. Thirdly, it would hold responsible not only the publishers, but also individual writers, for any offences caused by their work.[58] The bill passed its first reading on 6 July 1999,[59] in spite of strong protests inside and outside the Majlis.

On the same day, *Salam* ran a front page report, saying that amending the press law had been recommended by Saied Eslami,[60] also known as Emami, a senior Intelligence Ministry official who had been named as the chief culprit in the assassination of the Forouhars, Mokhtari, and Pouyandeh. Two weeks before the Majlis vote, Saied Emami had been officially reported to have committed suicide while in prison. Not only was the *Salam* report not able to cause the defeat of the bill, but it also led to the Special Court for the Clergy ordering the paper's publisher, Hojjatoleslam Khoeiniha, to stop its publication immediately, pending trial.[61] The decision was criticized by many, including the Minister of Culture and Islamic Guidance, Mr Mohajerani, who said that rather than being banned, *Salam* should have been given an award for having exposed a 'trend that began with threatening intellectuals, the press and writers and ended in killing the writers'. Mr Mohajerani also said that under the Constitution, press offences could only be dealt with by the Press Court, rather than by the Special Court for the Clergy or the Revolutionary Court.[62] *Salam*'s closure led to four days of protests by students at Tehran University's halls of residence, followed by another two days of riots in central Tehran, which were put down by the police and plainclothes security agents. At least one person was killed.

'Immunizing the youths'

Later, in 1999 and early 2000, there were many more criticisms of the press by Ayatollah Khamenei and senior religious figures based in Qom.[63] In August 1999, Ayatollah Khamenei repeated his call on officials to 'immunize' the young generation 'against the enemies' poisonous forces'. He said he could not accept that the press would 'lie to the people' and become 'the mouthpiece of Radio Israel or Radio America in the country', and suggested that the death sentence could be imposed on anyone denying an Islamic principle, such as *qesas*, a clear reference to the controversial pieces in *Neshat*. At a meeting with members of the Supreme Cultural Revolution Council in December, Ayatollah Khamenei said he was not 'satisfied with the Ministry of [Culture and Islamic] Guidance'. He pointed out that the Minister, Mr Mohajerani, himself a member of the Council, did 'not appear to be at the meeting, having relieved himself of hearing these words', and added that it did 'not matter whether or not' the Minister was there, but it did matter that the Ministry had done 'nothing Islamic' during the two years that Mr Mohajerani had been in charge. Ayatollah Khamenei said although he was protesting to the national radio and television 'once a week or less frequently, sometimes in a strong tone', the organization had made plenty of Islamic programmes, whereas halls affiliated to the Ministry of Guidance were displaying 'one hundred per cent anti-religion and counter-revolutionary' works. Two days later, addressing the Friday Prayers meeting in Tehran, he said some of the domestic media belonged 'to the enemy' and were 'lying' and 'crying out all the time, complaining of oppression'.[64]

Ayatollah Khamenei's next comment on the press followed the assassination attempt in March 2000 on a leading reformist politician, Saied Hajjarian, a key figure in the reformists' landslide victory in the Majlis elections held the same month.[65] In a letter to President Khatami, Ayatollah Khamenei said the 'criminal agents' involved in the attack had to be uncovered and prosecuted, lest the attempt 'should lead to ambiguities and rumours as was the case with the serial killings' of dissidents in November 1997. He added that there were 'tongues and pens intensively creating turbulence and rumours [...] levelling unfounded accusations against named individuals and even raising doubts about responsible organizations such as the [Revolutionary] Guards [Corps] and the *baseej*'.[66] Those who had carried out the attack on Mr Hajjarian were tried later and received light sentences.[67]

The Berlin Conference

Political tension in Iran rose further in April 2000 with the disruption of a conference in Berlin that had been aimed at discussing the reformists' victory in the Majlis elections. The conference had been organized by the German cultural organization, the Heinrich Böll Foundation, which had invited 17 prominent public figures, including several journalists, from Iran. On the first day of the conference, some Iranian opposition activists based in the West shouted abuse at the Islamic Republic's leaders and at the guest speakers. At one point, a woman protestor disrobed down to her underwear and a scarf and began dancing in the isles and a man took all his clothes off, ostensibly to show the marks of torture on his body. Attempts by the organizers to establish calm failed and the meeting could only be held the following day under strict security. The disruption, including the naked protests, was covered in a report on Iranian television that suggested the speakers had silently observed the verbal attacks on Iran's leaders and the display of nudity. In fact, several of the speakers had defended the Islamic Republic, at the cost of having more personal abuse hurled against them. Others had not been in the conference hall at the time of the protests and footage of their appearance on other panels had been edited in with scenes from the first day.

There were widespread protests against the misleading television coverage, but the political storm was intensified when the daily *Kayhan* carried the Persian translation of a German newspaper's interview with one of the speakers, the campaigning journalist, Akbar Ganji, with a headline attributed to him, saying that 'Ayatollah Khomeini will go to the museum of history.' Mr Ganji denied that he had made such a statement and the German newspaper said that it, rather than the interviewee, had chosen the words used in the headline. However, all the participants were summoned by the Revolutionary Court to be tried on charges of having undermined national security. Of the 17 participants, 2 did not return to Iran. The rest were tried and acquitted, even though 6 of them, including 2 of the 4 women participants, were imprisoned briefly. Three men, Ezatollah Sahabi, Akbar Ganji, and Ali-Reza Afshari, received longer prison sentences, on charges not related to the Berlin Conference.[68]

'Enemy bases' in the press

Meanwhile, another battle was raging in the country, with the conservative majority at the Fifth Majlis preparing to have the new press law approved in the last days of its term, and the reformist winners of elections to the Sixth Majlis declaring that changing the law would be one of their highest priorities. In a speech on 14 April, four days before the Majlis vote, Ayatollah Khamenei condemned foreign radio stations that had been set up 'to create tension in Iran and divide the Iranian people', and spoke of the 'truly sad story' of 'some who trust the enemy more than their friends' and would 'repeat the enemy's words in order to spite the friend'. On 20 April, two days after the bill had been passed, Ayatollah Khamenei said although there were 'good people working in many newspapers', some papers had become 'enemy bases.' There were '10 or 15 newspapers', he said, that appeared 'to be directed from the same centre', with the aim of 'making the people pessimistic about the system', running headlines that would make anyone 'think everything in the country had been lost.' He described this as 'journalistic charlatanism', which did not exist even in the West.[69] Within a week of the speech, the Judiciary had closed down 16 reformist newspapers, including *Mosharekat* (Participation), organ of the National Participation Front, using a 1960 law aimed at crime prevention.[70]

On 28 April, *Mosharekat's* licence holder and party leader and President Khatami's brother, Mohammad-Reza Khatami, as well as six other reformist newspaper publishers attended a meeting with Ayatollah Khamenei, who strongly criticized 'the state of some newspapers and the presence of counter-revolutionary and opposition elements' in them. 'One deviant tendency in the press', he said, was

> causing anxiety and disturbing the public's mind, avoiding the people's main issues and problems [...] The approach adopted by some friends towards this deviant trend is wrong and inefficient and in effect makes it possible for the enemies of the system to abuse the press. Therefore, it is necessary to review that approach.[71]

The Sixth Majlis was inaugurated on 27 May 2000, dominated by reformists, including 10 journalists, three of whom were elected to the Majlis's presiding board.[72] Three weeks later, the Majlis approved the single urgency of a bill to amend the press law that had been passed by the conservatives during the previous term. However, the Speaker of Majlis, Hojjatoleslam Mehdi Karroubi, later removed the bill from the agenda upon receipt of a handwritten letter from Ayatollah Khamenei, dated 6 August 2000, which said,

> should the enemies of Islam, the Revolution and the Islamic system take the press in their hands, a great danger would threaten the people's security, unity and faith and I do not consider it permissible for myself or for other authorities to remain silent in this vital matter. The present law has been able to some extent to prevent this great calamity from occurring and it would not be legitimate or in the interests of the system and the country to change it in line with what has been stipulated by the Majlis Committee.[73]

Thus failed the first of many attempts by the reformists to introduce new legislation during their four years at the Majlis.

Mourning at the Festival

Because of the sudden closure of a large number of newspapers, for the first time since its inauguration in 1994 the Press Festival could not be held in spring and opened instead on 7 August 2000, Iran's Reporter's Day,[74] named after Mahmoud Saremi, a correspondent for the national news agency, IRNA, who had been killed by the Taliban in Afghanisthan in 1998.

There were now two women on the jury, compared to only one the year before, but fewer women among the award winners – 6 out of 52, or 11.5 per cent, compared to 17.4 per cent the previous year. One jury member, Ahmad Zeidabadi, himself the top award winner at the Fifth Festival, was detained shortly before the winners were to be selected. Two of the award winners went to prison soon after the ceremony: the political columnist, Mohammad Qouchani,[75] and Seyyed-Ebrahim Nabavi,[76] whose entries had satirized the official reports about the suicide of the former senior Intelligence Ministry official, Saied Emami. The winning pieces included 19 entries from the daily, *Aftab-e Emrouz*, and 11 from *Neshat*, both of which had been shut down by the time the awards were announced. Eleven winning pieces had been entered by the weekly *Iran-e Javan*, which was closed down less than two months after the Festival. The monthly *Payam-e Emrouz*, with two award winning pictures of the 1999 student protests and five feature reports, including the most detailed background on Saied Emami, was closed down several months later. While the award winning photographs and graphic arts entries were sharper and more lucid than the previous years, the political and economic commentaries were long, ponderous and convoluted, reflecting the complexities of the time and, perhaps, the writers' efforts not to commit themselves directly to anything that could lead to their incrimination. The jury members themselves acknowledged the point, saying 'with certainty' that 'many valuable articles, editorials, reports, news stories, interviews, analyses, etc. must have been written in the past year, some of which did not find their way into the Festival for various reasons.'[77]

In the interval between the Fifth and Sixth Press Festivals, May 1998–May 1999, a total of 9 newspapers had been banned, 2 of them by the Press Court, and the rest by the Special Court for the Clergy, the Revolutionary Court, and the Press Supervisory Board, which was dominated by the Ministry of Culture and Islamic Guidance. By the time the Seventh Festival's awards were handed out (12 August 2000), 23 other publications had been banned – 21 of them by the Press Court[78] – with a total loss of circulation of about 3 million copies.[79] About 1,450 people had lost their jobs.[80] In his speech at the awards ceremony, the President of the Association of Iranian Journalists, Ali Mazru'i, said it would have been more appropriate to call the event 'The Press Funeral'.[81]

6   The second fall (2001–04)

Mr Mohajerani resigned as Minister of Culture and Islamic Guidance early in 2001, without any official explanation being given. He was appointed by President Khatami as the head of a recently established centre that was meant to pursue the President's call for dialogue among civilizations. The appointment led to speculation that Mr Mohajerani would repeat the experience of Khatami who had become President after heading Iran's National Library, following his resignation as Minister of Culture and Islamic Guidance in 1992. However, Mr Mohajerani resigned from the International Centre for Dialogue Among Civilizations in July 2003 amid press reports of problems in his personal life, because of which he was later imprisoned briefly.[1]

By May 2001, when the Eighth Press Festival was inaugurated by Mr Mohajerani's successor as Minister of Culture and Islamic Guidance, Ahmad Masjed-Jame'i, 23 more newspapers had been closed down. Fifteen closures had been ordered by the Judiciary, nine of them based on the 1960 crime prevention law which, in the words of President Khatami and other government officials, had been originally aimed at 'knife-wielders', thugs, and bandits, rather than the press.[2] The Judiciary defended the legislation as 'one of the progressive laws in the world' and said the banned newspapers had been staffed by communists,[3] and many complaints had been filed against them.[4] The Press Supervisory Board, which had been accused of negligence in preventing moral decline, had closed down seven newspapers, mostly for violations of Article 2 of the Press Law that instructs the press to promote the goals of the Islamic Republic's Constitution, or Article 10 that bans 'the instrumental [i.e. exploitative] use of individuals – men or women – in pictures or content and the denigration of women, promotion of ostentatious displays and illegitimate and illegal luxuries'. Seventeen journalists had also been imprisoned, although some of them were later released.[5]

Disappointment among journalists was clearly displayed when only a few attended a meeting on 'Job Security and Professional Independence', organized as part of the 2001 Press Festival.[6] At a meeting on 'The Press and the Law', a member of the Majlis Judicial Committee said newspapers had become 'politicized and personalized', carrying more critical material about Islam and religious personalities than about corruption and red tape in the government.[7] The most positive assessment of the state of the press came from a politician–journalist,

Mohsen Armin, who had entered the Majlis in the 2000 elections and was now one of its two deputy speakers. Mr Armin said political development in Iran had 'started with the Islamic Revolution and reached a turning point' with President Khatami's election. 'Now', he added, 'we see that instead of turning up as corpses in wastelands, writers such as Mr Ganji or Mr Shamsolva'ezin go to prison. This shows that the society has reached a high level of political development and can achieve higher goals.'[8]

The awards at the Eighth Press Festival demonstrated the continued under-representation of women, although they had won 15.8 per cent of the prizes, a rise over the Seventh Festival's 12.2 per cent. Deficiencies were evident in journalists' professional education and training. While 85 per cent of the award winners at both festivals had had university education, the share of journalism graduates had fallen from 14 per cent to 4.8 per cent, once again raising the question whether the country's universities were 'unable to produce qualified human resources for the press', or the press was operating in 'a non-specialized fashion, as is the case in other sectors' of the country's economy. However, 78.6 per cent of the award winners had considered journalism training, especially the use of the internet, to be essential and had asked for journalism education to be brought up to date. Seventy per cent of the winners at both festivals were under the age of 35, and 60 per cent had spent less than 10 years in journalism, both figures 'potentially confirming the point that many of the damages suffered by the country's press' had resulted from 'the immaturity of many of the journalists'. The large numbers of people who had entered the rapidly growing press since President Khatami's 1997 election could 'in the not too distant future turn into a specialized and skilled workforce', if the state could 'increase its tolerance of journalistic errors, and newspapers would not be shut down on the slightest pretexts'.[9]

'Nationwide disappointment and frustration'

The depressed state of the press was matched by a decline in public participation in politics that was demonstrated a few weeks later, in the 2001 Presidential election. Although President Khatami won a second term with 22 million votes, even more than his first victory, some 14 million eligible voters did not go to the polls. By autumn 2001, *Rasaneh*, the Ministry of Culture and Islamic Guidance's quarterly on media studies and research, was describing an atmosphere of 'rejection, dismissal, aggression, violence and sometimes hatred' between some statesmen and the press, which the statesmen regarded as 'irritating, rebellious and hostile' and in need of being 'got rid of'. Newspapers, said *Rasaneh*, had tried to say instantly what should have been said during several years, because there were no guarantees that they would last that long. A sense of security, stability, and permanence could lead to greater calm and moderation governing the behaviour of the press. If the press were to be weakened, *Rasaneh* warned, 'the mutually understood rationality favoured by Habermas, which is based on the strengthening of the society's verbal skills, will be replaced by the rule of an instrumental rationality and an instrumentalized human being, and humanity and spirituality would fade away'.[10]

Habermasian views notwithstanding, a few months later, the Judiciary banned the press from discussing the subject of negotiations with the United States, leading *Rasaneh* to wonder if the newspapers were indeed so important that they could affect an issue by merely talking about it. If they were, asked the journal, why were they treated disrespectfully at times? And if they did not matter, why take 'such harsh action against them?'[11]

By winter 2002, *Rasaneh* was reporting visible 'disappointment, passivity or a "crisis of participation" ' with respect to the profession of journalism. Very few journalists were attending speeches, discussions or training courses, including online journalism courses which they themselves had described as a priority. They were spending very little time reading specialist material, 'including *Rasaneh* or research documents and books that are produced with so much toil and trouble'. There was almost no contact between journalism colleges, with graduates who had not been to any editorial offices, and newspapers with mostly young and inexperienced managers, senior editors, and editors. While the lack of interest in learning could be partly blamed on some journalists' 'professional arrogance', it was also true that 'fear of the future' dominated the minds of newspaper publishers who were fighting for survival. Such an atmosphere, said the journal, was not conducive to investment in training, research, and development.[12]

The banning finger moves on

Between the Eighth and Ninth Press Festivals, May 2001–August 2002, 20 more newspapers were banned.[13] One paper had been closed by the Special Court for the Clergy;[14] five by the Press Supervisory Board for 'excessive coverage of crimes, sensational headlines, and promotion of material contrary to public decency', failing to promote the goals of the Islamic Republic's Constitution, or disregarding the ban on 'the instrumental use of individuals' and 'dissemination of rumours, untruthful material or distorting the works of others'.[15] The other 14 titles had been closed down by Judiciary, using the 1960 crime prevention law in only two cases,[16] and banning the rest for reasons including 'publication of lies to disturb the public's mind',[17] ignoring instructions from the Supreme National Security Council,[18] or insulting the President.[19] The weekly *Asr-e Ma* (Our Age), organ of the Organization of the Mojahedin of the Islamic Revolution, led by the Majlis deputy speaker, Mohsen Armin, was banned for 'insulting the religious sanctities and beliefs, propaganda against the system, and publishing lies and insults'. Tehran Municipality's monthly *Hamshahri-ye Mah* (Monthly Hamshahri) was banned, 12 months after its launch, for 'not having had a publication licence'. The daily *Iran*, the licence for which was held by the Ministry of Culture and Islamic Guidance, was banned on 3 May 2002 for 'insulting the religious sanctities and beliefs and promoting vice', but the Press Court's decision was overturned the following day by the head of the judiciary, Ayatollah Hashemi-Shahroudi.[20]

Two of the closures by the Press Court were related to the new daily newspaper of the Islamic Participation Front, the biggest party supporting President Khatami, which had replaced the party's banned paper, *Mosharekat*. The new daily first appeared in April 2001 as *Nowrouz* (New Day, the name of the Iranian

New Year's Day), with a licence in the name of the party leader, Mohammad-Reza Khatami. *Nowrouz* was stopped in July and was banned a year later, following the longest press trial in the Islamic Republic, having been found guilty of 'propaganda against the Islamic Republic and slandering its officials; publishing lies with the aim of disturbing the public's mind; supporting and defending anti-religious elements; cleansing the image of louts and hooligans involved in street riots and encouraging them to riot and disturb law and order'.[21] Two weeks later, the paper's planned successor, *Rouz-e Now* (also meaning New Day), was banned because 'its name was similar to *Nowrouz*'.[22] On the same day, the one-week old daily *Ayneh-ye Jonoub* (Mirror of the South) was also banned for having employed opposition activists.[23] The decisions came on Iran's Reporter's Day, 7 August 2002, hours after the end of the Ninth Press Festival.[24]

The jury at the Ninth Festival said the works they had reviewed had shown the need for professional independence, job security and continuous training. First prizes could not be awarded in some categories because of the dearth of investigative reporting, critique and analysis, and technical weaknesses in structure and clarity. The top awards for news coverage, investigative reporting and interviewing were given to the monthly *Payam-e Emrouz*,[25] which had been banned months before and whose editor, Amid Naini, had been detained for nearly three months in 2001.[26] Three journalists – Akbar Ganji, Emadeddin Baqi, and Hojjatoleslam Abdollah Nouri – were in prison at the time of the Festival.[27]

Exploitation in the provinces

Soon after the Festival, the poor conditions of journalists working on the country's provincial press were discussed in a *Rasaneh* editorial which said only a few 'mature and financially sound' papers in the provinces did not 'exploit' their writers. There were publishers who paid only some of their writers well, and those who did not pay at all. 'Quite a few family-run papers', some with good finances, were 'exploiting eager journalists'. There were papers poor in finances, management, and content, unable to pay 'acceptable' fees to their contributors. Some of these were about to close down, while their survival could at least provide employment, 'albeit limited.' Many provincial journalists had not been paid 'for years'. Designers of crossword puzzles were receiving 250 toomans ($0.30) a piece and pictures, cartoons, and graphic art works were being published without any royalties. The publishers, however, were using subsidized newsprint and printing facilities and running ads supplied by the government, and some of them had sound revenues. The article argued that the government should only support publishers who provided their staff with pay, insurance, and other benefits.[28]

Two years later, in May 2004, concern was expressed again about the very poor conditions of the press in the provinces, where national newspapers sometimes could not be found.[29] Isfahan, one of the country's richest provinces, had 48 papers, including two dailies, with 'low quality, compared to the national level, because of their use of semi-professional or unprofessional reporters'. Support provided by the government, in the shape of one training course, had not been enough.[30]

The much less prosperous province of Hormozgan, on the Persian Gulf coast, had eight local papers with young reporters, many of them students, without any training, insurance cover, or other benefits. They did not have up to date news sources or electronic production facilities. The papers had to be printed some 1,500 kilometres away, in Tehran,[31] which had about 10 per cent of the country's population, but 95 per cent of its newspaper printing machines, 51 per cent of them in the state sector.[32]

Authoritarians and libertarians

The winter 2003 editorial in *Rasaneh* spoke of the need for the convergence of two approaches to the press among Iranian statesmen. One group saw the press as a 'tool for political propaganda, the multiplication of its own discourse, and the preservation of the status quo', and wanted to impose more constraints on the press than there should be in a democratic society. The other group, with an 'open' definition of press freedom, considered the newspapers as the 'public's eye, watching over the government', that had to be 'critical, reformist, frank and courageous'. Iran needed a 'comprehensive media framework', the editorial argued, based on the rule of law, with guaranteed freedoms, professional independence, and security; specialist and professional training; a convention on professional ethical principles; a self-regulatory mechanism; and special regulations governing the profession. As an example of the problems resulting from the absence of such a framework, *Rasaneh* pointed out that while newspaper licences were being granted after checks with the intelligence and security organizations, the police and the judiciary, there were still those who did not appear to regard such authorities as competent and qualified. There were also economic challenges, including the press's lack of financial independence, unequal competition between the state and private sectors, low circulation, inadequate technical facilities, poor investment in material, intellectual and human resources, and distribution problems. The combined effect had turned newspapers into uneconomic enterprises that could not develop into credible and strong organizations with competent management. Because of weak professional and civil institutions, the press had fallen into lethargy and recession, creating a vicious cycle of media underdevelopment, which could not serve the cause of national development.[33]

The conservative press, however, believed that the profession was caught between the pair of 'scissors' of 'dogmatists' who could not accept progress and 'deviant intellectuals' incapable of creating an 'indigenous literature'.[34] The conservatives accused the reformists of pegging democracy to secularization, which had 'no place in our culture',[35] and of having abused the right to criticize by publishing a cartoon that showed a leading conservative clergyman, Ayatollah Mohammad-Taqi Mesbah-Yazdi, as a crocodile. The conservatives were also not convinced that the reformists had really suffered from the ban on their papers because the closure of one paper, 'with a couple of other licences in the pocket', was not only affordable, but would also bring one political credit.[36]

Death in custody

During the spring of 2003, more journalists were arrested or attacked by the police and plainclothes agents while covering student protests.[37] At the time of the Tenth Press Festival, in August 2003, several hundred journalists took part in a sit-in at the offices of the Association of Iranian Journalists (AOIJ) to protest against the treatment the Iranian press had received and to commemorate the Iranian–Canadian journalist, Zahra Kazemi, who had died on 10 July because of head injury sustained after she had been detained while taking photographs outside Tehran's Evin prison.[38] The meeting also heard the names of 19 imprisoned Iranian journalists.[39] During the Press Festival's final ceremony several award winners returned their prizes to the Minister of Culture and Islamic Guidance, Ahmad Masjed-Jame'i, in protest against the continued detention of journalists, Zahra Kazemi's death in suspicious circumstances, and the fact that awards had been given to reporters from national television, which the reformist print journalists regarded hostile to them and their cause.[40]

The Festival jury once again highlighted the qualitative decline of the Iranian press. While reporting an 'encouraging growth of Islamic studies articles, in-depth interviews, art critique, descriptive and analytical reports', the jury said there had been a 'dramatic fall in independent news production', with 'noticeable weaknesses in news coverage, headlines, political articles and analysis, investigative reporting, satire, and cartoons', and a decline in writing technique and style. Provincial newspapers in particular were suffering from 'severe weakness of scientific and specialist journalistic techniques'.[41]

'Writing for the dead'

Shortly afterwards, *Rasaneh* reported that the country's national newspapers, 'with the partial exception of two or three', were producing 'almost no original news items', relying instead on news agency or online reports, 'exactly replicating' all of their errors. Some newspapers had been carrying reports with anonymous sources or no source at all, or presenting other papers' material as their own. The headlines were often misleading, badly written, convoluted, unrelated to the main news point in the report, and visually unattractive. Most reports were too long, badly structured, and confusing, even when produced by the paper concerned. There was poor use of the Persian language in 'all but a few newspapers', with plenty of spelling, grammatical, and punctuation errors, overuse of Arabic, English, and French words. Some newspapers were 'too absolutist and negative, projecting a black and violent image, as if they were being produced for a dead society.'[42]

Newspaper closures and detentions of journalists continued in 2004. In February, the dailies *Shargh* (East) and *Yas-e Now* (New Jasmine) were closed down for publishing a critical letter to Ayatollah Khamenei signed by 144 Majlis deputies,[43] although *Shargh* was later allowed to reappear. *Yas-e Now* was succeeded by *Vaqaye'-e Ettefaqiyeh* (Happening Events), named after the first regular Persian language newspaper, launched in 1850 by the reformist Qajar Prime Minister,

Amir Kabir, who was killed two years later on the orders of the monarch, Nassereddin Shah.[44] The new *Vaqaye'-e Ettefaqiyeh*, published by the AOIJ President and Majlis deputy speaker, Ali Mazru'i, was banned within months of its launch because, said the judiciary, its journalists had been the same as those in *Yas-e Now*. The paper remained closed in spite of protests based on the absence of any law prohibiting such employment. Two more dailies, *Jomhouriyat* (Republic) and *Nassim-e Saba* (North-Eastern Breeze) and the monthly *Aftab* (Sunshine) were banned shortly afterwards.

In April 2004, the speaker of the Association for the Defence of Press Freedom, Mashaallah Shamsolva'ezin, reported that during the previous year, there had been 343 violations of press rights; one journalist, Zahra Kazemi, had died in custody; 35 newspapers had been banned or temporarily closed; 74 journalists had been tried, most of whom were awaiting their sentences; 108 journalists had been summoned and indicted; 16 had been sentenced; 32 had been detained; six persons had been banned from working as journalists; 500 files were awaiting judicial review; 1,433,000,000 toomans [$1.8m] had been put up as bail for journalists; and 187 websites had been blocked.[45]

In June, 300 journalists and lawyers gathered at the AOIJ offices for a 3-hour protest against the continuing trend of newspaper closures and the ban on *Vaqaye'-e Ettefaqiyeh* and *Jomhouriyat*. Speakers at the meeting included the lawyer and Nobel Peace Prize Laureate, Shirin Ebadi, who was acting on behalf of Zahra Kazemi's family, and the previous year's press award winner, Azadeh Akbari, who had been the youngest journalist working on *Vaqaye'-e Ettefaqiyeh*. Ms Akbari said journalists were worried about unemployment, while another speaker, Arash Hassan-nia, described journalism as a 'disposable' occupation. Iran's Reporter's Day, 7 August, was marked by an 8-hour sit-in at the AOIJ offices to protest against the continued detention of journalists.[46]

Fear eats the soul

The Eleventh Press Festival was also opened in August, with a message from President Khatami who was abroad at the time. The country's press, said the President, needed political, judicial, and professional security, and he was 'sorry that in practice, our press community is far from this required status'. The AOIJ President, Mr Mazru'i, told the awards ceremony that during the previous five years 110 newspapers had been closed on a 'temporary' basis, a ruling for which there had been no legal grounds. Only 10 cases had been reviewed, most of them resulting in cash fines, though some of the papers had not reappeared. He said journalists no longer 'dared approach news stories'; some former Festival prize winners had left the profession; and some had left the country.

The statement by the jury said conditions for efficient and coherent team building, development of professional identity, formation of strong newspaper organizations, and accumulation of experience and its transfer to the younger generation were at their lowest, leading to investment problems and a loss of public confidence. There had been a fall in quality in areas where journalists had to take risks to discover and tell the truth, or to have a strong intellectual and scientific background to be able to comment. News production was at a low level, except for the coverage of accidents. There was a scarcity of articles on religious thought and Iran's politics, and a shortage of high quality editorials and commentaries. There were gross weaknesses in investigation, confirmation of information, structure, and headline writing. The high points were in reporting, foreign affairs, in-depth interviews and photography.[47]

A Ministry of Culture and Islamic Guidance survey conducted at the time of the Festival and carried in a Ministry newsletter indicated that nearly half the journalists in the country did not know about the annual festival that had been held in their name for 11 years, and most had never been to one.[48] In September, another report in the same newsletter said journalists were working in an environment dominated by 'fear, poverty, lack of access to information, lack of recognition as professionals, a tightening political atmosphere, lack of freedom, unclear job prospects, incompetent managers, lack of a true trade union, discrimination, and a glaring [income] gap between managers and the editorial staff'. Many journalists needed second or third jobs, sometimes low-paid work on the newly emerging papers where they would not be given contracts and would be sacked the moment they voiced any criticism.[49] The editor of a sport daily told the newsletter that only 'three of four managers' could make a living out of a newspaper, and suggested that poorly paid reporters covering the huge payments received by football stars who appeared on advertising billboards could well be tempted into corruption to raise their incomes.[50] A veteran political activist and journalist, Lotfollah Maisami, warned that financial pressures were undermining editorial values.[51]

Not many left to ban

In June 2004, the Ministry of Culture and Islamic Guidance said its discussions with the judiciary had resulted in a reduction of newspaper closures.[52] While the talks may well have had some effect, it was also true that by then the Judiciary had closed down most of the young reformist papers[53] and had little more to do with the press. Those that had survived would say openly, as in the case of the government-owned daily *Iran*, that newspapers were 'not publishing the whole truth',[54] or in the case of the independent daily *Shargh* that they were 'exercising self-censorship',[55] something about which the Ministry expressed concern, saying that much of it was 'subjective'.[56] The journalists' calls for unemployment support resulted in President Khatami providing a fund for interest-free loans,[57] and the Cabinet allocating 20 billion rials [$2.3m] to insure writers, artists and journalists.[58] The Ministry of Labour provided the licence holder of the banned daily, *Vaqaye'-e Ettefaqiyeh*, Ali Mazru'i, with money to pay 3 months' salary to his staff.[59]

The Ministry of Culture and Islamic Guidance also announced that a research group chaired by Dr Kazem Mo'tamednejad had been working on four documents that would be presented for legislation with the aim of setting up a comprehensive media system in the country. One document was a draft bill for the formation of a Press Council (later renamed the Media Council); another was a Convention on the Ethical Principles of Professional Journalism; the third would draw up 'The Legal System of Professional Journalism'; and the fourth would set out 'The Collective Code of Employment of Journalists'.[60]

The 'cheap newsprint habit'

The Ministry also began efforts to make 'economic enterprises' out of newspapers, arguing that many of the damages inflicted on the press had 'resulted from the newspaper managers' lack of awareness of professional standards and legal codes.'[61] Very few of the publishers had ever drawn up a business plan or conducted an audience research to find out what their potential readers would want. Most of the public, said a senior official with a background in business journalism, were more concerned with their economic needs than with politics and wanted to have 'a calm life, free from tension'.[62] The Tehran Stock Exchange reached an agreement with the Ministry of Culture and Islamic Guidance to find 'scientific ways' to transform newspapers into large commercial concerns, hoping that 'at least two or three of them' would be represented on the Stock Exchange 'in the next two years'. The Stock Exchange would also support the newspapers by supplying them with financial information free of charge, even though the sales of such data made up to '22 per cent of the global stock exchange revenues'.[63]

A sharp rise in newsprint prices in the summer of 2004, caused by a domestic production cut and import prices driven up by increased demand in China, showed how dependent the Iranian press was on the government and how difficult it would be to remove the subsidies which had been in place since 1989 with the aim of keeping newspaper prices down. In an open letter to President Khatami, a group of private sector publishers said the Ministry of Culture and Islamic Guidance had not provided them with enough newsprint and warned that the newsprint shortage could force their closure. In its reply, the Ministry said the newspaper owners had been receiving foreign exchange 'for many years' to purchase paper directly, but there had been 'rumours that the foreign currencies and the government-subsidized newsprint were being sold on the free market'.[64] Although the implied accusation was directed at the private sector newspaper publishers, the Ministry's own figures made it clear that during 1989–2003, it had given the press a total of $368.8m in aid, of which $282m, or 77 per cent, had gone to the state-owned papers. During that period, *Kayhan* had received $107.205m in cash; *Ettela'at* had received $111.156m; and the *Iran* group $8.797m. The newspapers were also provided with mobile phones, cameras, scanners, film, and zinc and newsprint.[65] A more detailed examination of state support to a number of daily newspapers between 1998 and 2003 (Table 6.1), showed that two reformist newspapers, *Sobh Emrouz* (This Morning) and *Khordad* (third month in the Iran calendar partly covering May–June), both of which reached very high circulations (100,000 to 300,000), before being closed down by the Judiciary, had received much smaller support from the government.

The other banned reformist papers had also had very high circulations. *Jameah* and *Tous* had sold up to 300,000 copies a day and the political biweekly *Iran-e Farda*

Table 6.1 State subsidies to newspapers, 1998–2003[a]

Paper	Type of aid	1377 (1998–99)	1378 (1999–2000)	1379 (2000–01)	1380 (2001–02)	1381 (2002–03)	Total	Per year
Ettela'at	$	3,124,000	2,092,000	2,434,000	2,095,000	1,375,000	11,120,000	2.224m
	Rls	520,000,000		4bn				
	Paper (tons)	350	900	1,860	950	1,000	5,060	1,012
Kayhan	$	2,664,000	1,789,000	2,065,000	2,058,000	1,376,000	9,952,000	1.99m
	Rls	1.005bn						
	Paper (tons)	450	900	1,413	450	850	4,063	812
Hamshahri and Aftabgardan	$	2,457,000	1,407,000	1,903,000	1,685,000	1,427,000	8,879,000	1.776m
	Rls	900,000,000						
	Paper (tons)	100	900	1,425	750	400	3,575	715
Iran	$	1,111,000	946,000	1,532,000	1,553,000	1,151,000	6,293,000	1.26m
	Rls	324,000,000						
	Paper (tons)	200	600	1,450	900	1,050	4,500	900
Jomhouri-ye Eslami	$	517,000	389,000	611,000	570,000	436,000	2,523,000	504,600
	Rls	208,000,000						
	Paper (tons)		414	271	280	370	1,335	267
Sobh Emrouz	$	127,000	597,000	260,000			984,000	196,800
	Paper (tons)	300	790	260			1,350	270
Khordad	$	127,000	358,000				485,000	97,000
	Paper (tons)	350					350	70

Note

a Author's tabulation of figures in Mass'oud Kazemi, 'Doshvari-haye Nashriyat-e Mostaqel dar Barabar-e Gostaresh-e Nashriyat-e Dowlati ya Mowred-e Hemayat-e Dowlat' (The Difficulties Faced by the Independent Publications with respect to the Expansion of Publications owned or Supported by the State), *Rasaneh Quarterly*, vol. 14, no. 4, Winter 2004, pp. 18–19.

(Tomorrow's Iran) had had a circulation of 50,000,[66] several times more than most other periodicals. The success of the independent papers was especially notable since they had higher cover prices and faced greater distribution problems. In contrast, the circulations of the state-owned newspapers, with prices kept low through heavy subsidies, fell sharply when the independent newspapers were able to operate. Just as the ability of the reformist newspapers to offer a wider range of news and a critical point of view had helped their finances, the newspaper closures and the tighter restraints imposed on the remaining papers resulted in the loss of that comparative advantage. This, in turn, would lead to lower circulations and smaller advertising revenues, possibly forcing some small independent publications into closure.[67]

The 'specialist haven'

The deepening depression of political journalism was accompanied by a rise in financial reporting and a rapid growth of the specialist and technical periodicals. In the words of Dr Kazem Mo'tamednejad, in the early years after the Revolution, 'death notices were the only ads appearing in the papers, because the society was not looking favourably at advertising.' The 'tendency in society towards prosperity' that followed the end of the war led to the emergence of business newspapers, first in the shape of supplements published by the dailies.[68] In spite of a number of setbacks in the first half of 1990s, the country's general economy improved in the second half and picked up speed thanks to the rise in oil revenues following the 2003 US-led occupation of Iraq. The period 1997–2004 saw a quadrupling of Iran's annual accumulation of fixed capital per active head of population.[69] The improved economic conditions were reflected in the appearance of 250 newspapers covering industries, technology, business and management, 70 per cent of them licensed after President Khatami's election in 1997.[70]

While most of the 80 or so economic and financial monthlies appeared secure in 2004, thanks either to state backing or advertisements, the 10 business dailies had a precarious existence, lacking trained staff and especially short of 'reporters with a sense for economic news'.[71] With circulations of between 6,000 and 32,000 copies per day, they were fighting for advertising revenue, with complaints that they had been undercutting each other's rates. The Ministry of Culture and Islamic Guidance spoke of 'less than proud' relationships developing between the papers and their advertisers, with the papers promoting the commercial firms through advertisements, and the firms paying the newspapers' bills.[72] Business journalism was also affected by politics when, in July 2003, the editor the business daily *Asia*, Iraj Jamshidi, was arrested after running a photo of a leader of the Mojahedin-e Khalq Organization, Maryam Rajavi. Mr Jamshidi was released on bail in August 2004, having appeared in court to face charges of 'acting against national security, insulting the official figures of the system, publishing lies with the intention of disturbing the public's mind, disrupting the country's economic system, and providing information to foreign countries'. The court verdict was not made public.[73]

By the end of 2004, Iran had more than 700 specialist periodicals, amounting to 60 per cent of the country's newspaper titles. There were 155 titles covering arts, culture and literature; 154 dealing with medicine, health and hygiene; 148 on engineering, architecture, technology, and computers; 93 on religious studies and philosophy; 49 on cultural heritage, the police force, libraries, and other public services; 38 on education; 31 on basic sciences; and 8 titles each on the environment and tourism. The smallest groups of newspapers, with five titles each, were the 'Holy Defence Literature' and 'Satire and Cartoons.'[74]

Some of the specialist papers were among the best produced in the country, with high cover prices and expensive advertisements.[75] Others were suffering from a shortage of skilled staff, limited financial and technical resources and a small audience.[76] Early in the year, the Ministry of Culture and Islamic Guidance had set up a 'Specialist Press Centre' to provide such papers with editorial and technical support, including photography, layout, lithography, and printing.[77] Reformist journalists whose jobs were threatened by political restrictions or economic pressures were advised that instead of giving up journalism or entering public relations, they 'should join the specialist papers, because these conditions are temporary and the press spring will come back again'.[78]

7   Women and journalism

The first Iranian newspaper for women, the weekly *Danesh* (Knowledge), appeared in 1910, 73 years after the appearance of the first Persian language newspaper in the country, but only four years after the Iranian women's first experience of mass political action during the Constitutional Revolution. Published by a woman optician, Dr Kahhal, *Danesh* was a non-political paper, offering advice on 'feeding one's husband on time', 'keeping his room warm', using make-up to secure his affection and, hence, ensuring 'a blissful family life'. It also ran articles on health, childcare and managing the servants, as well as fiction and reports on girls schools which were a great novelty at the time. Small circulation in a poor nation of 10 million, 95 per cent of them illiterate, and most of them dispersed in inaccessible villages, led to the closure of *Danesh* in less than a year.[1]

By the mid-1950s, thanks to rises in population, urbanization, literacy, and standards of living the press had considerable advertising revenues. Iran's first commercial women's newspaper, the weekly *Ettela'at-e Banovan* (Ladies' Ettela'at), was published in 1956. The rival *Kayhan* group's *Zan-e Rouz* (Woman of the Day) appeared in 1964, by which time Iran had a population of 24 million, 40 per cent of them living in cities. National literacy rate had risen to 30 per cent, and women made up one-third of the country's literate population.[2] In 1966, the first journalism training course for women was offered at the Farah College of Arts for Girls (named after the then Queen Farah), covering the laws and regulations governing journalism, the history of the press, reporting skills and reporter's ethical and social responsibilities. The three-year course, offered to students with middle school certificates, also included typing and photography and internships at newspapers and periodicals. The course was so well-received that the College also organized a four-year programme with 100 hours of training per year.[3] During the 1960s and 1970s, women's presence in Iranian journalism was 'fully noticeable, especially in Tehran', and they engaged in writing, translation, reporting, management, and editing of publications, and 'even technical matters such as layout'. In 1971, Iranian women journalists formed a professional organization, *Anjoman-e Zanan-e Rouznamehnegar-e Iran* (The Association of Iranian Women Journalists), to 'support the rights of lady journalists'. The Association carried on its publicity 'slowly but surely', and by the time of the 1979 Revolution it had '38 permanent and 50 associate members'.[4]

Women, Islam, socialism

In the first year after the Revolution, more than 500 new papers appeared in Iran, about 30 of them published or edited by women. Some were Islamic, including *Nehzat-e Zanan-e Mosalman* (Muslim Women's Movement); *Zan-e Mosalman* (Muslim Woman); *Rah-e Zaynab* (Zeynab's Way), named after the Prophet Mohammad's grand-daughter; and *Payam-e Hajar* (Hagar's Message), named after the Prophet Abraham's wife. Most, however, were tied to left-wing organizations, with titles such as *Bidariy-e Zan* (Woman's Awakening), *Paykar-e Zan* (Woman's Struggle), *Rahai-ye Zan* (Woman's Emancipation), and *Sepideh-ye Sorkh* (Red Dawn). In addition to articles about the conditions of Iranian women, especially from the working class, these magazines had articles on leading socialist women in the West, such as Rosa Luxemburg, Alexandra Kollontai, and Nadezhda Krupskaya. In the case of the last, sometimes there would also be a debate on her life with her husband, Vladimir Ilich Ulyanov Lenin, and the exact nature of his relationship with the French-born socialist, Inessa Armand. Anxiety about sexual attraction between male and female activists impacting on organizational hierarchies led organizations with underground, paramilitary structures to issue instructions on managing personal relationships. One left-wing group published a pamphlet called '*Proletarian Guidelines for Choosing Your Partner*', originally issued by the Communist Party of the Philippines (Marxist-Leninist).

For the third time since the 1906 Constitutional Revolution, the question of women's rights was being discussed by the Iranian society, this time with an astounding range. On the one hand, street demonstrations against the imposition of the Islamic dress code were attacked by club-wielders shouting, '*Ya rousari, ya tousari*' (either a scarf on your head, or a punch in your head). On the other hand, on national radio, a spokeswoman for a socialist group would read the group's election manifesto which included women's right to use their bodies as they wished. By the early 1980s, the sharpening of domestic political conflicts and the onset of the war with Iraq had led to the closure of all opposition newspapers and only the few Islamic women's papers were being published. After the war, a market developed for popular journalism, focusing on sports, entertainment, youths, families, and women, but it also became possible for the Islamic system to be subjected to gender-focused critique, by its own women.[5] In 1996, there were 27 Iranian publications managed by women, including academic quarterlies on nursing and midwifery and the publications of the women-only Al-Zahra University on basic sciences, painting, sculpture, literature, psychology, and politics.[6] Women's small share of the press, 4.9 per cent of the 544 titles, was criticized in February 1996, when a conference on 'Women, the Press, the Status Quo and the Desired State' was held at Al Zahra University.[7] In October, 'The First Congress of Specialist Women's Press' was held at the Khavaran Cultural Centre in the working class south Tehran in order to 'familiarize the managers of women's press with women's social needs, and familiarize the public with women's press.' The event included workshops on writing for newspapers and magazines.[8]

Male owners, female editors

Women's presence in journalism rose rapidly after the victory in May 1997 of their, and young people's, favourite presidential candidate, Mohammad Khatami. By the end of Mr Khatami's second term in 2005, women were publishing, managing or editing a total of 130 newspapers, 10.6 per cent of the country's total. These included 20 periodicals about women and 12 about families which will be discussed in some detail below. Others covered: cinema, fashion, photography, and other arts (14); literature, culture, and education (14); engineering, architecture, computers, and basic sciences (14); medical sciences (13); entertainment, young people's lives, and crossword puzzles (13); children and adolescents (7), including *Teenager*, Iran's only English-language paper for young people;[9] politics and economics (7); and general knowledge (4), including *Danestaniha*, one of the oldest and most popular, independent, post-Revolution monthlies, published, managed and edited by a woman, Faraneh Behzadi.[10] There were far fewer women in charge of publications covering religion, tourism or environment, daily news, social affairs, or satire and cartoons.[11]

Women were not only under-represented in the mainstream Iranian press, as will be discussed later in this chapter, but they were not even fully in charge of the 20 'specialist' women's papers, whose titles speak of their non-political character. Women were the licence holders and managers of only 6 women's papers: *Poushesh* (Garment), *Hoqouq-e Zanan* (Women's Rights), *Zanan* (Women), *Farzaneh* (Wise), *Madaran* (Mothers), and *Madaran-o-Dokhtaran* (Mothers and Daughters). Eight other women's papers were managed and/or edited by women, but owned by organizations, for instance Kayhan group's *Zan-e Rouz*; the Islamic Association of Women's *Irandokht* (Daughter of Iran); *Ketab-e Zanan* (Women's Book), published by the Women's Cultural–Social Council, affiliated to the Supreme Cultural Revolution Council; and *Zan-e Sharghi* (Eastern Woman), published by the Baseej (Mobilization) Resistance Force of the Islamic Revolutionary Guards Corps. The remaining six were published and edited by men, including *Banou* (Lady), 'a monthly on healthcare and beauty'; *Payam-e Zan* (Woman's Message), published by the Qom Seminary's Islamic Publicity Bureau; and the Islamic Culture and Communication Organization's English language monthly, *Mahjoubah* (The Modest Woman).[12]

Women made up the majority of the contributors to the specialist women's press, most of whose coverage dealt with childcare, family, violence against women, crime, health and hygiene, women's social status, and politics, including women's expectations from the Islamic Majlis. Household management, emotional relationships between women and men, relations between girls and boys, marriage, divorce, alimony, dowry, inheritance, child custody, and violence took up less than 10 per cent of the space. Most of the content was focused on issues, rather than personalities, although there were interviews with politicians, artists, football players, and other public figures. About 75 per cent of the coverage dealt with Iranian women's lives, and women's health and hygiene around the world were the most prominent international subjects. Very little attention was paid to regional women's issues.[13]

The most significant women's publications have included the veteran weekly *Zan-e Rouz*, one of the few titles to have survived the Revolution; the monthly *Zanan* that grew out of a political dispute at *Zan-e Rouz* in the early 1990s; and the short-lived daily, *Zan* (Woman) (August 1998–April 1999).

Zan-e Rouz

In the oil-rich 1960s and 1970s, *Zan-e Rouz* had many pages with titles such as 'Love', 'Make-up', and 'Movie Stars'. It also serialized novels with romantic, sometimes thinly veiled erotic themes. The front-cover picture would often be that of a glamorous entertainer, or some other female celebrity. Advertisements took up around one-third of the pages.[14] On 13 January 1979, a month before the overthrow of the monarchy, *Zan-e Rouz*'s front cover was given to the picture of a *chador*-clad woman, shouting slogans. The weekly's editorial pointed out that it now contained 'only a few pages as reminders' of 'a certain state and social system with which everyone is familiar', but 'has now been thrown much further away by the nation's Revolution'. The new-look *Zan-e Rouz*'s content was a mix of the old-style pictures and tales of romance, alongside articles about political prisoners, torture and the Revolution, and pictures of women in anti-Shah demonstrations. The next few issues indicated the influence of the left, but after the *Kayhan* group's change of ownership in the summer of 1979, *Zan-e Rouz* said it would be 'unattached to any group, and follow the path of the Islamic Revolution', that it would 'say nothing but the truth', but also that 'not all the truth need be told.' Photographs and drawings of women wearing the hijab continued to appear in *Zan-e Rouz*, but there were no images of fashion models during the war years.

Zan-e Rouz's editor after the war, Shahla Sherkat, introduced changes to its content and appearance, including a sewing supplement with patterns, which survived her departure in 1991, after President Khatami had left as the supervisor of *Kayhan* group. Ms Sherkat, who soon started her own monthly *Zanan*, was replaced as the editor of *Zan-e Rouz* by the weekly's legal advisor, Ashraf Geramizadegan, who in turn left in 1997 to start the monthly *Hoqouq-e Zanan* (Women's Rights). In spite of these and subsequent changes of editors, *Zan-e Rouz*'s character remained stable.[15] A typical issue in 2004 carried an editorial with a religious theme, followed by a report – this time on the roots of stubborn behaviour; news about women in Iran and abroad; advice on marital or personal, emotional problems; health, hygiene and beauty; childcare; recipes, including one for 'macaroni and cheese casserole', hardly a traditional Iranian dish; sewing, with the aid of patterns copied from foreign publications, but with ink-drawn, scarf-wearing heads superimposed on pictures of the original models; and poetry, short stories, and serialized novels.[16] By now, *Zan-e Rouz* had a lower-middle-class readership whose income was reflected in the paper's few pages of advertisements for cooking and tailoring classes, slimming and beauty clinics and inexpensive cosmetics and sweets. The main reason why *Zan-e Rouz*, and its daily sibling, *Kayhan*, can survive without much advertising is that they are owned by the state, with public funds covering their costs.

Zanan

The monthly *Zanan*'s character was made clear in its first editorial which said the key to women's problems had to be found in 'religion, culture, law and education'. The paper said it would do all it could 'with the help of masters of thought and love, to prepare the ground for women's elevation in all affairs'. The paper said it had 'not come to fight against men', but that it would 'not shy away from that either'.[17] Among the specialist women's papers, *Zanan* has had the highest coverage of politics, 7.61 per cent of the content; women's education, 8.46 per cent; and social participation, 10.77 per cent. It has also had more pictures of women in politics, in Iran and Afghanistan; the largest share of women contributors, 86 per cent; and one of the highest shares, 11.28 per cent, of 'critical material' about the conditions in the country. *Zanan*'s legal coverage, at 7.48 per cent, has also been among the highest.[18] For several years, *Zanan* had a column by a woman lawyer, Mehr-Anguiz Kar, who was imprisoned after speaking at the Berlin Conference of April 2000. Ms Kar's husband, Siamak Pourzand, was arrested later in 2000,[19] while she was having medical treatment in the United States, where she stayed and became a founding member of a campaign calling for a referendum to change the Iranian constitution. Another contributor to *Zanan*, Shirin Ebadi, won the Nobel Peace Prize in 2003.

In its 1997 pre-election issue, *Zanan* devoted 10 pages to the presidential race, leading with an interview with Mr Khatami, whose smiling photograph appeared on the front cover. Another interviewee was Ms A'zam Taleqani, publisher of Iran's oldest post-Revolutionary women's magazine, *Payam-e Hajar*, and the first woman to nominate herself for presidency in Iran. Ms Taleqani, daughter of the late Ayatollah Mahmoud Taleqani, said the nomination was primarily aimed at seeking clarification of Article 115 in the Islamic Republic's Constitution which says the President should be elected 'from amongst the *rejal* of religion and politics.' Though the Arabic word *rejal* and its singular *rajol* are commonly used in Iran as synonyms for the Persian words *mardan* (men) and *mard* (man), respectively, Ms Taleqani argued that in political or social discourse, *rajol* or *rejal* could mean 'personality' or 'personalities'. In the *Zanan* interview, Ms Taleqani also pointed out that other Islamic countries, such as Pakistan and Bangladesh, had had women heads of state or government. Mr Khatami said in his interview that many experts believed women could reach presidency in Iran, but added that the 'esteemed Council of Guardians are the official interpreters of the Constitution.' He also said he saw no problem with women joining the cabinet, but that he disagreed with the idea that there should be a ministry for women's affairs, arguing that the growth of non-governmental organizations would be more effective in improving Iranian women's conditions.[20] The Council of Guardians later rejected Ms Taleqani's nomination without stating the reason.[21]

Zanan has carried the third largest share of advertisements among the women and family magazines, after the health and beauty bimonthly, *Banou*, and the monthly *Arous* (Bride), published by the Arts Department of the Islamic Publicity Organization.[22] The ads in *Zanan* speak of the monthly's well-off readership.

The November 2004 issue, with a cover picture of the Hollywood star, Meryl Streep, and 7 pages about her, carried a total of 26 pages of advertisements, compared to 71 pages of editorial content. There were 21 pages of full-colour ads – 15 for household appliances, 5 for perfumes, cosmetics and beauty, and 1 for laptop computers – and 5 black and white pages promoting yoga, more household appliances, and English, French, Italian, Russian, and Spanish language classes.[23]

Zan

Shortly after President Khatami's election, former President Rafsanjani's daughter, Faezeh Hashemi, obtained her long awaited licence to publish a daily newspaper, *Zan* (Woman), which appeared in August 1998. Writing in the first issue, Ms Hashemi said *Zan* did not aim to

> achieve domination by women, nor to set man and woman against each other, but to create a balance between the two, with equal values [...] *Zan* intends to write from a woman's point of view for women, but not only about women [...] It intends to create conditions in which our young girls do not feel inadequate because of 'being girls' [...] We must not forget that historically, rights have been there to be taken, not to be given.[24]

Zan quickly established itself as an innovative paper, both by its tabloid size and relatively simple and elegant layout, and by its lively approach and wide range of subjects, including, naturally, women's rights. Ms Hashemi's advisors during the preparation for *Zan*'s launch had all been men, as were the paper's senior editorial staff. Women made up one half of the staff of about 80, very few of whom, Ms Hashemi later said, could have been appointed to editorial positions.[25] The paper did have a number of young woman journalists with great enthusiasm and determination who wrote incisive reports. One highlighted a man's legal power to divorce his wife in her absence, without her knowledge.[26] Another focused on the very mild punishment that a man could receive for murdering his offspring,[27] a point that Iran's leading children's rights advocate, Shirin Ebadi, also discussed in depth in an interview with *Zan*.[28] The daily also published an interview with Mehr-Anguiz Kar, who said Iran's family rights legislation had moved backwards since the Revolution.[29]

In a later interview with *Zan*, Ms Hashemi said although the paper would write more about women, 'because there are more cases of injustice against women in our society', there was no distinction between men and women 'on the day's news pages, where the society's general issues are discussed'. She said surveys had shown that most of the paper's readers had been men, 'proving that there has been no confrontation'[30] with men on the pages of *Zan*.

The general, the queen, and the mugger

In January 1999, when *Zan* was barely six months old, Ms Hashemi appeared before Tehran's Press Court to defend the paper against the charges that it had libelled the Police Force's Counter-Intelligence Chief, Brigadier–General Mohammad-Reza Naqdi, and insulted his department. The libel accusation had resulted from a report saying that General Naqdi had been seen near the site of a September 1998 mob attack on two reformist members of the cabinet, the Minister of Culture and Islamic Guidance, Ataollah Mohajerani, and the Minister of Interior, Abdollah Nouri. The insult had allegedly been caused by the paper's publication of a phone message from a reader who had likened the Counter-Intelligence division to a wolf, given the task of protecting lambs. Defending the paper against the former charge, Ms Hashemi produced only one witness to testify that General Naqdi had been at the scene of the attack on the two ministers, while the General produced several witnesses to prove that he had not been there. The Court did not make it clear whether it had dismissed, or accepted, the General's alibi, but it did not accept the libel accusation. It did, however, find *Zan* guilty of having insulted the Police Force's Counter-Intelligence division, ordered Ms Hashemi to pay a cash fine, and closed the paper for two weeks.[31]

In April 1999, the Revolutionary Court closed the paper down indefinitely for publishing excerpts from the Iranian New Year's message of the former Queen Farah, who had been living in exile since the 1979 Revolution, and a cartoon with a man pointing to his wife and telling an armed assailant to kill her, 'because her blood money is less than mine.'[32] The Ministry of Culture and Islamic Guidance declared the closure out of order, saying the Revolutionary Court was not authorized to deal with press offences.[33] A similar point was made by a leading legal expert who also cast doubt on the continued validity of the Revolutionary Court, many years after the victory of the Revolution.[34] Other critics said the Court's decision had been politically motivated, because reports of the former Queen's message had appeared in a number of other papers, without it leading to legal action.[35] Nonetheless, *Zan* remained closed.

Women and family papers

The 12 women and family publications published in 2004 included biweeklies, monthlies, and a bimonthly. Women provided most of the content for these papers, while owning only 5 licenses and editing only 4 titles.[36] The papers gave plenty of coverage to women's social relationships, artists' lives, health and hygiene, parents' relationships with children, and 'social crimes' – including violence and harassment, homicide, running away from home, prostitution, burglary, suicide, and addiction.[37] A survey of women and family publications in 2002 found that they had paid little attention to women's education, social and political participation, employment, child custody, inheritance, alimony, and marriage payments. Eighty per cent of the content had been focused on Iran, and 60 per cent of all content had a positive tone. The papers had carried more pictures and images of artists, sportsmen, young people and students, clothes patterns, and health and hygiene products,[38] and had not covered politics at all.

The recent rise in Iranians' standards of living has increased the demand for beauty aids, including medications and cosmetic operations, advertised in the family journals. Asked about health and safety concerns, the male publisher of one family journal said medications and surgical operations were 'definitely inspected, but this is not the case for other products. Look at television. They cannot investigate every ad that they broadcast'. Advertising, he said, 'is only about introducing a product, not about guaranteeing it'.[39]

In 1995, an official seminar on 'Women and the Media' heard that 'only about 3 per cent of the news carried by newspapers was related to women'.[40] Five years on, a survey of Iran's 10 main dailies found that the coverage of women's news had risen to an average of 10 per cent, exceeding 15 per cent in *Abrar* and in *Iran*, the only paper to have a special women's page, later expanded into a weekly supplement. News had made up two-thirds of the material. A detailed examination of the content revealed that less than 20 per cent had dealt with women's political and economic participation and employment, while more than 50 per cent had gone to family matters, arts, and cultural subjects. The coverage had had little planning and care, and most of the news reports had been provided by agencies.[41] Since then, coverage of women's lives has increased in the Iranian dailies, many of which now have women's pages.[42] More attention is paid to women in the region, especially Afghanistan, where women have been cabinet members and have run for president since the fall of the Taliban in 2001.[43] However, the overall picture of women in the Iranian dailies is largely negative. 26.5 per cent of the content about women in August 2004 consisted of news and articles about violence and harassment, with women as the victims (44 per cent of the total), and homicide, with women as the perpetrators (11 per cent). Next came cultural items, 22.6 per cent, followed by news and social affairs, 17.3 per cent, and politics, 7.6 per cent.[44]

The same image, with the political coverage in a subdued, implied language, was on display in the nine main dailies on 28 December 2004. *Iran*, that had had the biggest share of women's news in 2004, had brief reports on the continued trials of two Iranian women accused of murder. One, who said she had killed a man to defend herself against rape, was eventually spared execution. The other, the temporary wife of a football star, was sentenced to death for having murdered his permanent wife. Pictures of the two defendants were among the few photographs of women appearing in the dailies. Others were those of conservative members of Majlis, the wife of the recently elected President of Ukraine, Iranian female students in a group marriage service, grieving tsunami survivors, and the reformist former Majlis deputy and the General Secretary of the Iranian Women Journalists' Association, Jamileh Kadivar.

The strongest demonstration of Iranian women in this sample of daily journalism was provided by *Shargh*, which carried nine pieces by named women journalists. These included an article which described women's presence in Iran's political parties as little more than 'window-dressing';[45] a feature on women's lives in a convent in Florence, Italy;[46] an analysis of the falling prices of cement industry shares on the Tehran stock exchange;[47] and a report, albeit in translation, on 2004 having been a bad year for Spanish football.[48] Early in 2005, women made up 35.4 per cent of *Shargh*'s named contributors,[49] considerably higher than the 23 per cent that was women's share of the overall community of Iranian journalists.[50]

Women journalists have been prominent in the business dailies that have recently emerged in Iran,[51] and have carried out some of the strongest interviews with men in senior administrative positions.[52] Outside the editorial offices, computerized typesetting and design have opened the way for women's involvement in the technical side of journalism. One of the best books on the Iranian Press Law, published in 1991, was written by Shirin Ebadi,[53] and the publisher of *Jameah*, Hamid-Reza Jalaiepour, was defended by another woman lawyer, Fariba Tavakkoli, when he appeared before the Press Court in June 1998.[54]

23% of workforce, 10% of management

The number of women in Iranian journalism has risen rapidly since 1972 (Table 7.1), when the only comprehensive record of Iranian journalists included the names and biographies of 50 women, 6.2 per cent of the 800 entries.[55] In January 2005, the Association of Iranian Journalists had 2,706 members, 623 or 23 per cent of them women, a rate of growth 4.8 times faster than that of the overall membership, and 6.4 times faster than men's. With the Association estimating the total number of Iranian journalists at around 5,000,[56] the total number of women would probably be around 1,150. Compared with the 88 members of the Association of Iranian Women Journalists before the Revolution, the number of women journalists had risen 6 times faster than Iran's population.

Table 7.1 Numbers of women journalists in Iran

Year	Total	Men	%	Women	%
1972, recorded total numbers[a]	800	750	93.8	50	6.3
1992, total numbers[b]	2,145	1,867	87	278	13
2002, union members[c]	1,846	1,439	78	407	22
2004, union members[d]	2,706	2,083	77	623	23
1972–2004, average annual growth %	7.4	5.6		35.8	• 4.8 times faster than total • 6.4 times faster than men

Notes
a Gholam-Hossein Salehyar, *Chehreh-ye Matabou'at-e Mo'asser* (The Image of the Contemporary Press), Tehran: Press Agent, 1973.
b Mehdi Mohsenian-Rad and colleagues, 'Payam-Afarinan-e Matbou'at-e Iran' (The Message Creators in the Iranian Press), Part 1, in *Rasaneh Quarterly*, vol. 4, no. 2, Summer 1993, p. 6. The research found that women's ratio of journalists was almost the same among full-timers (13.3%) and part-timers (12.8%), but there were about twice as many women journalists in Tehran (13%) than in the provinces (7.6%).
c Vice President of the Association of Iranian Journalists, Dr Karim Arghandehpour, interviewed by the author, Tehran, 8 January 2002.
d Secretary of the Association of Iranian Journalists, Mass'oud Houshmand-e-Razavi, interviewed by the author, Tehran, 4 January 2005.

At the annual Press Festivals, women increased their share of awards from 8.8 per cent in 1995 to 14.3 per cent in 2004, with a peak of 17.4 per cent in 1999, when the jury had its first woman member (Table 7.2). There have also been awards for Outstanding Women Reporters organized by the Iranian Women Journalists' Association.[57]

However, Table 7.2 also shows that women's awards have been disproportionately low compared to their numbers. Since women journalists were better educated than the men,[58] the underperformance could only have been due to their more limited opportunities to practise and improve their skills. A September 2004 survey found that while 70 per cent of Iranian journalists had had less than 10 years of experience, women were less experienced than men. There were more male cartoonists and more men in senior positions.[59]

Women's under-representation in the press was also evident at the stage where applications for newspaper licences were submitted to the Press Supervisory Board whose seven members did not include any women. Table 7.3 shows that in March 2003 women made up 13 per cent of the applicants but only 8 per cent of their applications had been accepted. Men's share of licences granted was higher than that of applications they had submitted.

An examination of the structure of ownership, management and editorial direction at newspapers in 2004 (Table 7.4) shows women's continued under-representation. While 10.6 per cent of the country's newspapers were published, managed or edited by women or addressed women and their families, women managed 8.2 per cent

Table 7.2 Women award winners at Press Festivals[a]

	1	2	3	4	5	6	7	8	9	10	11
Year	1994	1995	1996	1997	1998	1999	2000	2001	2002	2003	2004
Women on jury	0	0	0	0	0	1/7	2/7	N/A	1/7	1/7	1/7
Awards	N/A	57	63	40	72	46	52	49	57	86	70
Women		5	8	4	9	8	6	6	9	12	10
Share %		8.8	12.7	10	12.5	17.4	11.5	12.2	15.8	14	14.3

Note

a Press Festival reports and various issues of *Rasaneh Quarterly* and *Rouznamehnegar.*

Table 7.3 Newspaper licences in March 2003[a]

Category	Total	Men	Men's share (%)	Women	Women's share (%)
Licence applicants	2,628	2,296	87	332	13
Licences granted	2,421	2,222	92	199	8

Note

a *Matbou'at az Negah-e Amar* (Press through the Statistical Viewpoint), Tehran: Ministry of Culture and Islamic Guidance, August 2004.

Table 7.4 Senior women in Iranian newspapers, April 2004[a]

Type	Total	Woman licence holders, managers, or editors	% of total	Woman licence holders	% of total	Woman managers	% of total
National dailies	61	1	1.6	1	1.6	1	1.6
Social issues	27	0	0	0	0	0	0
Law	19	0	0	0	0	0	0
Holy Defence	5	0	0	0	0	0	0
Satire and cartoons	5	0	0	0	0	0	0
Women's papers	20	20	100	6	33	13	65
Families	12	12	100	5	42	4	33
Popular papers	18	10	55	9	50	9	50
Children and adolescents	19	5	26.3	3	15.8	3	15.8
Literature	35	8	23	8	23	8	23
Arts	63	14	22	11	17.5	11	17.5
Crossword puzzles and leisure	18	3	17	3	17	3	17
Youths	12	2	16.7	1	8.3	1	8.3
General knowledge	27	4	15	3	11	2	7.4
Computers	28	3	10.7	2	7.1	2	7.1
Medical Sciences	154	13	8.4	6	3.9	12	7.8
Engineering and industries	89	7	7.9	5	4.2	7	7.9
Education	38	3	7.9	2	5.2	1	2.6
Architecture, urban planning	31	2	6.4	0	0	2	6.4
Political	78	5	6.4	4	5.1	5	5.1
Sports	38	2	5.3	2	5.3	2	5.3
Specialist information	49	2	4.1	2	4.1	2	4.1
Culture	57	2	3.5	2	5.7	2	5.7
Basic Sciences	31	1	3.2	0	0	1	3.2
Religious studies	93	3	3.2	0	0	3	3.2
Economics	82	2	2.4	2	2.4	2	2.4
Agriculture, animal husbandry, poultry farming and nutrition	68	2	2.3	1	1.5	1	1.5
Environment	8	1	1.3	0	0	1	1.3
Tourism	8	1	1.3	1	1.3	1	1.3
Religious minorities	8	1	1.3	1	1.3	1	1.3
Total	1,229	129	10.6	79	6.4	102	8.3

Note
a Author's compilation from *Shenasnameh-ye Mowzoui'-ye Matbou'at-e Keshvar.* 'Licence holder' and 'manager' are the only two people whose names must be published by law. Both these positions, and the editor's, are sometimes held by the same person.

of the papers and their share of licence ownership was 6.35 per cent. Women edited only 65 per cent of the specialist women's journals and held the licences for only 33 per cent of them. Their share of owning and managing the family-oriented papers was 42 per cent and 33 per cent, respectively. The situation was worse in papers covering literature, culture and arts, where women's share of senior positions ranged between 10.1 and 17.5 per cent, and in children and young people's papers, where women had a 13 per cent share. It was much worse in education, with 5.2 per cent ownership and 2.6 per cent management, even though women made up the vast majority of the workforce in education. By March 2005, only one of the country's 61 national dailies was owned, managed, and edited by a woman.[60] Women had little or no role in directing publications that dealt with politics, economics, agriculture, the environment, sports, computers and basic sciences, and humour.

Commenting on the small numbers of women's newspapers in Iran, the manager of the Islamic Ladies' Association's monthly *Irandokht*, Fatemeh Karroubi, said the reason was not a shortage of women writers, but the country's general economic and financial problems. Asked why women were not rising above the reporter or service editor's level, Ms Karroubi said the same problem existed across the country, where 'women's presence at senior management levels does not exceed 3 per cent.' It was, therefore, 'natural that the same conditions should prevail in the press'.[61] Ms Kadivar also said that 'in spite of specialization, experience, competence and capability comparable to their male colleagues, women journalists do not have opportunities for advancement and promotion.' She said the 'most important goal' of the organization she headed, the Iranian Women Journalists' Association was 'to try to elevate women journalists' conditions'. She said her organization had 'spent a lot of effort on pursuing welfare issues, such as the provision of housing, vehicles, and insurance, organizing music concerts, training courses and sports events'.[62]

Online views

Real change in the conditions of Iranian women journalists would require a much wider degree of debate and participation than has taken place in the Iranian press so far. To make up for the shortfall, discussions have been taking place on the internet. In recent years, Iranian women journalists have started several online news bulletins, including *Women of Iran*,[63] the *Iranian Feminist Tribune*,[64] and *Badjens*,[65] the last one with a name that literally means 'naughty' or 'bad-natured', but is often used as a term of endearment. Women's websites were among the organizers of an April 2004 protest against the 'clichéd image of women' on national Iranian television.[66] Late in 2004, a group of women members of the Islamic city councils launched the internet-based Iranian Women's News Agency (IWNA).[67]

Some of the most beautifully designed and best-written Persian-language 'weblogs', or online personal diaries and discussion pages,[68] were produced by women 'from all age groups, with different levels of education and social and class backgrounds'. Women weblog writers, or bloggers, were 'more individualistic and extrovert than the previous generation of Iranian women,' and spoke 'about their real, private lives much more openly than their mothers and grandmothers do'. Weblogs were seen as an environment 'much freer than the other media, based on gender equity, virtually without censorship'. They were also seen as suitable for the publication of 'analyses that might not get printed in the papers because they are not very well developed',[69] because the weblogs seemed to operate in a legal vacuum. The feelings of freedom and security received a blow late in 2004, when the Judiciary ordered the closure of websites which it said were 'immoral or heretical or publish lies',[70] and several weblog writers, including a woman, Mahboubeh Abbasqolizadeh, were detained before being released on bail.[71] Nonetheless, the gender debate continued, even if with varying degrees of openness, in the relative privacy of thousands of weblogs, waiting for another opportunity to become public.

8   The electronic media

Iranian radio, founded on 24 April 1940,[1] has always been owned by the state. Television first appeared as a private station, Iranian Television, in 1958, but was bought by the state in 1966 and later merged with the newly founded state-owned station, National Television,[2] to form the National Iranian Television (NITV).[3] NITV was in turn merged with Radio Iran in 1972 to form the National Iranian Radio and Television (NIRT).[4] The structure was preserved after the 1979 Revolution but renamed, in Persian, as *Seda va Sima-ye Jomhouri-e Eslami-ye Iran* (Voice and Vision of the Islamic Republic of Iran), and in English as the Islamic Republic of Iran Broadcasting (IRIB). According to the Islamic Republic's Constitution, radio and television should be 'aligned with the course of perfection of the Islamic Revolution and serve the promotion of Islamic culture and to this end benefit from the healthy collision of different ideas and seriously avoid spreading and propagating destructive and anti-Islamic tenets.'[5]

The IRIB's political significance is demonstrated by the fact that its management is the subject of one of only 3 chapters out of 14 in the Islamic Republic's Constitution with a single article (Article 175), the other two chapters covering the formation of the Supreme National Security Council (Article 176) and the mechanism for revising the Constitution (Article 177). Under the Constitution, the Supreme Leader appoints the head of the IRIB and the organization is meant to be overseen by a Supervisory Council with six members, two each representing the President, the Head of the Judiciary and the Majlis.[6] Although there is no constitutional ban on private broadcasting, the IRIB's 1983 Charter gives it 'the monopoly over setting up stations and broadcasting radio and television programmes anywhere in the country', adding that any 'real or legal person attempting to set up or use such installations will be stopped from doing so and will be prosecuted legally'.[7]

Iran's radio and television network began to expand during Mr Rafsanjani's presidency, slowly at first while the war was on and the organization was headed by his brother, Mohammad Hashemi, and much faster following the 1994 appointment of Ali Larijani,[8] who had been the Deputy Chief of Staff and the Acting Chief of Staff of the Islamic Revolutionary Guards Corps, the Deputy Minister of Post, Telegraph and Telephone and Minister of Culture and Islamic Guidance.[9] After Mr Larijani's appointment, the IRIB was given 50 per cent of the budget allocated to fighting the West's 'cultural offensive',[10] much more than the combined share of the Ministry of Culture and Islamic Guidance and the Islamic Publicity Organization. By the year 2000, the share of the national budget allocated to the IRIB, with a workforce of 25,000,[11] was one-third that of the country's health service,[12] which employed more than 290,000,[13] or nearly four times higher on a per capita basis.[14] The Majlis further supported the IRIB by a 1994 legislation banning the use of satellite dishes and receivers and instructing the Interior Minister to 'cooperate with the Ministry of Intelligence to prevent the imports, construction and distribution of satellite reception equipment, seize any equipment uncovered and turn its agent over' to the Revolutionary Court.[15] Satellite programmes, a senior Majlis deputy said, would 'cause a metamorphosis of identity, transform an individual's personality and divert societies and human beings from their history, culture, character and divine identity'.[16] The Minister of Culture and Islamic Guidance, Seyyed-Mostafa Mir-Salim, said that while not all satellite programmes were 'harmful', uncontrolled use of the receiver would cause harm. Therefore, 'suitable programmes' broadcast via satellites had to be selected for transmission on Iranian television. 'The satellite', said Mir-Salim, 'is in our clutches and we have no worries in this regard'.[17] An earlier, ineffective, ban on the use of video recorders was lifted at the same time as the ban on satellite receivers was being imposed.[18]

The leader praises the IRIB

Ayatollah Khamenei repeatedly expressed his satisfaction with Mr Larijani, who was reappointed to his post for a second five year term in 1999. Privately, Ayatollah Khamenei was reported to have praised television programmes including the press review, a nightly satirical magazine, and a Thursday evening programme aimed at encouraging young people to attend the Friday prayers.[19] Publicly, such as during a 1996 visit to the IRIB's headquarters, Ayatollah Khamenei described Mr Larijani and his staff as 'committed, god-fearing and competent'. He said 'some parts' of the organization had made 'progress in writing and reading properly', but advised that 'all programmes should fully observe the standards of Persian language and literature' and 'films and other products should have native Iranian features.' He also said satire was weak in radio, television, and the press.[20]

By the end of Mr Larijani's second term at the IRIB in 2004, the organization had 'more than 15 provincial, national and international television networks' and more than 30 radio networks, with a combined daily output of 1,100 hours.[21] Iranians at home were spending an average of 156 minutes a day, 42 per cent of their leisure time, watching domestic television, compared with 20 minutes per day spent on reading newspapers,[22] although they trusted the papers more than television as a source of news.[23] Iranians abroad could watch television programmes in Persian from home carried by satellite, a service launched on Ayatollah Khamenei's instruction, 'with the aim of promoting the values and achievements of the Islamic Revolution.'[24] The IRIB also had several channels in other languages, including the 24-hour Arabic news and current affairs channel, *Al-Alam* (The World), 'launched at the cost of $2m, compared to the $250m spent on the leading Arab channel,

Al-Jazeera,' which was broadcasting from the Persian Gulf emirate of Qatar.[25] At the same time, in spite of the official ban on satellite receivers, many in Iran were able to watch hundreds of TV channels from other countries,[26] 21 of them in Persian, some with a commercial nature and others hostile to the Islamic Republic.[27] Many more Iranians could listen to Persian radio broadcasts from Beijing, Bonn, Jerusalem, London, Moscow, Paris, Prague, Tokyo, and Washington,[28] and read many of their reports on the internet.

'Friendly fire' on late scholar

During Mr Larijani's tenure, Iranian television came under strong attack by critics of the Islamic Republic and by the reformist faction that took shape after Mr Khatami's 1997 election. The main subjects of criticism included newscasts which were described as biased against President Khatami and his administration and several programmes against the country's secular intellectuals. The first programme to cause protests was a 1996 series called *Hoviyyat* (Identity) that accused a large number of secular intellectuals of having been subservient to the West and the Shah's regime. It was later revealed that the programme had been produced by the senior Intelligence Ministry official, Saied Emami, who was officially implicated in the 1997 assassination of four political activists and writers. The killings themselves were the subject of another controversial broadcast, a live 1999 programme called *Cheragh* (Light), in which a clergyman, Rouhollah Hosseinian, said the victims had been opponents of the Islamic Republic, some had been apostates and some had insulted the Shi'ite Imams, actions which under religious law could lead to execution.[29] The third television programme to cause widespread protest was the coverage of the 2000 Berlin Conference, in which blurred clips of naked protestors and pictures of the speakers invited from Iran had been edited in such a way that the speakers appeared to have watched the protests.[30]

On 17 May 2004, Mr Larijani's deputy, Ezatollah Zarghami, a former officer in the Islamic Revolutionary Guards Corps, was named as his successor as the Director of the IRIB. On the same day, during a visit to the IRIB's headquarters, Ayatollah Khamenei praised Mr Larijani's ten-year record and said that 'political currents' would attack the organization because of 'the same strengths'.[31] Speaking to the press after he had left broadcasting and was preparing himself for the 2005 presidential election, Mr Larijani defended all the controversial programmes as legitimate, with the exception of *Hoviyyat*'s attack on the late literary historian, Dr Abdol-Hossein Zarrinkoob, who later received homage in other programmes on Iranian television. Mr Larijani described the attack on Dr Zarrinkoob as a case of 'friendly fire', using the English words in a Persian language interview.[32] He also repeated his denial of the charges of financial misappropriation at radio and television raised in a report by the Sixth Majlis in April 2003,[33] saying that the IRIB was 'amongst the purest organizations' and a planned court hearing would clear the matter.[34]

However, criticism of Mr Larijani's record had begun even before the end of his term and increased noticeably after Mr Zarghami took office. In April 2004,

300 women's rights activists gathered at the office of the Association of Iranian Journalists (AOIJ) to protest against TV's 'clichéd image of women'. They demanded that television end all programmes with an 'anti-woman content', 'truly reflect' women's activities by giving a platform to independent women's groups, and cover women's activities worldwide to secure their human rights. They also demanded legislation that would provide punishment for women's negative portrayal on television and place the organization under judicial, as well as 'popular', supervision through women's NGOs and civic organizations. Another demand was for private radio and television networks to be set up and for independent productions by women's NGOs and other civic organizations to be carried by national television.[35]

In January 2005, the Iranian Women's News Agency, established by women members of the Islamic city councils, carried a report that accused television of portraying traditional marriages as dysfunctional, tension-ridden and short-lived and promoting remarriage and polygamy.[36] And in February, a woman Majlis deputy accused the IRIB of 'male chauvinism', saying that it had broadcast only a few minutes of news and reports about women deputies.[37]

A group of religious officials and Friday prayer leaders meeting Mr Zarghami in November criticized the 'vacuous content' of some television programmes, crime and violence in 'many films', and children's lack of respect for parents and elders in some TV series. They called on television not to show popular programmes at prayer times, and instead try to encourage the public to visit the mosques, something that television 'had to do', now that it had been able to support 'sports, the culture of observing traffic regulations, and even the Qoran', to which one television channel was devoted. There was also a call for a 'mosques department' at television, as well as a television network to counter the '7,000 doubts raised about Shi'ite' Islam since the Revolution'.[38] At another meeting, the production team working on a TV drama based on Joseph's life were warned by more senior religious authorities that dealing with such a subject amounted to 'walking on the edge of a razor blade, with morality and immorality on the two sides'. The film-makers were warned about the two types of love in Joseph's story, the 'pure love for Joseph of people such as his father', and the 'impure love' of the Pharaoh's wife. The story, they were advised, had to be dramatized in such a way that those who fond of Joseph would see him like 'rose and jasmine and take the beauty of that love to their hearts and souls'.[39]

The leader sets IRIB's mission

In December 2004, Mr Zarghami, his managers and some of the IRIB staff members were received by Ayatollah Khamenei who said the Islamic Republic was the only 'resistance group' standing in the face of a 'global, authoritarian, wealth-centred class' that was 'occupying the Middle East and the Islamic region economically, culturally and politically'. The 'media war', Ayatollah Khamenei, said was the 'true war in today's complex world', and the 'national medium', that is, television, had an important role to play in the confrontation. Ayatollah Khamenei set ten major goals for the IRIB to follow:

> (1) elevating enlightened religious understanding; (2) immunizing the society's mind against the foreign media's destructive offensive; (3) deepening public faith in the regime's effectiveness; (4) strengthening the country's executive management; (5) promoting public solidarity, empathy, and affection; (6) promoting the movement to generate science, ideas, and theories; (7) meeting the public's need for smiles, leisure, and entertainment; (8) keeping alive the concern with justice; (9) strengthening the movement to awaken the Islamic world; and (10) promoting public morality.

The IRIB Director said quality improvement was the organization's top priority, for which a 5-year plan had been drawn up. He said planning was also underway to ensure maximum participation in presidential elections in a healthy environment.[40] Another senior IRIB official told the media that the organization had committed itself to impartiality in the elections.[41]

Mr Zarghami may have decided that the organization had succeed in 'supplying smiles' when, soon after the meeting with Ayatollah Khamenei, he described a Friday morning show on the radio, *Iranian Friday*, as the 'peak of radio satire', adding that 'making the faithful happy is a form of prayer'.[42] His colleagues, however, appeared to be doubtful that all of Ayatollah Khamenei's instructions would be carried out. Writing in the organization's own daily *Jam-e Jam* (Jam's Chalice), a senior television film-maker and advisor to the IRIB Director, complained that he had heard 'such statements from His Excellency time and time again on various economic, political, cultural, social and even military matters during meetings with top level officials and various managers. But who's listening?'[43] Several years earlier, in 1999, Ayatollah Khamenei himself had spoken of protesting to the national radio and television 'once a week or less frequently, sometimes in a strong tone',[44] a situation that need not have arisen if he did have the command over the organization that his position would suggest.

By the time Mr Zarghami was in charge of the IRIB, the organization appeared to have taken on an even more independent position. Thanks to their majority in the Majlis, the conservatives occupied four of the six seats on the IRIB's Supervisory Council and were reported to believe in the Director's 'total control' over the organization.[45] The government, now in a minority, would complain that the Director would not consult the Council about his decisions or actions.[46]

Commentators criticized the shortage of interesting programmes other than football on the most popular television network, Channel 3,[47] where sports reporters and commentators regularly mispronounced foreign names; referred to the Persian Gulf as 'the Gulf'; or made up phrases and sentences in violation of Persian grammar or its common usage.[48] TV series produced for the fasting month of Ramazan were described as 'not very successful in attracting the audience', with sequences about breaking fast inserted into the programmes merely to give them a religious flavour.[49] Overnight programmes 'underestimated the intelligence of the audience', were 'old-fashioned' and 'less imaginative than the test card.'[50] The IRIB's music policy also came under indirect criticism when it was announced that its Music Production Department would help create 3-member music teams, in a break with the past practice where the lyrics had to be approved by the Poetry Council, which would then commission a composer to make the music. A singer would then record the song. Sometimes, the three would never meet. The new teams, it was hoped, would generate more harmony,[51] even though musicians and their instruments would still not be shown on television, in keeping with the organization's music broadcast policy.[52] In comments that implicitly challenged Mr Larijani's record, IRIB staff members advised Mr Zarghami to deal with the 'obesity and lack of planning and ideas' at the organization, ' "one fifth of whose staff" was adequate for a well-run and orderly organization.'[53] And in a curious twist to the debate over the morality of the 'Berlin Conference' nude clips, opponents of Mr Larijani's presidential bid were reported to have sent copies of a CD with 'indecent and immoral scenes from television programmes' to religious authorities in order to damage his chances as a Presidential candidate.[54]

In 1966, under the monarchy, Iranian print journalists had complained that the 'limitations that are placed on the press do not apply to radio, television, and cinema, which often carry freely what is considered unsuitable for the press.'[55] The same complaint was made nearly 40 years later, after the Islamic Republic's television began broadcasting imported and locally made police series and war movies with plenty of scenes of violence, while a highly successful newspaper specializing in crime coverage quickly lost its licence.[56] Reformist journalists accused television of trying to 'eliminate' them by ignoring their newspapers in its press reviews, broadcasting programmes hostile to them, without giving them the right to reply, and censoring the defence statements of journalists appearing before the Press Court.[57] Following the newspaper closures that began in 2000, the leadership of the Association of Iranian Journalists would openly say that the union did not have good relations with radio and television as an organization, although it did have respect for its reporters.[58] Union activists, however, would express suspicion about television reporters covering events held in protest against newspaper closures.[59]

Ethnic and cultural 'discrimination'

The IRIB has also been criticized for failing to represent Iran's cultural and linguistic diversity. Writing in *Rasaneh* in spring 2003, using very cautious figures on Iran's population, the communication scholar, Dr Mehdi Mohsenian-Rad, showed (Table 8.1) that while accounting for slightly more than 50 per cent of Iran's population, Persian speakers had more than 90 per cent of the IRIB's airtime. The Azarbaijanis, who made up an estimated 22.5 per cent of the population had a 4.45 per cent share of the airtime; the Kurds' 7.5 per cent share of the population gave them 1.79 per cent of the airtime; Iran's Arabs, with 3.5 per cent of the population, had been on the air for 0.49 per cent of the time; and the remaining 14 per cent of the public had been able to use 0.77 per cent of the airtime. All ethnic minorities had had a significantly smaller share of the airtime on the much

Table 8.1 Iran's ethnic and linguistic communities and their representation on national radio and television[a]

Language	Population share (%) (approximate)	RTV share (%)	Radio share (%)	TV share (%)
Persian	52.5	92.5	90.66	95.71
Turkish	22.5	4.45	5.03	3.44
Kurdish	7.5	1.79	2.5	0.53
Arabic	3.5	0.49	0.68	0.17
Others	14	0.77	1.13	0.15
Total	100	100	100	100

Note

a Dr Mehdi Mohsenian-Rad, 'Zarourat-e Tavajoh beh Maqouleh-ye Ertebatat-e Mian-farhangi dar Jame'eh-ye Iran beh Manzour-e Movajeheh-ye Sahih ba Tahavolat-e Jame'eh-ye Ettela'ati' (The Necessity of Paying Attention to the Concept of Inter-cultural Communication in Iran for the Purpose of Correctly Dealing with the Developments in the Information Society), *Rasaneh Quarterly*, vol. 14, no. 1, Spring 2003, pp. 19–26.

more powerful television than on radio, while the Persian speakers' exposure on television had been more than 5 per cent higher than on radio. There was concern that by focusing heavily on Persian, the IRIB was alienating other linguistic communities in the country, thereby damaging the status of Persian language among them. According to one report, quoted by Mr Mohsenian-Rad, Iran's largest Azari-speaking province, East Azarbaijan, had ranked third in the country in terms of Persian literacy in 1976, but by 1991 had fallen to the twenty-third place. There was also concern over the IRIB's inadequate sensitivity to the religious beliefs of Iran's Sunni Moslem population.[60]

Mr Mohsenian-Rad pointed out that in spite of Iran's ethnic diversity, Shi'ite Islam and Persian language had been acknowledged as agents of national unity and national solidarity. He went on to say that while the long-held view of religion and language as agents of national unity had not been challenged seriously, it was 'certainly' going to be questioned because of global developments, 'especially during the next two decades'.[61] By early 2005, ethnicity had already appeared as an important subject in the forthcoming presidential elections. At a meeting in Tehran in January, Kurdish reformists demanded, among other things, Sunni representation among 'members of the cabinet, provincial governors and ambassadors'.[62] Arab political activists meeting later on said the reformist movement had not done enough for ethnic communities during the previous eight years and the reformists needed to increase their efforts to meet ethnic rights.[63]

In February 2005, the IRIB faced an international challenge when France banned the satellite relay of the Iranian, Arabic language channel, *Sahar* (Dawn), accusing it of carrying 'anti-Semitic material', including a film about Israel's actions against the Palestinians, and an interview in which a French commentator had said that 'most of the images depicting the bodies of Jews in World War II were in fact pictures of Jews killed by infectious diseases.'[64] The French action had been predicted by Iran's communication officials in December 2004, when

France stopped satellite broadcasts of the Lebanese Hezbollah's *Al-Manar* (Beacon) channel, accusing it of carrying anti-Semitic material.[65] Iranian officials had then urged the government to move towards launching an Iranian satellite,[66] planned in 1996, when Iran's National Security Council instructed the Ministry of Post, Telegraph, and Telephone[67] to secure Iran's three internationally agreed orbital positions and purchase a satellite. In January 2005, Iran signed an agreement with Russia for the construction and launch of the satellite *Zohreh* (Venus), within two-and-a-half years. The cost of the project was not announced, but it was said that with a 15-year lifespan, the satellite would save Iran $163m in rental fees.[68]

Online news

In the meantime, a conflict between an Iranian news organization and a United States internet service company focused attention on Iran's fast growing online news services. On 14 January 2005, an American web-hosting company terminated its contract with the Iranian Students News Agency (ISNA) for what it described as legal restrictions and gave the news agency 48 hours to find another host. The press freedom group, Reporters Without Borders, and other critics said the move

Table 8.2 A selection of online news and information sources in Iran[a]

	Name	Address	Funder
1	Aftab News	www.aftabnews.ir/	Reputed to have been launched by the Expediency Council, chaired by former President Rafsanjani
2	Azad University Students News Agency	www.ana.ir/	Islamic Azad University
3	Baztab	www.baztab.com/	See note under *Baztab* below
4	Cultural Heritage News Agency	www.chn.ir/	Cultural Heritage Organization
5	Fars News Agency	www.farsnews.com/	N/A
6	Ghavanin, legal website	www.ghavanin.ir/	Tehran Justice Office
7	Ghest News Network	www.ghest.net/News.jsp	Judiciary
8	Iranian Agriculture News Agency (IANA)	www.iana.ir/	Ministry of Agriculture
9	Iranian Quran News Agency (IQNA)	www.iqna.ir/	Jihad Daneshgahi, Centre for Quran Activities
10	Iranian Students News Agency (ISNA)	www.isna.ir/	Jihad Daneshgahi, Ministry of Sciences and Technology
11	Iranian Women's News Agency (IWNA)	www.iwna.ir/	Women members of Iran's Islamic Councils
12	Iran Labour News Agency (ILNA)	www.ilna.ir/	Worker's House

Table 8.2 Continued

	Name	Address	Funder
13	Iran Oil and Energy News Agency (SHANA), in Persian, or Petroenergy Information Network (PIN), in English	www.shana.ir/	Ministry of Petroleum
14	Iran Pas News Agency (IPNA)	www.ipna.ir/	Police Force and its Football Club, Pas
15	Islamic Republic News Agency (IRNA)	www.irna.ir/	Ministry of Culture and Islamic Guidance
16	Islamic Republic of Iran Broadcasting (IRIB), Central News Unit	www.iribnews.ir/	National radio and television organization
17	Mehr News Agency	www.mehrnews.com/	Arts Council of the Islamic Publicity Organization
18	Mowj News Agency	www.mojnews.com/	'Private'
19	Pupils Association News Agency (PANA)	www.irpana.ir/	Islamic Republic News Agency and the Students Association
20	Rooydad	http://rooydadnews./ blogspot.com	Islamic Iran Mosharekat (Participation) Front [blocked by the Judiciary in summer 2004]
21	Shabestan News	www.shabestannews. com/	Ministry of Culture and Islamic Guidance
22	Shahokooh, first Iranian village to go online, followed by its neighbour, Gharnabad	www.shahkooh.com/ www.gharnabad.com/	Local communities
23	Sharif University's News site	http://sharifnews.com/	N/A
24	Society of Iranian Youth News Agency (SYNA)	www.syna.ir/	National Organization of Iranian Youths
25	Students News Network (Baseej)	www.snn.ir/	Baseej-e Daneshjouyi (University Student Mobilization)

Note
a *Rasaneh Supplement*, vol. 1, various issues, October–December 2004, and the websites concerned. All sites accessed last on 15 August 2006, unless otherwise stated.

was politically motivated and concern was expressed in Iran about many other Iranian websites hosted by the same company. Reporters Without Borders said internet users in Iran were already facing heavy government censorship, so the role of web hosts outside Iran's borders was even more important. The Iranian Students News Agency eventually moved to another host.

ISNA, set up in 1999, is the oldest of more than 30 online news sources that have since emerged in Iran. The names and addresses of some news agencies and a selection of other news sites are listed in Table 8.2. Brief descriptions of a representative selection follow.

1 *Aftab* (Sunshine) was launched early in 2005, reputedly by the Expediency Council, chaired by former President Rafsanjani, to disseminate information about Iran's nuclear programme. However, it gradually turned into a general news site, aiming to 'firstly to display Iran's rich, several thousand year old culture' to Iranians and 'secondly to promote and symbolize "ethics" in all arenas – especially politics'.[69]

2 *Baztab* (Reflection) is widely believed to have been launched by the former Commander of the Islamic Revolutionary Guards Corps, Mohsen Rezaie, who has served as Secretary of Iran's highest decision making body, the Expediency Council. The belief that *Baztab* enjoys strong political support has been reinforced by the fact that it carries some of the most varied and outspoken online reports about allegations of corruption and mismanagement, open discussions of religious issues, such as critical comments on Shi'ite mourning services during the month of Moharram, and sharp political satire. In March 2005, the director of *Baztab* said the site supported the 'entirety of the Islamic Republic', was not tied to any political faction, and was funded by advertising and 'charitable donations'.[70] The site has been suspended by the authorities on several occasions.[71]

3 *Fars* news agency, launched in February 2002,[72] is close to conservative forces.

4 *Ghest News Network* was set up by the Judiciary following a 2001 instruction by Ayatollah Khamenei for 'correct, serious, consistent, guided, rational, and considered publicity about the fight against economic corruption'.[73]

5 *Iran Agriculture News Agency* (IANA) went online on 15 November 2005 to cover agriculture and rural development. [74] Its areas of coverage include agricultural economics, non-governmental agricultural organizations, research and development, international agricultural news, and rural culture and arts.[75]

6 *Iran Labour News Agency* (ILNA) was established by the Islamic Republic's equivalent of a trade unions federation, *Khaneh-ye Kargar* (Worker's House) in February 2002 with the aim of 'information dissemination for the toiling stratum of labourers, and with justice-centred discourse as its motto'.[76]

7 *Iranian Quran News Agency* (IQNA/IKNA) was established on 10 November 2003, with the aim of promoting 'Quranic culture among various social strata; comprehensive and up-to-date Quranic information dissemination across the country and internationally; and reflecting and recording Quranic material'. The agency has 36 full-time staff members, and has issued Honorary Reporter cards for President Khatami and his second Minister of Culture and Islamic Guidance, Ahmad Masjed-Jame'i, Nos. 001 and 002, respectively.[77]

8 *Iranian Students News Agency* (ISNA) was established in 1999. By July 2005, it had 19 separate news departments, 80 full-time staff members – managing editors, senior editors, editors, reporters, translators, typists, support, and technical staff – and 70 part-time reporters. ISNA is supported by the

Ministry of Sciences and Technology with an annual budget of Rls 6–7bn [$700,000–800,000].[78] The agency also offers training courses.[79]

9   *Iranian Women's News Agency* (IWNA) was started by a group of women members of Iran's Islamic city councils in order to 'disseminate information about women's abilities and the obstacles they face'.[80]

10 *Islamic Republic News Agency* (IRNA) is Iran's official and oldest news agency. It was set up in 1934 as Agence Parse, a department of the Ministry of Foreign Affairs, with the task of providing news to officials, the public and the press. Renamed as Pars News Agency, it was incorporated into the newly established Ministry of Information in 1964 and began a 24-hour operation. In 1981, it was renamed the Islamic Republic News Agency. IRNA has national, regional, and international news teams in Iran, 30 bureaus abroad and a service for monitoring international radio, television and online news services. It was the first news organization in Iran to have an online news service.[81]

11 *Islamic Republic of Iran Broadcasting* (IRIB) Central News Unit supplies news to the radio and television networks and the daily *Jam-e Jam*.[82]

12 *Pupils Association News Agency* (PANA) was set up in May 2003 by the ministries of Culture and Islamic Guidance and Education. Operations began in the summer of 2003, with software enabling student reporters to file from anywhere in the country. Former President Khatami is an honorary member of staff.[83] In January 2005, the government announced plans to bring 5,000 schools online by the end of the Iranian year, 20 March 2005, and to raise the number to 130,000 by the end of the Fourth Development Plan in 2009.[84]

13 *Shabestan News Agency*, supported by the Ministry of Culture and Islamic Guidance, covers the programmes at 45,000 mosques across the country.[85]

14 *Shabakeh-ye Akhbar va Ettela'at-rasani-ye Naft va Enerji* (SHANA) (Oil and Energy News and Information Network) or, in English, the Petroenergy Information Network (PIN), carries news and information about fossil fuel and nuclear energy sources.[86]

15 *Sharifnews* went online in August 2004, 'following the work done by the Political Studies Office at the Sharif University of Technology', Iran's most prestigious university for engineering, but with reporters studying at 'all the universities in Tehran'. The agency says its goals are 'the same as those of the Islamic Revolution. We cherish independence and value freedom and our red line is defined by ethics and religious principles'.[87]

Apart from the much older IRNA, the IRIB news service and ISNA, the other online news services in Iran have emerged in recent years following the closure of reformist newspapers. Several sites are operated by factions whose newspapers were closed down and are staffed mostly by journalists who worked on those papers. The online services, therefore, share some of the weaknesses of the press, as well as having their own problems of using a new medium, without any subscription or advertising revenues.[88] Not surprisingly, their output has been criticized as falling short of professional standards, 'lacking analytical depth', and being 'politically biased'.[89] The new services are also Tehran-based and, according to some critics, have 'nothing' to offer the people in the provinces, 'unless there is an earthquake and someone is sent to cover it'.[90] At newspaper offices, with their inexperienced and low-paid staff who have to work for several papers to make ends meet, the abundance of news from online services has led to journalists 'buying ready-made material' rather than producing their own.[91]

Six million internet users

Personal use of the internet has also grown very rapidly in Iran since 1995, when the country's first Internet Service Provider (ISP), Neda Rayaneh, was set up by Tehran Municipality.[92] The number of users rose from 250,000 in the year 2000, the beginning of the Third national Development Plan, to 6 million in January 2005.[93] The number was set to rise further, given the fact that the country had 16.9 million fixed telephone connections.[94] The government had granted licences to 600 ISPs, with 80 more to come. Other companies had been given licences to set up high capacity connections that would raise the speed of online communications by nearly 40 times.[95] Most internet users were to be found in Tehran and other large cities, but the service was also spreading to the countryside, where all villages with more than 100 inhabitants had telephone connections.[96] One village, Shahkooh, near the north-eastern city of Gorgan, went online in 2000, followed by the neighbouring Gharnabad, the site of Iran's 'first comprehensive rural communication and information technology centre', and of a conference on the application of communication and information technology for national development. The experience gained at the two villages has been used by the Ministry of Communication and Information Technology to draw up plans for bringing 10,000 villages online.[97] In parts of the country, private companies applying for the new licences for high-speed internet connections were asked to provide equipment for villages in exchange for using government facilities.[98]

While the growth of the internet in Iran has been impressive, the 2005 figures were modest by global standards. The absolute number of internet users did not place Iran among the top-twenty countries, where the lowest position was occupied by Sweden, with more than 6.7 million users. Iran's per capita usage, or internet 'penetration' level, of 7 per cent[99] was less than one tenth of Sweden's 74.3 per cent, the highest in the world.[100] Regionally, Iran was doing much better than Afghanistan, Pakistan and all the countries in Central Asia and the Caucasus, with penetration levels of between 0 per cent and 3.6 per cent, except for Armenia's 6.7 per cent.[101] Iran also stood well ahead of Palestine (West Bank), Syria, Yemen, and Iraq, and at about the same level as Jordan, Oman, Turkey, and Saudi Arabia and Lebanon, but well behind Qatar, Kuwait, Bahrain, Israel, and the United Arab Emirates, where the penetration levels ranged form 16.4 to 29.6 per cent.[102] Given the speed at which the internet had grown worldwide and in Iran, the Islamic Republic's target of a 30 per cent penetration level by the end of the Fourth Development Plan in 2009[103] was likely to be achieved, if not surpassed, not least because of the fall in the prices of computers, globally, and of internet connections in Iran, where local phone calls at less than 0.2 cents per minute were already very low by most Western standards. At a time when Iranians were complaining of the rising price of everything, the government promised that the cost of using the internet would be halved by 21 March 2005, the beginning of the Iranian New Year.[104] By the end of Iran's Fourth Development Plan, of course, other countries may also have moved much further ahead.

'Blogging'

Weblogs, or personal online diaries, have grown even more rapidly since appearing in Persian for the first time in 2001. By October 2005, there were an estimated 100 million weblogs wordwide,[105] 700,000 of them produced by Iranians, of which about 40,000–110,000 were active. Most of the Iranian weblogs were in Persian,[106] reportedly the fourth most widely used language by weblog-writer in the world after English, French, and Portuguese.[107] More than 85 per cent of the Persian language weblogs were said to have been hosted by the Iranian company, Persianblog.[108] In November 2006, Persianblog hosted 32 categories of weblogs, including: 'General' (29,612), 'Computer and Technology' (8,427), 'Literature' (7,763), 'Life' (7,535), 'Education and Research' (6,662), 'Satire' (4,932), 'Business and Commerce' (3,251), 'News' (2,260), 'Cinema' (1,553), 'Journalism' (918), 'Afghanistan' (801), 'Sports' (642), and 'Tajikistan' (147).[109] Many weblogs are in formal Persian of a high quality, but there are also writers who use the spoken language, sometimes with vocabulary that others might consider vulgar or obscene.[110] While most weblog writers are anonymous, some are well-known personalities, such as the former Vice-President Mohammad-Ali Abtahi, who publishes his diaries and comments, as well as photographs of ministers and other officials, sometimes in their private lives.[111]

Just as the proliferation of newspapers in the second half of the 1990s led to a collision between the Judiciary and the press, so did the expansion of internet journalism in the following five years. And just as the first confrontation led to newspaper closures and detention of journalists, the internet clash led to the closure of websites that the authorities considered immoral, sacrilegious, or detrimental to national security, and the detention of people who had produced or written for them. The conflict became particularly intense in the run-up to the parliamentary elections in February 2004, with the authorities requiring internet service providers to restrict access. According to Reporters Without Borders, about 10,000 sites had been blocked by the end of 2004.[112] Even Persianblog and Orkut, a site affiliated to the internet search company, Google, that is used to locate old friends and set up virtual clubs, were briefly blocked by the judiciary in January 2005.[113] While many of the blocked websites are based abroad, two of the most prominent closures, in August 2004, were those of *Emrouz* (Today) and *Rooydad* (Event) that had been launched by reformists inside Iran.

Between August 2004 and February 2005, a total of 18 people were arrested for having 'acted against the system by working on illegal internet sites', including *Rooydad* and *Bamdad*, and *Gooya* (Vocal or Articulate) that is based abroad.[114] Most were released on bail after spending up to three months in prison, without a date having been set for their trials,[115] but one person was given a 14-year jail sentence,[116] and one a 6-month sentence.[117] Two detainees issued statements after their release saying they had repented what they had done.[118] Later, they and several other detainees had meetings with a committee that reported to President Khatami, the head of the Judiciary, Ayatollah Mahmoud Hashemi-Shahroudi, and the Commander of the Police Force, General Mohammad-Bagher Ghalibaf, and said they had been mistreated while in detention. During the meetings, which were reported by Mr Abtahi on his weblog, the journalists said they had been put under long interrogations, beaten up and asked questions about their sex lives in order to force confessions out of them. One journalist, Fereshteh Qazi, also said she had suffered a broken nose during her detention.[119] The Police Commander apologized for what had happened and said he would look into their complaints against the police.[120] On 16 January, the Head of the Judiciary, Ayatollah Hashemi-Shahroudi, appointed a special committee to examine the confessions and report its findings. On 9 March, the Ayatollah announced that the Committee was 'still reviewing' the cases filed against judges and judiciary bailiffs, including 'the weblog writers' files.'[121] In April, the Judiciary announced that only four of the weblog writers were to face charges, which were not specified, and the others, including the women, had been 'acquitted'. The Judiciary also said that there had been 'irregularities' in the manner in which the detainees had been held and treated, and that these would be 'dealt with'.[122] In June, a 27-year-old weblog writer, Mojtaba Sami'inejad, was given a two-year prison sentence for 'insulting one of the authorities' in his weblog, but was acquitted of the charge of acting against national security. Significantly, the court said apostasy, with which he had been charged was 'not a crime', and Mr Sami'inejad had been tried for 'abusing the Prophet'.[123]

Challenging the faith, defending the heritage

A decade after the mid-1990s surge of enthusiasm about the internet and the freedom of expression that it was expected to bring along, governments around the world have imposed controls on the internet, and it has become clear that 'surveillance is much easier in cyberspace than in the real world.'[124] However, new technology has expanded the space for public debate and 'opened the way to greater democracy, albeit at a relatively slow pace'.[125] In the case of Iran, online communication has not only led to a high degree of open political debate, but Islam itself has been subjected to unprecedented scrutiny. The internet has made it possible for the critical views of Ayatollah Khomeini's former successor designate, Ayatollah Hossein-Ali Montazeri, to reach a far wider audience than would have been possible in print. In addition to Ayatollah Montazeri's own website,[126] his views are also reflected on other sites, including that of the BBC's Persian Service, which also carries fresh pictures of the Ayatollah.[127] Another notable religious site is the weblog of the reformist cleric, Ahmad Ghabel, who has overturned the common view of Islamic jurisprudence that reason will govern only in cases where religion has not provided any rules, by declaring that religious laws need be resorted to only where human reason cannot provide a satisfactory answer to a question.[128] The views of Mr Ghabel, who for a while took up residence in Tajikistan after being imprisoned in Iran, have also been carried online by the BBC's Persian Service.[129]

While the Iranian government has been widely accused of disregarding the views of its citizens, in November 2003 Iranian public opinion, expressed through the internet, helped bring about a change of policy abroad, forcing the American magazine, the *National Geographic*, to alter its recently published online atlas on which the Persian Gulf had also been given the 'alternative' title of 'Arabian Gulf'.[130] The Iranian government banned the reporters and sales of *National Geographic*,[131] which had been extremely popular in Iran for decades, and more than 90,000 people signed an online letter of protest to the magazine.[132] *National Geographic*, whose own 2003 style manual had explicitly banned the use of 'Arabian Gulf' for the Persian Gulf,[133] rapidly issued a 'clarification' and amended the online map.

The clash between the state and the internet journalists was reminiscent of the earlier, unsuccessful, attempts to ban the use of video recorders in the 1980s and satellite receivers in the 1990s. In early twenty-first century, while the Iranian Judiciary was busy closing down websites on religious or political grounds, another communication upheaval was taking place with the increasing use of mobile telephones capable of sending text, using Short Message Service (SMS),[134] as well as photographs. As in other countries, mobile phones in Iran were seen as a powerful means of earning revenues, especially from young people, estimated at rials 100,000 [$11.2] per month per phone.[135]

By the end of 2004, 3.5 million Iranians were using mobile phones and 5.6 million had paid deposits for the new connections that were to be made available in the following few years.[136] It was expected that the number of mobile phone users would exceed 25 million by the end of the Fourth Development Plan, 2009.[137] Services promised by the authorities – including weather reports, football scores and university entrance exam results – were unlikely to satisfy the young people who were going to make up a substantial proportion, if not the majority, of the mobile phone users. Much of their conversation and SMS traffic was likely to consist of social and, perhaps, political chat, with unpredictable consequences. Political text messages were already widely in use by the time of the June 2005 Presidential election, many of them attacking former President Rafsanjani in the run-up to the first round, and then trying to rally support for him in the second round, against the Tehran Mayor, Mahmoud Ahmadinejad.

9 Organization, education, and training

The Iranian journalists' largest pre-Revolution trade organization, *Sandika-ye Nevissandegan va Khabarnegaran-e* Matbou'at (The Syndicate of Newspaper Writers and Reporters), was formed in 1962, with the 'special support' of Mohammad-Reza Shah,[1] and backed by his longest-serving Prime Minister, Amir-Abbas Hoveyda.[2] A member of the Syndicate's first elected board of management, Daryoush Homayoun,[3] was to become Minister of Information and Tourism in 1978 and oversee the publication of the article in the daily *Ettela'at* that insulted Ayatollah Khomeini, setting off the cycle of protests that culminated in the Shah's overthrow.[4] Even though the Syndicate organized two strikes by journalists during the Revolution,[5] the backing it had received by the Shah's regime could not have endeared it to the revolutionary regime. The Syndicate was not officially banned by the Islamic Republic, but it fell into disuse since the new law provided for workers' 'associations', but not for syndicates.[6]

The first organization to represent the interests of the press under the Islamic Republic was formed in 1989, after a group of newspaper publishers met the then Minister of Culture and Islamic Guidance, Hojjatoleslam Seyyed-Mohammad Khatami, and asked for permission to set up a Press Cooperative 'to defend their rights'. The publishers of 32 newspapers and magazines later met and selected a five-member board of directors for the Cooperative. In 1991, the Cooperative secured President Rafsanjani's approval for providing the newspapers with 100 vans and later arranged for Bonyad-e Mostaz'afan to provide a number of motorcycles for the smaller papers. The Cooperative secured 300 housing units for the staff of its member publications; replaced the newspaper kiosks around Tehran with new ones; obtained lower rates from printers for newspapers; secured government credits to set up its own print works to print the smaller newspapers; obtained a plot of land from the Ministry of Construction Crusade to build a press club, recreation facilities and a print works; and started a biweekly, *Karnameh-ye Matbou'at* (The Press Record) to cover the events related to the press.[7]

However, journalists responding to a 1990 survey said it was necessary for them to have a trade union to deal with the problems of job insecurity, lack of professional or financial protection, lack of contact and understanding among the journalists and the absence of an authority to resolve trade disputes. Another survey, in 1994, found that the journalists considered the absence of a trade union as one of the biggest problems they faced. The demand for a union grew stronger in the following years, with journalists describing it as not only a 'necessity, but a legitimate requirement of the times'. They also said that they would have to overcome several obstacles before they could establish a union, including

> divisions among journalists; the belief held by some that a union would be a political organization, causing new difficulties; structural problems that impeded the creation of civil society institutions in the country; the general inability to accept criticism; the extremely centralized and paternalistic nature of government organizations; the intrusion of political biases into the community of journalists; individualism; lack of professional independence; the affiliation of the press to the centres of power; lack of awareness of professional rights; lack of a rich, deeply rooted press culture and the less than favourable history of trade organizations in the country.[8]

Newspaper publishers and editors responding to a 1996 survey were much more positive, with the majority saying that circumstances were right for setting up a union because of factors including the quantitative and qualitative growth of the press, the rise in the numbers of journalists, and the presence among them of veterans of the profession. However, most respondents also thought that the problems of political factionalism, inter-generational conflicts, lack of trust, and lack of awareness of common interests among the journalists needed to be overcome. Forty per cent of the respondents thought the union should be set up by the journalists themselves, while 60 per cent believed the first step had to be taken by the Ministry of Culture and Islamic Guidance.[9]

Newspaper publishers organize

The idea of setting up a journalists' union had emerged in 1995, after a group of newspaper publishers had been received by the Supreme Leader, Ayatollah Khamenei, who said 'explicitly that it would be very effective for the press community to have an organization'. Two years later, in September 1997, soon after President Khatami's election, the Association of Iranian Journalists (AOIJ) was inaugurated at a general assembly with more than 500 participants who also ratified the Association's constitution. Although the Association had been founded by the publishers of six daily newspapers, the general assembly elected a board of directors that did not include any publishers.[10] The publishers were later excluded from membership altogether when the Association's rules and regulations were drawn up.[11]

The AOIJ, which describes itself as Iran's 'only nationwide and inclusive journalists' trade organization', is recognized by Iran's Ministry of Labour and Social Affairs. It is open to journalists who have been working for the press for three consecutive years and can present 10 samples of their work for each year, from different months. They also have to produce a letter of accreditation from their place of work. By January 2005, the Association had 2,699 members in three categories: 2,510 full members, with three years of experience, who had the right to vote; 189 associate members, with less than three years of

Table 9.1 The Association of Iranian Journalists –
membership details[a]

Year	2002	2004
Total	1,846	2,699
Full	N/A	2,510
%	N/A	93
Men	1,429	2,083
%	78	77
Women	407	623
%	22	23
Dailies	1,164	N/A
%	63	N/A
Provinces	N/A	276
IFJ members	N/A	1,004
%	N/A	37

Note
a Author's interviews with the AOIJ Vice President,
Dr Karim Arghandehpour, 8 January 2002 and the
union's Secretary, Mr Mass'oud Houshmand-e-Razavi,
4 January 2005.

experience; and 7 honorary members, who may not have been journalists, but had provided services in the field of journalism (Table 9.1). The Association has been registered with the United Nations as a non-governmental organization (NGO). It has also been accredited by the International Federation of Journalists which many AOIJ members have joined. Unlike the pre-Revolution Syndicate which had members at newspapers and at radio and television,[12] the AOIJ's membership is open only to print journalists,[13] excluding their colleagues at news agencies, radio and television and online publications. In spite of a call by the union's leadership in June 2002 for proposals to amend the constitution and allow expanded membership,[14] no change had been made by the time of this writing.

Much of the Association's efforts since its establishment have consisted of protesting against the closure of newspapers and detention of journalists, subjects that have featured on the front pages of most issues of its newsletter, *Rouznamehnegar* (Journalist), which first appeared in September 1999. However, the organization has also been able to take measures to improve journalists' pay and working conditions, including the creation of an arbitration committee to resolve the differences between journalists and their employers. In line with its predecessor, the Syndicate, it has also provided its members with subsidized housing. The Association has organized leisure tours for its members; supplied them with mobile phones; set up a fund that has been issuing interest-free loans of between 2,000,000 rials [$240] and 5,000,000 rials [$600]; and set up a fund to support the families of jailed or unemployed journalists.[15] It has also set up a college of journalism with a degree validated by the Ministry of Science and Higher Education (of which more below).

While the AOIJ is the largest trade organization of Iranian journalists, several other unions have also been set up, some as early as 1990, to represent special groups of journalists or promote specific issues related to the profession. These include the following:

1 The Association for the Defence of Press Freedom, set up in 2000, which has about 100 members and aims to support the 'free flow of information and the constitutional rights of the press and journalists'.[16] (An organization of the same name was founded in the summer of 1978, but did not survive long after the Revolution.)[17]

2 The Association of Children and Youths' Writers, formed in November 1999, has about 250 members, 30 per cent of them women. The Association's tasks are to secure insurance cover for its members and improve their pay and working conditions.[18]

3 The Association of Cinema Critics and Writers was founded in November 1995, 'following a request presented to the Ministry of Culture and Islamic Guidance by about 100 cinema writers and critics'.[19]

4 The Association of Crisis Photographers was formed in June 2004 with the aim of helping with the mobilization and delivery of national and international relief aid to areas affected by 'natural or unnatural crises to which Iran is very vulnerable'.[20]

5 The Association of Holy Defence Writers was set up in 2004, on Iran's Reporter's Day, 7 August, to 'redress the weakness that had existed in presenting a true image of the martyrs of the imposed war to the world'.[21]

6 The Association of Iranian Graphic Artists was established as a housing cooperative in 1997 and became a trade union the following year. It has 348 full members and some student associate members.[22]

7 The Association of Iranian Press Photographers, established in 1997, has 469 members, 252 of whom are full-time professionals working with various news organizations and the rest are freelancers. The Association's main service has been to provide its members with accreditation. It also has plans to offer training courses later in 2005.[23]

8 The Association of Moslem Journalists, with 350 members – 60 of them women – is aimed at 'promoting the ethics of journalism, based on Islamic teachings'.[24] The Association is registered with the Ministry of Interior as a political organization.

9 The Association of Sports Writers and Photographers was set up in November 1995, at a general assembly attended by 89 out of the country's estimated 150 sports writers and photographers. The Association was licensed by the Interior Ministry in 1997,[25] under a law that regulates Iran's political parties.[26]

10 The Association of Tehran Freelance Journalists, formed in January 2002, has 300 members, more than 60 per cent of whom are women. The higher ratio of women among freelancers compared to the members of the much bigger AOIJ is accounted for by the fact that the Association of Freelance Journalists recruits not only writers and reporters, but also typists, graphic artists and

layout artists, most of whom are women. The Association has been established in accordance with guidelines from the International Labour Organization that 'require the formation of city trade unions, before provincial and national ones could be established'.[27]

11 The Association of Young Journalists was formed in February 2004 by journalists from a number of weekly and daily newspapers and young sports writers, to raise 'problems such as insurance, salaries, ranks, training and promotion opportunities', and to support young journalists who had lost their jobs following the closure of reformist newspapers.[28] In February 2005, the Association had 200 members, 50 per cent of them women.[29]

12 The Iranian Women Journalists' Association was registered with the Interior Ministry in February 1999 as the nucleus of a women's political party, but later also developed as a trade organization. It has 460 members.[30]

13 The National Centre for Theatre Critics was founded in 1990 and within six months had 167 full and honorary members.[31]

A survey of journalists in September 2004 found the following shares of union membership among them: the Association of Iranian Journalists, 39.4 per cent; the Association of Moslem Journalists, 6.5 per cent; the Association of Iranian Press Photographers, 6.5 per cent; the Iranian Women Journalists' Association, 5.3 per cent; the Association of Children and Youths' Writers, 2 per cent; the Association for the Defence of Press Freedom, 1.6 per cent.[32]

Relations between the Association of Iranian Journalists and the Association of Moslem Journalists were so bitter that neither group attended a session about trade unions at the Third Seminar to Study the Problems of the Iranian Press in March 2005, each protesting against the other's presence. It was left to the Women Journalists' Association and the Association for the Defence of Press Freedom to protest against the detentions of journalists and newspaper closures which had led to 'insecurity among journalists, especially women.'[33]

From ad-hoc training to College of Communication

The first training course for Iranian journalists was offered in 1939 by the Ministry of Culture, after it had been learned during a visit by a group of foreign journalists to Iran that there were very few journalists in Tehran who could speak any foreign languages or had had any professional training. The programme was organized by the editor of the Ministry's magazine, Mohammad Moheet-Tabatabie,[34] who later became one of Iran's most highly regarded academic figures and the author of one of the best histories of the press in Iran. The courses were taught by some of the leading literary figures of the time, including the novelist, Mohammad Hejazi; the writer and literary historian, Saied Nafissi; and the writer, Abdorrahman Faramarzi, who in the 1950s became one of Iran's most influential commentators as the editor of *Kayhan*. The course came to an end with the Allied invasion of Iran and the fall of Reza Shah in September 1941. The next series of journalism courses was offered by American trainers in the 1950s as part of the aid programme the United States had made available to the Shah's government, following the overthrow of Dr Mosaddeq's government in 1953.

The next round of journalism training, in 1964, was organized by the publisher of *Kayhan* newspaper, Dr Mostafa Mesbahzadeh. The courses were taught by a number of *Kayhan* journalists whom Dr Mesbahzadeh had sent abroad for training. These included Hamid Molana, the first Iranian to obtain a PhD in journalism, who studied in the United States, and Kazem Mo'tamednejad, who received his doctorate in France. In October 1965, Dr Mesbahzadeh was allowed by the government to set up a college, *Moassesseh-ye Ali-ye Matbou'at va Ravabet-e Omoumi* (Advanced Institute of the Press and Public Relations), with four-year BA courses in journalism, public relations and publicity, translation, photography, and film-making. The first entrance examination was attended by 6,000 applicants, with 300 admissions. Two years later, the institute was renamed *Daneshkadeh-ye Oloum-e Ertebatat-e Ejtema'i* (College of Social Communication Sciences).

Shortly after the February 1979 Revolution, the College of Social Communication Sciences fell victim to the general closure of universities. Communication re-emerged in late 1980 as a subject within the College of Social Sciences, when 30 colleges and university departments specializing in literature, humanities and social sciences were amalgamated in what finally became known as the Allameh Tabatabaee University. MA courses in communication were launched in 1990, and PhD courses in 1996,[35] to train 'managers and advisors who would improve the operations of communication organizations, in particular the press, news agencies, radio and television networks' and 'specialists to confront the global media domination through communication activities on national and international levels'.[36] In December 2004, the Department turned into the College of Social Communication Sciences to offer courses in journalism, public relations, and communication and information technology studies.[37]

The pre-Revolution College of Social Communication Sciences had been highly selective in its admissions policy and very demanding in its academic programme, with BA students required to complete 36 credit units in English as well as French, German or Italian. MA students were supplied with 'the best resources' and had to perform to very high standards of achievement.[38] Students admitted to the mid-1990s BA communication programme at Allameh Tabatabaee University had had communication among the lowest of the 75 choices they could make when taking the general university entrance examination. Most had had high school grade averages of between 10 and 12 out of 20, with the highest achievers among them reaching 14.05.

The BA programme's 126 credit units included a total of 9 units in foreign languages, 5 of them in Arabic and an unspecified 'foreign language', and 4 in 'specialist language', which consisted of 'reading social communication texts' in English. Journalism itself took up 28 credits, or 22 per cent of the programme, with the rest going to communication theories, Islamic studies, demographics, statistics, politics, management, and law. The programme had three credit units on 'mass communication laws', but no course on Iran's Press Law that had been at centre of the conflicts between the press and the state in Iran since the 1906 Constitutional Revolution. The University had no facilities for photography, recording, or producing student newspapers, nor could it afford adequate fees to bring in working journalists to teach practical skills.[39] The programme did not include any courses on computers.[40]

The Radio and Television College

Iranian radio and television's *Daneshkadeh-ye Seda va Sima* (College of Voice and Vision) is the country's second oldest media training centre, having been established in 1969 as *Madresseh-ye Ali-ye Cinema va Televizion* (The Higher School of Cinema and Television).[41] In the academic year 2004–05, the College had 430 students on courses in various areas of radio and television programme production, and 202 studying news for radio and television, mass communication research, media management and advertising.[42] The IRIB has also published more than 40 titles on the media.[43] However, the education offered by the radio and television College does not appear to have had much direct impact on the press, first because much of it has been of a technical, rather than editorial, nature. Second, while the conservative newspapers, especially *Kayhan*, have had a close relationship with the broadcast media, especially television, the interaction between radio and television and the reformist press has been hostile, as pointed out in the preceding chapter.

The Centre for Media Studies and Research

The first post-Revolutionary media training institution, the Centre for Expansion of Media Education, was established in October 1989, as part of the office of the Deputy Minister of Culture and Islamic Guidance for Press and Publicity, to 're-train the editorial staff of the newspapers and train competent staff for the press'. At the same time, the Ministry established a Centre for Media Studies and Research, 'with the primary aim of carrying out research in communication, with particular emphasis on press and journalism'. The two were merged in 1996, under the collective title of the Centre for Media Studies and Research, with the primary educational aim of 'training and retraining the staff working at the newspapers and then, capacity permitting, to train other applicants'. The Centre offers short courses in journalism and graphic arts for the press during two terms in an academic year. The journalism branch has included practical courses such as Persian language for the press, writing, editing and managing news, writing reports and articles, interviewing techniques, as well as theoretical courses such as the fundamentals of mass communication, international communication, and the press law. There are also optional courses for journalism students in photo-journalism, graphic arts, and layout design. The graphic arts branch has covered basic and specialist drawing, graphics, photography, layout, printing and publishing, and image-making for the press.

The Centre has also organized intensive courses in provincial capitals for local journalists, representatives of large-circulation newspapers, and staff members of public relations offices. Between September 1997 and January 2004, the Centre organized 69 journalism courses, with 2,763 graduates, and 15 graphics courses with 111 graduates. The Centre's publications include *Rasaneh*, a quarterly journal of media studies and research, first published in 1990; more than 50 books on media training, media theories and the history of the press in Iran; and more than 100 reports on the Iranian press. In 2005, the Centre had a library with more than 3,500 titles in Persian; nearly 2,000 titles in foreign languages; and collections of university dissertations and Iranian and foreign newspapers and journals.[44] In 2005, the Ministry of Culture and Islamic Guidance announced that it was planning to transfer journalism training to the private sector, under the Ministry's supervision.[45]

Islamic Azad University

Between 1993 and 1999, the Islamic Azad (Free) University, a nationwide network of 'non-governmental, non-profit making'colleges,[46] had a total of 220 journalism admissions, with an enrolment pattern matching the rise and fall of journalism in Iran during the same period. The intake was a total of 4 for the first 3 years, 1993–95, well before the newspaper boom that followed President Khatami's 1997 election. It rose rapidly in 1996, 1997, and 1998, reaching 22, 50, and 121 respectively. In 1999, the intake fell to 23, and no new admissions were listed for the following years.[47]

Tehran University

Since 1994, Tehran University's Faculty of Social Sciences has been offering 'practical journalism' and 'specialist journalism' as subjects that are taken by some 400 students a year at its Social Communications Department. The Faculty does not offer any degree courses in journalism.[48] In the spring 2005 semester, the 'practical journalism' course was dropped due to 'lack of demand', but 'specialist journalism' was still being offered.[49]

Falling academic standards

A 1994 review by the Centre for Media Studies and Research of dissertations written by communication graduates at various Iranian universities noted that, with the exception of a few 'worthy works of scientific value', the rest demonstrated a 'declining trend' in academic standards. Most of the dissertations had been translations of foreign texts, or copies of earlier dissertations, some by authors who had died, or copies of dissertations written at other colleges. The widespread copying, said the review, may well be the reason why college libraries were not lending dissertations for outside use.[50] The extent to which journalism college courses before or after the Revolution had contributed to the quality of the country's press is debatable, since one of the leading figures in the field, Dr Mohsenian-Rad, found in 1994 that out of 1,000 graduates in 22 years of journalism education in Iran, only 60 had joined the press.[51] Ten years later, the communication scholar Dr Mo'tamednejad estimated that at 'the very best', only 10 per cent of journalism students would have learned the skills that would prepare them for work at newspapers. That was the reason why the newly established College of Social Communication Sciences was going to have either a separate entrance examination or a specialist one following the main university entrance examination. 'Journalism', said Dr Mo'tamednejad, 'is not something you do accidentally'.[52]

Following a speech in April 1996 by the Supreme Leader, Ayatollah Khamenei, who strongly criticized the quality of the press,[53] an editorial in *Rasaneh* said it was 'painful to witness publications with numerous technical weaknesses', even though there were specialist journalism courses at 'three major centres, Allameh Tabatabaee University, the Islamic Azad University and the Centre for Expansion of Media Training, but we must accept that such weaknesses exist'. The editorial said journalism education at universities had to include 'practical experience' to allow the students to have their first 'trials and errors' while producing student publications, rather than after they had started professional work. It also called for training workshops to be organized for working journalists. One option, said *Rasaneh*, would be for workshops to be set up by universities, but it added that knowing the facilities at the universities, such a proposition was 'in effect asking for the impossible'. Alternatively, newspaper publishers themselves could organize training for their editorial staff and 'plan for it, just as they plan for the provision of paper and printing material'. Success, said the editorial, would require 'close and sincere cooperation between the educational centres and press institutions', something which had been talked about over the years, without 'any serious move' having been made. The editorial ended with a rather desperate 'call on all those involved in professional journalism training and on the large and small press organizations to think about this important matter and try to find a solution to this big problem'.[54]

Cartoon training

One of the brightest spots in Iranian journalism training seems to have been the Iran Cartoon House, an affiliate of the Arts Organization of Tehran Municipality, which was established in 1996 to support 'the recognition, upgrading and propagation of cartoon and caricature in Iran' and help Iranian cartoonists to 'introduce their works in Iran and the world'.[55] Between May 1999 and March 2005, the Cartoon House had had more than 6,000 trainees on its courses. The Centre houses an archive of cartoons produced in Iran and other countries.[56]

The News College

In 1998, the state-owned Islamic Republic News Agency (IRNA), inaugurated its *Daneshkadeh-ye Khabar* (News College), also known as the School of Media Studies, with a four-year BA programme that includes specializations in the coverage of economic, political, cultural, arts, strategic sciences, and sports news.

According to the College's constitution, women have to make up 30 per cent of its students. 50 per cent of the seats are allocated to IRNA staff; 20 per cent to the staff of the other media organizations and the public relations staff of state organizations; and the rest go to other applicants. The College, affiliated to the University of Scientific–Applied Studies, also runs short-term training courses for IRNA's staff and those of other media organizations.[57]

The AOIJ College

The Association of Iranian Journalists is the latest organization to have launched a college offering degree courses in journalism. The college, known as the Centre for Scientific–Applied Training, is affiliated to the University of Scientific–Applied Studies, and grew out of short-term training courses offered at the Association's offices. The college began in 2002 with 16 students of photojournalism. By the end of 2004 it also had courses in English translation, reporting and public relations, with a total of 150 students.[58] The Association says that because of their specialized nature, the courses offered by its college and by IRNA provide the students with guarantees of employment. However, the Association acknowledges that the absence of any courses in media economics and media management is a major shortcoming in its curriculum, as well as in those of all other schools and colleges offering education in journalism.[59]

Between theory and practice

In the summer of 2004, the editor of IRNA's sibling, the daily *Iran*, Kasra Nouri, repeated the oft heard view that Iran's 'journalist training system has not yet been able to produce graduates who can easily move from the theoretical world into the practical one'. Working journalists might not have a great chance of learning on the job either, because 'when a publication is having trouble meeting its very basic needs, it will try to recruit the cheapest human resources possible and it cannot possibly pay any attention to training.' On the other hand, said Mr Nouri, there were many successful journalists in the specialist press who had studied subjects other than journalism. The educational system, 'with textbooks 20 or 30 years old', had to be brought up to date, and a remedy had to be found for a 'major weakness of the newspapers', namely the fact that very few members of staff knew English'.[60]

In January 2005, an article in *Shargh* remarked that many journalists did not know Persian very well either. The article spoke of the 'bitter truth' of 'extremely ill-read and illiterate journalism students' at universities being taught by instructors few of whom were journalists. 'Our student and our novice reporter', said the article, 'know as much as the unenthusiastic instructor who merely reads out what he has just read' and who would also 'pick up a pen and write thick books' about journalism. 'This', said *Shargh*, 'is the great pain: students and journalists who study very little; scarcity of professionals; ignorance of vocabulary and syntax; unawareness of Persian literature; and the lack of a personal prose style'.[61]

The gap between Iranian journalism's academic establishment and the practising journalists was demonstrated starkly at the poorly attended Third Seminar to Study the Problems of the Iranian Press, 1–2 March 2005. Journalists made up one-third of the 18 speakers.[62] There were no senior editors, prominent journalists or newspaper managers among the audience. Nor were there any senior officials from the Ministry of Culture and Islamic Guidance present throughout the two days.[63] The Minister, Ahmad Masjed-Jame'i, attended the Seminar towards the end of its second day, to deliver a speech which highlighted, once again, the quantitative growth of the press. The Minister did, however, have the chance to hear an unscheduled, detailed presentation about the severe problems faced by provincial journalists,[64] to which he responded by calling for a special seminar to discuss the subject.[65]

10 One hundred years of legal confusion

The Iranian state's first commitment to press freedom, within rather narrow bounds, came in the Constitution adopted on 30 December 1906, Article 13 of which said newspapers 'are free and authorized to publish useful material of common benefit such as the Majlis debates and the public's comments on them', as long as the content would not 'disrupt any of the principles of the state or of the nation', adding that publishers of 'tendentious material opposed to the above or committing accusation and libel' would be 'legally interrogated, prosecuted and punished'.[1] The Amendment to the Constitution, adopted on 8 October 1907, contained three references to the press, all rooted in the Belgian Constitution. The Amendment's Article 20 said 'all publications, except misleading books and material harmful' to Islam would be 'free and their censorship banned, but should anything opposed to the Press Law be seen in them, the publisher or writer will be punished in accordance with the Press Law. When the author is known and resident in Iran, neither the publisher, nor the printer, nor the distributor can be prosecuted.' The last sentence was a verbatim translation from the Belgian Constitution,[2] with the name of the country changed to 'Iran'. According to the Amendment's Article 77, there had to be a 'unanimous vote' for 'political and press wrongdoings to be tried in secret'.[3] Article 79 of the Amendment, calling for the jury to be 'present at the courts, with regard to political and press wrong-doings', had been adopted from the Belgian Constitution's Article 98,[4] omitting the reference to 'all criminal matters', which under the Belgian law also had to be heard by a jury.

The 1906 Constitution's lack of clarity as to what would 'harm' Islam or 'disrupt' the 'principles of state or the nation', and the incongruity of having jury trials for 'political and press wrongdoings' but not for criminal offences, survived the change of royal dynasties in 1920 and the Islamic Revolution in 1979 and has deeply affected the legal status of the Iranian press. 'Press and publications', says Article 24 of the Islamic Republic's Constitution, 'are free to express matters unless it is contrary to the principles of Islam or public interests. The details of this are to be determined by law.'[5] According to the Constitution's Article 168, 'political and press offences will be examined in public with a jury present in the courts of law. The procedures for selection, the conditions and powers of the jury and the definition of political offences shall be determined by law, on the basis of Islamic standards.'[6] Not only did the law fail to provide any definition of 'press offences', but its explicit instruction for the definition of 'political offences' had not been carried out either at the time of this writing. Matters were not helped when in 2001, more than 22 years after the establishment of the Islamic Republic, the 'principles of Islam' were officially described very broadly as the body of its 'beliefs, moral codes, rulings and rituals', and the 'rights of the public' as 'all the obligatory laws accepted in Islam and the Constitution for the individual, society and the state, in the varied personal and social relationships that include the private rights governing the relationships between individuals and also the public rights in the realm of the relationship between the people and the state'.[7]

The chaos and the flames

The ambiguity has been central to many of the conflicts between the press and the judiciary that have been covered in the preceding chapters. The spirit, and some-times the letter, of the journalists' protests in the past decade could be found in a 1915 address to the Majlis by the deputy and Poet Laureate, Malek-o-Sho'ara Mohammad-Taqi Bahar, himself the publisher of the newspaper *Nowbahar* (New Spring). Since the Constitutional Revolution, he complained, there had not been a 'day when the government has been happy with the press and the press happy with the government.' The press was 'engulfed in the flames of chaos', Parliament was silent, and the government was 'fanning the flames'. Newspapers were being banned without trial, with the Interior Minister saying the summary closures resulted from '*politiques generales*' [*sic*], while the country did have a press law 'on the basis of which the affairs can be run extremely well'.

Bahar called on the Majlis to 'discipline the newspapers' without allowing them to be 'executed', because that would amount to 'executing the spirit of the country's literature and culture'. Even if the government did not think so, Bahar argued, it could 'at least consider a newspaper publisher to be as important as a shopkeeper' whose business could not be shut down without a trial. Although the press did on occasions 'commit injustice', he said, for instance, 'hitting at Parliament's rights and being impertinent towards a freedom-seeking deputy', he would not be happy to see these newspapers being closed down 'in front of the Majlis' eyes without due process of law.' Warning that 'the blows dealt at the press' would eventually strike the Majlis, he called on the 'the Ministry of Justice to immediately establish a legally sanctioned court that is qualified to try the press, with a jury, at the Ministry of Justice and put an end to this chaos'.[8]

The state's case then and now can be seen in a 1918 article in the semi-official daily, *Iran*,[9] which said that 'instead of being guides to a blissful future', the country's newspapers had turned into 'tools for swindling, extortion, picking pockets', carrying the 'novel literature of abuse and insults', and being used by 'the ringleaders of daylight robberies'. The article wondered if the government officials' '"lack of courage in making useful decisions and taking action" was not "largely" due to their being intimidated by what was being published by the press', some of which could not be published 'in countries with several hundred years of freedom of the pen', without the writer facing prosecution. 'In the name of the Constitution', said the article, 'a naked sword' had 'fallen into the hands of drunkards'. The press would say newspaper closures were illegal and the court hearing the cases of newspapers was not qualified, but they would not consider any 'scandalous behaviour' of their own to be illegal or detrimental to national interests. Why, wondered the article, did the nation read such newspapers? Why did it want them? 'To hear abuse and insults' from 'known and unknown authors?' It was incumbent on the Government, the article said, to try to uproot 'this corruption from the country and to put an end to this abuse of freedom of the pen decisively and seriously', without being hindered by any obstacles found 'in the path of taking a bold and courageous decision for the sake of the country's and the nation's happiness'.[10]

The Press Law referred to by Bahar had been passed on 8 February 1908, based on France's Press Law of 29 July 1881, and had undergone changes similar to those that happened to the Belgian Constitution when it became Iranian. On the one hand, the 1908 Iranian Press Law required only the submission of a declaration before a newspaper could be published, as did the French law. On the other hand, the Iranian law also demanded that the publishers pledge in writing to observe the Press Law, thereby in effect negating the freedom to publish without a licence that had been established in France. New legal restrictions were imposed on the press in the years to come, including the requirement for a publication licence to be obtained from the state, a condition that was retained in the Islamic Republic's Press Laws, the first of which came in 1979, in spite of the expectations of press freedom that had been created by the Revolution.[11]

Even more 'supervision'

The Islamic Republic's second Press Law, passed in 1986, provided for a Press Supervisory Board consisting of the Minister of Culture and Islamic Guidance or his representative, a Majlis deputy selected by the Majlis, a university professor chosen by the Minister of Culture and Higher Education, and a newspaper manager elected by the newspaper managers. The Board had the power to issue licences, 'examine the violations of the press' and, 'if necessary', arrange for legal prosecution by a court.[12] The composition of the Board gave the government decisive influence and the vague definition of its powers allowed it to withdraw newspaper licences without a court hearing. The 1986 law also contained three new sections. The first, the 'Mission of the Press', placed the press at the service of the state. The second, the 'Rights of the Press' allowed the press 'to publish constructive criticism' and 'disseminate news [...] to raise public awareness and protect the society's interests'. And the third, the 'Limits of the Press', forbade 'the publication of heresy' as well as 'spreading corruption', 'promoting extravagance', revealing confidential documents and instructions, insulting Islam or the Supreme Leader and the religious authorities, libelling state officials or religious authorities – even through the publication of pictures or cartoons – plagiarism, reproducing material published by 'deviant and anti-Islam' groups in a way that would promote them, and making 'instrumental' use of individuals and denigrating women.[13]

Restrictive as the changes to the Press Law were, they did not meet with any protest because of 'the extraordinary conditions created by the war'. After the war, however, conflicts developed between the press and the state both because of the law's limitations and because of its ambiguities, among them the absence of any definition of a press offence. Furthermore, the absence of any punishment stipulated for actions that had been described as an offence – for instance a newspaper 'encouraging actions against the country's foreign policy' (Article 25) – would leave the defendant's fate in the hands of the judge. The Law's presumed ban on censorship of the press by officials (Article 4) could not be enforced because such action had not been defined as an offence and was therefore not liable for any punishment,[14] whereas the 1979 Press Law had provided a lifetime ban from public service as well as a prison sentence for such an offence (Article 29).[15] In 1995, widespread protests led to the withdrawal of a bill that aimed to amend the 1986 Press Law by adding a teacher from the Qom Seminary to the Press Supervisory Board and giving it the legal right to revoke newspaper licences.[16]

Jury trials

Press trials in the presence of a jury, as required under Article 20 of the Amendment to the 1906 Constitution, began in 1909 and continued until 1928, well into Reza Shah's rule. There were no more trials with a jury under Reza Shah, especially after a May 1931 law had declared that the publication of 'insults', 'abuse', and 'libel', especially against the monarch, would not be considered 'press offences', making it possible for the authorities to close down newspapers that carried such material without any court hearings,[17] a practice that continued after the Allied occupation of Iran and Reza Shah's fall in September 1941. The next jury trial of a newspaper publisher was held in March 1950, after the absence of a jury had been strongly criticized during the month-long trial earlier in the year of the nationalist leader and opposition newspaper publisher, Dr Mozaffar Baqai.

There were more jury trials, as well as trials without a jury, after Dr Mosaddeq had taken over as Prime Minister in March 1951 and introduced new Press Laws in December 1952 and February 1953, bringing back some of the offences that had been removed from the Press Law in 1931, and providing for jury trials in all cases. There were several more press trials in the presence of the jury after Dr Mosaddeq's overthrow, using his legislation. A new Press Law, introduced in August 1955, replaced Dr Mosaddeq's laws and divided press offences into non-political ones that were to be tried by common courts without a jury, and political ones that required criminal court trials in the presence of a jury. It also reduced the number of jurors from five to three. However, no more jury trials took place under the monarchy.[18]

Although the Islamic Republic's 1979 Constitution had stipulated that 'political and press offences will be tried in public and with a jury present in the court of law', and the 1979 Press Law had devoted eight articles to the formation and operation of the press jury, the provision first came into practice many years later, in the case of clerical publishers of critical newspapers. However, under a decree from Ayatollah Khamenei, issued in September 1991, such clergymen were to be tried by a special court, in the presence of a 'jury comprising clergymen approved by the prosecutor and the judge'.[19] The decree was issued within days of protests over the secret trial, without a jury, of a clergyman who had been publishing a daily newspaper in the city of Mashhad.[20] One of the most important jury trials of clergy newspaper publishers came in September 1993, when the Special Court for the Clergy found the licence holder and manager of *Salam*, Hojjatoleslam Seyyed-Mohammad Mousavi-Khoeiniha, guilty of publishing 'insults and lies' and banned him from journalism for three years, with the sentence suspended for five years.[21] The sentence, which was not challenged by Mr Khoeiniha, was cited against him seven years later, when he was tried again by the Special Court for the Clergy following the closure of *Salam*.[22]

At roughly the same time that Ayatollah Khamenei authorized jury trials for the clergy, lay publishers of 64 newspapers wrote to the head of the judiciary, Ayatollah Mohammad Yazdi, protesting against 'ambiguities faced by the press as it performs its mission' and asking for any 'confrontation with any publication to take place within the framework of the Press Law, in the presence of a jury.'[23] Their request was met four years later, with the July 1995 appointment of a jury of 7 main and 7 substitute members, all of them conservative public figures, for a two-year period.[24] The acquittal of the managing-editor of the conservative daily, *Kayhan*, was the most notable event during the first jury's tenure.[25] The next round of jury appointment, during President Khatami's first year in office, resulted in a jury with 7 reformists, 2 of them women, among the 14 members (Table 10.1).[26] A conflict developed between the jury and the Press Court judge, Saied Mortazavi, when he overruled their not-guilty verdict in the February 1998 trial of Ezatollah Sahabi, the managing editor of the biweekly, *Iran-e Farda*, and ignored their recommendation for leniency at his retrial in November 1998.[27] In protest, five reformist members of the jury refused to attend the February 1999 trial of *Kayhan* managing editor, Hossein Shariatmadari,[28] and were disqualified by Judge Mortazavi from sitting on the jury for two years. One of the five, the lawyer and journalist, Kambiz Nowrouzi, later said that the dismissals had in effect stopped the court from functioning, achieving what 'some tendencies', implying the conservatives, had been trying to do for a year.[29]

The third group of press jurors, with a solid conservative majority, were appointed under the amended Press Law that was passed by the conservative-dominated Fifth Majlis during the last days of its term, on 26 April 2000. The new law added the head of the Islamic Publicity Organization and the representative of the Friday Prayer Leaders' National Policy Making Council to the panel in charge of selecting the press jury, which until then had consisted of a senior official from the Ministry of Culture and Islamic Guidance, a senior judiciary

Table 10.1 Press jury members appointed under the 2000
Press Law

Main members	Substitue members
Seyyed-Ja'far Shobeiri	Homeira Hosseini-Yeganeh
Mohsen Do'agou	Marzieh Vahid-Dastjerdi
Habibollah Asgar-Oladi	Ali Fazeli
Mohammad Agha-Nasseri	Mohsen Qomi
Jamal Shourjeh	Ja'far Mar'ashi
Sha'ban Shahidi-Moaddab	Shahaboddin Sadr
Reza Rahgozar	Abbas Salehi
Mojtaba Rahmandoust	Hamid Ansari
Mohammad Mirbaqeri	Ali-Akbar Kassaian
Fatemeh Karroubi	Ali-Reza Zakani

Source: Kashi, Gholam-Reza, *Matboua't dar Asr-e Khatami, Mordad
76–Mordad 79* (Press in Khatami's Era, August 1997–August 2000),
Tehran: Selk, 2000, pp. 180–181. Advice on the jury's political composition provided by Dr Hassan Namakdoost-Tehrani.

official and the chair of the City Council (Article 36). The new law also allowed
judicial authorities to appoint members of the press jury directly, should
their selection by the panel not have been completed by the due date (Article 36,
Note 1); and provided for the press jury's secretariat to be funded by and use the
resources of the Judiciary (Article 38, Note 30).

Tighter bounds

Other important changes to the Press Law included banning the publication of
any material against the Constitution (Article 6, paragraph 12); holding the
writer, in addition to the editor, responsible for the content of a publication
(Article 9, Note 7); demanding clearance from the Ministry of Intelligence, the
Ministry of Justice and the police for the publisher and editor of a newspaper for
which a licence application had been filed with the Press Supervisory Board
(Article 9, Note 6); banning anyone opposed to the Islamic Republic or with a
record of conviction for such opposition from involvement in any form of jour-
nalistic activity (Article 9, Note 8); adding two new members to the Press
Supervisory Board, a seminary professor selected by the Supreme Council of the
Qom Seminary and a member of the Supreme Cultural Revolution Council
(Article 10, paragraphs F and G) – achieving what the withdrawn 1995 bill had
failed to do and building into the Board a potential conservative majority; giving
the Board the right to stop a publication before its case had been heard by a court
(Note to Article 12); and banning the replacement of a banned publication with
one with a similar name, appearance or logo (Article 33, paragraph B).[30] An
attempt by the reformist majority in the Sixth Majlis to amend the law once again
and remove the new restrictions failed because of opposition by the Supreme
Leader, Ayatollah Khamenei.[31]

Meanwhile, two other legally significant developments had also taken place. First, the Revolutionary Court had become directly involved with the press, closing the daily, *Zan* (Woman), in April 1999.[32] Second, the judiciary had prosecuted individual journalists for what they had written for the press, at criminal courts without a jury, arguing that the Press Law's provision for jury trials applied only to the managing editor who was to be held responsible for every item in the publication. Writers, said the judiciary, were responsible for their own act of writing, rather than for publishing it. They were therefore covered by the Islamic penal code (Article 697) that provided for the punishment of anyone writing or publishing anything criminal.[33] The Judiciary maintained that its actions had been fully based in law, as had been demonstrated by the prosecution of two journalists, Emadeddin Baqi and Mashaallah Shamsolva'ezin, whose convictions had been upheld by the appeal court and the Supreme Court.[34]

Legal unawareness

While the Iranian press by and large has criticized the judiciary as being politicized and acting against press freedom, publishers and journalists themselves have been criticized, by their supporters, for their dealings with the country's legal system. Speaking at the Second Seminar to Study the Problems of the Iranian Press in 1998, Kambiz Nowrouzi, a lawyer with expertise in press cases, said journalists had often taken political action, for instance by mobilizing public opinion, rather than defending their rights by using the guarantees provided by the law, thereby further weakening the press and allowing the law's 'protective function' to fall into disuse.[35] According to President Khatami's reformist Ministry of Culture and Islamic Guidance, the legal problems of the press had been compounded by the fact that many journalists and publishers did not know what was contained in the Press Law, a shortcoming which in 2001 was the cause of 'one third of the Ministry's notices to the press'.[36] There was also a shortage of specialist lawyers to defend the press, because the Press Law had not been taught at the faculties of law, although there were plans to introduce the subject at post-graduate level.[37]

However, reformist legal experts maintained that even with knowledge of the law, journalists would still be at risk because, there was no clear definition of concepts such as the principles of Islam;[38] newspapers could be closed down by a variety of authorities, sometimes without any court hearing; and laws such as the 1960 Public Security Law for crime prevention were being applied to the press without any legal justification.[39] Conservative legal experts rejected the accusation that reformist newspapers had been treated unfairly, saying such papers had been banned because they had questioned Islamic rules such as those on 'stoning, retribution, inheritance and testimony', while there had been no ban on newspapers that had not 'insulted Islam'.[40] The reformist journalists were also criticized by their conservative colleagues for 'abiding by the first part' of the Constitution's Article 24, which provides for press freedom, while ignoring its second part that bans the publication of anything 'contrary to the principles of Islam or public interests', as if 'they were living in London or Paris'.[41]

Plans for a 'media system'

Following a directive from President Khatami in 2003, a group chaired by Dr Kazem Mo'tamednejad set out to produce four documents to set up 'a comprehensive media system for the country' to guide the press 'into an active and dynamic phase, directed not by political biases, but by the principles of freedom of information dissemination and responsibility and accountability', so that it could 'prevent the government from making mistakes'.[42] The four documents, prepared in 2004, included a draft bill for the formation of a Media Council 'as an independent, public service institution aimed at expanding the public right of access to information, supporting and protecting the independence of the press, establishing and promoting scientific and professional standards for journalism and adherence to its professional ethical principles' (Article 1.A). The Council, funded by the government (Article 18), would have 9 members, 3 of them appointed by the President, the Judiciary and the Legislature, 3 representing the Bar Association, the Association of University Professors and the Supreme Provincial Council, and 3 representing the journalist's trade organizations (Article 8). The Council would provide training for journalists, advise governmental and non-governmental organizations on strengthening the freedom, independence and professionalism of the media, cooperate with the journalists' unions and media managers to develop a convention on the media's 'self-regulation', and would have the authority to deal with complaints from the public about the media's violations of the ethics of journalism (Articles 2–6).[43]

Another document, the Convention on the Ethical Principles of Professional Journalism, on the one hand sets out journalists' 'duties and responsibilities', including:

> providing accurate information and rational and fair analysis; viewing news as public goods, rather than a commercial commodity; refusing material rewards and resisting pressures and threats aimed at influencing the journalist's professional conduct; keeping journalism separate from advertising; respecting religious principles and beliefs, ethnic and national customs and traditions and good conduct and public decency; striving towards international peace and tranquility and nations' peaceful coexistence; confronting the spread of weapons of mass destruction; preventing environmental pollution; fighting against global cultural and communication domination; respect for democracy and human rights, linguistic and cultural diversity, nations' right to development and support for liberation movements; respect for individual dignity and personal privacy; avoiding insults, libel, and slander; providing special support for the rights of women, children and youths, and mobilizing support for the old, the sick, and the needy; and keeping the sources of confidential information secret, unless there is a court order for disclosure.

On the other hand, the Convention defines 'journalist's rights and privileges', including:

> freedom of access to all sources of news and information about all aspects of public life, except where there are legal restrictions; editorial independence;

the right to refuse any action in contravention of the general policies of the media organization as stipulated in its collective employment contracts; the prohibition of forcing journalists to act against their beliefs and conscience; participation in the ownership and management of the media organization; the right to set up trade unions; the creation of a Media Council with the participation of journalists, media managers and certain independent cultural and social institutions to protect the independence of the media; the right to receive regular professional training; protection of intellectual property rights; confronting any discrimination in employment with the aim of promoting women's participation in professional journalism; and national, regional and international laws to protect journalists against any threats to their personal safety and professional security.[44]

The third document is a draft bill for setting up a legal framework 'to help secure professional independence and impartiality for journalists and promote their public service in expanding the right of universal access to information for the purpose of enhancing the quality of public life and the country's social, economic and cultural progress'. The statement, in the document's preamble, is fundamentally different from the Press Law's requirement, cited above, for the press to be at the service of the Islamic Republic. The document's other distinction lies in offering a definition of professional journalism much wider than what has been commonly used in Iran in two respects. First, the definition would apply not only to print journalists, but also to those working for news agencies, radio and television and online news services. Second, the definition includes not only writers and reporters, but also calligraphers, graphic artists, photographers, and proof-readers (Articles 2–3), while leaving out 'advertising staff, casual contributors and managers' (Article 3, Note 1) and the 'designers of crossword puzzles and games' (Article 3, Note 3). If adopted, the new definition would increase the official size of the journalists' community enormously, potentially giving them greater social and political power. The emphasis in the document on the need for journalists' independence from 'governmental and political authorities' and from the 'special interests of the owners of commercial enterprises' (Article 1.2) could also help the media professionals. However, the efficacy of the document is likely to be reduced by the elaborate accreditation mechanism that takes up 15 of the bill's 37 articles.[45]

The fourth document produced by Dr Mo'tamednejad is a draft collective employment contract, in 42 articles and 25 notes, to be signed by 'representatives of media owners and managers and representatives of journalists' trade unions to establish the working conditions of editorial staff of newspapers and other media'.[46] Given the state of the Iranian press, as discussed in the preceding chapters, this document appears to have the least chance of success in the near future.

Sceptics speak

Doubts have also been expressed already about the effectiveness of the other pieces of draft legislation and regulations that are meant to create Iran's 'comprehensive media system'. Kambiz Nowrouzi, who has defended several newspapers and has also been on the press jury, believes that such laws 'cannot be effective in a society where the democratic system has not been institutionalized, and whose government is still a long way away from democratic principles applying to such an important arena as the press'. Mr Nowrouzi has argued further that 'without careful social consideration of the circumstances of the press, press bills could become counterproductive, turning a dynamic, independent and comprehensive press into a dependent and frail' profession.[47]

The reformists' long-standing call for the abolition of the newspaper licensing system did not appear to have any chance of being met soon either, in spite of their arguments that the system had failed to control the press; that it existed in only a few countries other than Iran; and that it was inherently conducive to corruption, with licences being issued to bring the state political or material gain, rather than to promote professional journalism.[48]

'Uneconomical' jury

In 2004, the reformists also saw the practical defeat of their only legislative success, the creation of a law for selecting a large pool of people – 500 in Tehran and 100 in the provinces – from among whom a 'more representative' jury would be selected. Soon after taking their seats in the Seventh Majlis in June 2004, the conservative majority argued that the new jury system could not be set up because the reformists' provision for meeting the costs of establishing it through 'donations' would make the system vulnerable to abuse. While a debate continued inside and outside the Majlis as to how the legal defect could be remedied, no press trials could be held because of the absence of a jury, leading to protests not only from the journalists' union and reformist political groups,[49] but also from the Tehran Prosecutor, and former Press Court Judge, Saied Mortazavi, who said the absence of a jury system was detrimental to the legal system and the journalists.[50] Finally, the Majlis announced in January 2005 that while 'preparations were being made' for the new jury to be funded through the government's budget and for its pool of members to be selected, a procedure that could take a year,[51] press trials would be held in the presence of the jury as stipulated under the 2000 Press Law, passed by the conservative majority in the Fifth Majlis.[52]

There were signs in March 2005 that the authorities had decided to adopt a softer approach towards the press, with the Head of the Judiciary, Ayatollah Hashemi-Shahroudi, advising the courts 'to try not to close down newspapers, but to deal with the offenders',[53] and the Commander of the Police, General Mohammad-Baqer Ghalibaf, announcing that police officers found to have physically attacked the reporters had been 'punished severely'.[54] Journalists' groups welcomed Ayatollah Hashemi-Shahroudi's instruction as an 'implicit admission' that the closure of more than 100 newspapers had been 'illegal' and demanded the resumed publication of such newspapers, 'the rehabilitation' of journalists who had been imprisoned, and the reimbursement of the financial losses that had resulted from the newspaper closures. However, they expressed scepticism about the effectiveness of the instruction, given the fact that as long as it had not been made into law by the Majlis, it could be disregarded by judges on grounds of their professional independence.[55] At the same time, the Majlis' Culture and Islamic Guidance Committee announced that the revision of the Press Law would be placed on the parliamentary agenda in the Iranian New Year (beginning on 21 March), with the aim of 'removing its defects'. There was also a suggestion that cash penalties, rather than prison sentences, would be imposed on journalists found guilty of press offences.[56]

The 'revision and reform' of the Press Law has been promised by the 4th Development Plan, 2005–2009, which also calls for 'the preparation of a bill on the professional security of those engaged in culture and arts' and the provision of a 'three-year unemployment insurance cover for those engaged in culture and arts, at the discretion of the government'.[57] The question was whether the reform would move in the direction of providing the legal structure called for by the Association of Iranian Journalists' legal advisor, Kambiz Nowrouzi, at the Third Seminar on the Problems of the Iranian Press, in March 2005. Mr Nowrouzi said a legal regime for the press in Iran would have to take account of six rights:

1. The right to publish freely, close to what had been provided under the 1986 Press Law, but had not been observed by the Press Supervisory Board, nor under the 'very strict regime' introduced by the year 2000 amendments;
2. The right to sustain publication, including the prohibition of the closure of newspapers, other than in very exceptional circumstances, and even then with very difficult conditions, a right which has not so far been protected by the regulations in force in Iran;
3. The right to obtain news form public sources, while respecting individual privacy, that had been acknowledged in the 2000 Press Law, but needed stronger guarantees for its application;
4. The right to disseminate news freely, as recognized by the Constitution, while acknowledging the government's right to impose censorship on the press, 'limited in time and content', as had been done in the United States at the time of its wars against Iraq;
5. Journalists' right to enjoy professional security, with heavy penalties stipulated for attacks on them;
6. The right to special judicial proceedings, which had been provided in the Constitution's Article 168 but had never been realized in full.

'In praise of compromise'

In line with his earlier criticism of the journalists' failures to use the law, Mr Nowrouzi concluded his speech by saying that although legal guarantees were needed for the development of press freedom in Iran, it was only through 'development from within' that the press and the journalists could become a community with an impact on how decisions were made in the country.[58] There are signs that such a development has been underway. Commenting on the

Iranian press in 1993, the writer and former *Ayandegan* journalist, Mohammad Ghaed, noted:

> More often than not, Iran's daily newspapers have paid little attention to technique, with the journalists believing in the existence of a 'truth' that has to be revealed as rapidly as possible. In practice, however, because of insufficient mastery of technique, inadequate or incorrect information, or the journalist's haste in conveying the 'message', many readers are led to believe that the newspapers' continuous hue and cry is, in fact, a smokescreen hiding certain issues.
>
> One could say that the most reputable newspapers in the world are those who recognize the established state and government as undeniable facts, but also acknowledge that there are those who, for whatever reason, do not share such recognition. In such a case, the press informs the public of the state's views, while at the same time informing the state of the views of its opponents. [...] If newspapers are able to provide a picture of the contradictions that exist in their own society and in the world, they will be read every morning both by the highest state officials and by their opponents.[59]

Although Iranian journalism is still some distance away from such a secure status, even some of the most passionate campaigning journalists who were inspired by President Khatami's 1997 electoral victory and the reformist movement that followed, and paid the price by losing their jobs or freedom, have since then modified their view of journalism in order to protect the newspapers in which they work. The new attitude was summed up in 2004 by Mohammad Qouchani, the editor of *Shargh*, the only major reformist daily to have survived the round of newspaper closures that began in April 2000. Speaking at a seminar on 'Scared Pen, Truthful News and the Journalist's Mission', Mr Qouchani defined the journalist's honesty as 'not lying to society'. This, he said, was because of 'uncharted red lines' that could not be crossed. His paper, he said, had consequently decided 'not to enter certain arenas', not because of 'lack of honesty', but because of 'lack of ability', with the aim of ensuring the paper's survival. 'Journalism', he said, 'is our job, our passion and our life, something that we don't want to lose, unless we reach the point where we cannot work honourably'. 'Life', said Mr Qouchani, 'is a compromise'.[60]

11 Conclusion

Iran's history has been characterized by repeated political convulsions that have led to the creation of a 'short-term society', without the opportunity to accumulate sufficient material and moral wealth for the well-being of all its citizens.[1] As far as journalism is concerned, the past quarter century could, at first sight, be seen as a continuation of the same pattern, with two periods of rapid growth, a very short one in 1979 and a longer one nearly two decades later (1997–2000), each described as a 'Spring of Freedom', each followed by the closure of dozens of newspapers by the State. The first closures led to the exclusion from the profession of many journalists who had learned their skills before the 1979 Revolution. The closures that followed the second 'Spring of Freedom' affected dozens of newcomers to the profession, as well as a smaller number of surviving veterans.

Behind this bleak image, however, a more complex picture has developed, with areas of significant progress. The most impressive advances have been quantitative, with a rapid rise in the numbers of papers during the reform movement that followed the 1997 election of President Khatami. In 2004, Iran had more than 1,200 newspapers, and more than 5,000 men and women who made most or all of their income from writing for the press. The numbers of newspapers and journalists were nearly 10 times greater than what they had been at the time of the Revolution, having grown five times faster than the country's population.

There has been an even faster rise in the number of women in the press, who make up about one quarter of the journalists. Women journalists have made major contributions to the advancement of women's rights in Iran, as well as breaking new grounds in journalism in general and, consequently, coming into conflict with the state. However, women have been under-represented at senior editorial and managerial positions in the press, holding less than 10 per cent of the licences. Recent years have also seen the appearance of newspapers in Iran's minority languages, but not on a scale that would match renewed demands for representation by Iran's diverse ethnic and religious communities. The disparity has been particularly sharp in radio and television.

There have been major improvements in newspaper design and layout, the use of graphic arts and photography, and the quality of printing, particularly in the more expensive, and more profitable, specialist periodicals that can afford to invest in more experienced staff and better technical resources. The quality of writing, however, has not risen at the same pace and most papers have a long way to go before they could provide their readers with accurate, fair, balanced, and comprehensive coverage. Daily newspapers have suffered badly from the repeated closures and the exclusion of many of the country's best journalists who would have been best placed to train their younger colleagues.

Journalism students, and practitioners, are in urgent need of training and education in journalistic and computer skills, Persian and other local languages, foreign languages, Iranian and world history, economics, and media management. With radio, television and the internet supplying the public with the basic facts about a whole range of issues, print journalists can only succeed if they can provide their readers with context, background and expert analysis, enhancing their ability to cope with the future actively, rather than being taken by surprise and merely reacting to developments. While there has been a rise in the number of journalism training and education centres in Iran, the quality of journalism taught at colleges is in need of improvement, having fallen due to the scarcity of resources, shortage of practical experience and an over-emphasis on abstract, theoretical subjects. Iranian journalists also need to learn through exchange of information and experience with colleagues around the world. The rise in the numbers of books and other teaching material on journalism, the practical courses offered by a number of journalism training centres, and training visits to media organizations abroad by groups of Iranian journalists have been promising moves in the direction of dealing with these problems.

Professional training can only be effective if it is followed and supported at the workplace. Real and sustained improvement in the editorial practices of several thousand journalists across Iran can only be achieved if higher standards are in place at the country's most influential media organizations: the Iranian radio and television (IRIB); the national news agency (IRNA); and Iran's major newspaper groups, including the oldest two, *Ettela'at* and *Kayhan*. Without such editorial reform, the majority of the Iranians will not have access to the reliable news and information service that a large, highly urban and literate, and increasingly industrialized society needs for a healthy life.

Following the change of management at the IRIB, its output has been subjected to much more professional critique, rather than purely political attacks on the organization. The organization itself has also adopted a more open approach, in contrast with the preceding years when it was accused by the reformists of being biased against them. Although the more diverse political coverage might have been intended to increase public enthusiasm for the 2005 presidential election, the change in behaviour seems to have outlived the immediate expediency. IRNA's coverage has improved in recent years, especially in competition with more than a dozen much younger news agencies, but it is still constrained by being part of the Ministry of Culture and Islamic Guidance and could operate more effectively as a public corporation. Higher editorial standards, and hence higher circulations, at *Kayhan* and *Ettela'at* would not only bring financial benefits to the two organizations which are now heavily reliant on public funds, but would also elevate the status of titles that are part of Iran's modern cultural heritage.

The emergence of some 15 journalists' unions has been another positive aspect of the development of professional journalism in Iran. Most of these organizations are too small to supply their members with anything more than personal accreditation and professional networking, but the largest union, the Association of Iranian Journalists, has been active in defending press freedom, as well as supporting its members in disputes with their employers and providing them with facilities such as subsidized housing. To increase their effectiveness, the unions would need to open thier membership to journalists from radio, television, and the large numbers of news agencies and other online news services. Overcoming the political divide that has always existed between the press and the broadcast media in Iran would enable journalists' unions to influence the editorial standards as the country's single biggest provider of news, information and entertainment, the national radio and television.

In addition to the political pressures, Iranian journalists have also complained of low salaries, lack of job security and poor working conditions, raising the possibility of corruption, for example, accepting payment for favourable coverage, especially in business and financial journalism. New documents setting out the ethical standards of journalism and employment practices at newspapers are expected to be turned into legislation in the next few years in order to counter such professional ills. Another draft bill calls for the establishment of a Media Council, with membership drawn from the journalists' unions and other relevant organizations, to protect the journalists against political pressure and secure their right to self-regulation.

The Media Council could also deal with two contentious issues: newspaper publishing licences, the abolition of which has been demanded by many journalists who consider the system to be politically biased; and press subsidies, the bulk of which have gone to state-owned newspapers, increasing their advantages over the independent press. Since both the licensing regime and the subsidies are likely to be in place for the foreseeable future, journalists might be better served by demanding involvement in their implementation, through the Medial Council, rather than campaigning for their removal. The Media Council could depoliticize the licensing and subsidization regimes and implement them under transparent criteria drawn up through wide-ranging consultations. Supporting the minority publications that cannot survive on their own sales and/or advertising revenues would have to be a top priority for the Media Council.

Six press laws have appeared in Iran in less than a century, each drawn up in highly polarized political conditions, and almost always seen by the press as being aimed at controlling, rather than safeguarding, its freedom. Efforts by journalists to reform the press laws have rarely succeeded, to some extent because they have been conducted largely as party political campaigns without sufficient public awareness or support. The present press law, enacted in 2000 by a conservative dominated-Majlis, has been described as inadequate even by some conservative politicians and its reform has been promised by the Fourth National Development

Plan, 2005–09. It should therefore be possible for reformist and conservative legislators, in consultation with journalists themselves, to find common grounds for removing the confusion and ambiguities of the present legislation.

Iranian journalists have also suffered because of their limited knowledge of the law in general and the Press Law in particular. Experts in Iran have said that greater legal awareness could well have prevented the papers from committing some of the offences for which they have been prosecuted, and enabled them to defend themselves more effectively against charges and to seek redress for the violations of their rights. This is an area where journalists could expect support from the State, perhaps even in the shape of legal training offered by the Judiciary, which has so far been seen as an enemy of press freedom, rather than its defender.

The implementation of the measures proposed here would require collective efforts by journalists, supported by their unions and other civil society organizations, as well as the public at large. Such collective action will only be possible if journalists have a common understanding of their occupation and their aspirations and how their goals could be achieved. For many decades, Iranian journalists were widely regarded as either 'mercenaries' or 'lackeys' of the State, or as 'heroes', 'saviours', and, perhaps, 'martyrs' to the cause of truth. Judging by what some of the most prominent Iranian journalists have said in recent years, the belief appears to have grown that while responsible journalists may not be able to offer miraculous solutions to the complex questions that their readers face, they can supply the readers with the information they need to find their own answers. The high degree of skill that is needed to deliver such a service can only be gained by working and learning for a long period of time, rather than being deprived of one's livelihood, liberty, or life after producing the first seemingly epoch making report. After more than a century of toil, trouble and struggle, the task of informing the public in Iran seems to have developed from a 'mission' into a 'profession'.

Notes

Introduction

1 The author is grateful to Mr Hadi Khorsandi for pointing out the usage of the term *khedmat* in the biographical notes of Iranian journalists compiled in Gholam-Hossein Salehyar's *Chehreh-ye Matabou'at-e Mo'asser* (The Image of the Contemporary Press), Tehran: Press Agent, 1973.

1 The Shah's last years (1977–79)

1 Projection from tables in *Salnameh-ye Amari-ye Keshvar* (National Statistical Yearbook), Statistical Centre of Iran, 1977, p. 173.
2 Hamid Molana, *Journalism in Iran – A History and Interpretation*, PhD dissertation, Evanston, IL: Northwestern University, 1963, p. 570.
3 1952 population of 18.47 million, 5.33 million urban, from Julian Bharier, *Economic Development in Iran, 1900–1970*, Oxford University Press, 1971, Persian translation, Tehran: Planning Organization, 1984, pp. 38–39. 1978 population of 35.8 million, 48.4 per cent urban, based on *Nemagarha-ye Jam'iyati-ye Iran* (Iran Population Index), Tehran: Statistical Centre of Iran, 1999, p. 10.
4 *Nemagarha-ye Jam'iyati-ye Iran*, p. 94.
5 Molana, *Journalism in Iran*, p. 581.
6 Mass'oud Barzin, *Seiri dar Matbou'at-e Iran* (A Survey of the Iranian Press), Tehran: Behjat, 1966, p. 8.
7 Ali Behzadi, *Shebhe Khaterat* (Pseudo Memoirs), Tehran: Zarrin, 1997, p. 793.
8 Assefnia Aryani, 'Negahi beh Qanoun-e Matbou'at az Aghaz ta Emrouz' (A Glance at the Press Law from the Beginning until Today), Part 12, *Ettela'at*, 2 August 1978.
9 Abbas Towfiq, *Ketab-e Hafteh* (The Book Weekly), no. 455, 22 June 2002, p. 21.
10 Aryani, 'Negahi beh Qanoun-e Matbou'at'.
11 Barzin, *Seiri dar Matbou'at-e Iran*, pp. 52–53.
12 The author is grateful to Dr Hassan Namakdoost-Tehrani for pointing out and commenting on *Paygham-e Emrouz* and *Bourse*. 13 Youness Javanroudi, *Tasskhir-e Kayhan* (The Seizure of Kayhan), Tehran: Hashieh, 1980, p. 217.
14 Ibid., pp. 217–218.
15 *Natayej-e Moqaddamti-ye Sarshomari az Kargahha-ye Bozorg-e San'ati, 1355* (Preliminary Results from the Census of Large Industrial Firms, 1976), Tehran: Statistical Centre of Iran, 1978.
16 10.5m rials out of total revenues of 2.7bn rials ($35.71m) – Javanroudi, *Tasskhir-e Kayhan*, pp. 217–219.
17 Ibid., pp. 37–38
18 Ibid., pp. 52–53.
19 Hadi Khorsandi, former *Ettela'at* columnist, interviewed by the author, London, 26 February 2002.

20 Mehdi Beheshtipour, 'Matbou'at-e Iran dar Dowreh-ye Pahlavi' (Iranian Press in the Pahlavi Era), *Rasaneh* (Medium) *Quarterly Journal of Media Studies and Research*, vol. 4, no. 4, Winter 1994, p. 76. The gifts would include caviar, sturgeon and other fish from the Shilat (Fisheries) Organization (Ali-Reza Taheri, former *Ettela'at* journalist, interviewed by the author, London, 26 February 2002), cash or houses or villas (Javanroudi, *Tasskhir-e Kayhan*, pp. 40–41), and gold plated fountain pens (Beheshtipour, Matbou'at-e Iran dar Dowreh-ye Pahlavi).

21 Beheshtipour, 'Matbou'at-e Iran dar Dowreh-ye Pahlavi', p. 47.

22 Ibid., p. 75.

23 Barzin, *Seiri dar Matbou'at-e Iran*, pp. 52–54.

24 Ibid., p. 19.

25 Beheshtipour, 'Matbou'at-e Iran dar Dowreh-ye Pahlavi', p. 73.

26 Barzin, *Seiri dar Matbou'at-e Iran*, pp. 185–187; Mehdi Beheshtipour, 'Tashakkolha-ye Senfi-ye Matbou'at' (Journalists' Trade Organizations), *Kilk* monthly, no. 84, March 1987, pp. 217–234; Daryoush Homayoun, 'Sad Sal az Rouznamehnegari beh Siyassat' (One Hundred Years of Passage from Journalism to Politics) in *Iran Nameh*, vol. 11, nos. 1–2, Spring and Summer 1998, p. 250; Mohammad-Ali Safari, *Qalam va Siyassat* (Pen and Politics), vol. 3, Tehran: Namak, 1998, pp. 627–634; Gholam-Hossein Salehyar, *Vijhegiha-ye Irani-ye Matbou'at* (Iranian Features of the Press), Tehran: Ministry of Information and Tourism, 1976, pp. 177–182, on 'one hundred per cent', etc.

27 The Persian third person singular pronoun, *ou*, is not gender specific.

28 Safari, *Qalam va Siyassat*, vol. 3, pp. 628–629.

29 Javanroudi, *Tasskhir-e Kayhan*, pp. 29–32.

30 Soroush Publications, *Taqvim-e Tarikh-e Enqelab-e Eslami-ye Iran* (Journal of the Islamic Revolution of Iran), Tehran: Soroush, 1991.

31 Ibid., pp. 14–124.

32 Homa Katouzian, *The Political Economy of Modern Iran*, Persian translation by Mohammad-Reza Nafissi and Kambiz Azizi, Tehran: Markaz, 1993, pp. 286–287.

33 Homa Katouzian, 'The Pahlavi Regime in Iran', in H. E. Chehabi and J. Linz (eds), *Sultanistic Regimes*, Baltimore, MD: The Johns Hopkins Press, 1997, pp. 204–205; Ervand Abrahamian, *Iran between Two Revolutions*, Princeton, NJ: Princeton University Press, 1982, pp. 498–500.

34 Safari, *Qalam va Siyassat*, vol. 3, pp. 621–622.

35 Aqeli Baqer, *Rouz-shomar-e Tarikh-e Iran az Mashrouteh ta Enqelab-e Eslami* (Chronology of Iran, 1896–1979), vol. 2, Tehran: Goftar, 1991, p. 325.

36 Abrahamian, *Iran between Two Revolutions*, pp. 501–505.

37 Souroush Publications, *Taqvim-e Tarikh-e Enqelab-e Eslami-ye Iran*, p. 38.

38 Safari, *Qalam va Siyassat*, vol. 3, pp. 584–588.

39 Ibid., pp. 598–606.

40 Souroush Publications, *Taqvim-e Tarikh-e Enqelab-e Eslami-ye Iran*, pp. 46–47.

41 Ibid., pp. 54–57.

42 Katouzian, *The Political Economy of Modern Iran*, pp. 271–273.

43 Souroush Publications, *Taqvim-e Tarikh-e Enqelab-e Eslami-ye Iran*, pp. 54–57.

44 Abbas Milani, *The Persian Sphinx: Amir Abbas Hoveyda and the Riddle of the Iranian Revolution*, London and New York: I.B. Tauris, 2000, pp. 286–287.

45 Safari, *Qalam va Siyassat*, vol. 3, p. 611.

46 Abrahamian, *Iran between Two Revolutions*, pp. 505–508.

47 Safari, *Qalam va Siyassat*, vol. 3, p. 621.

48 Ibid., pp. 621–627.

49 Ibid.

50 Ibid., p. 680.

51 Ibid., pp. 678–679.

52 Daryoush Homayoun, *Gozar az Tarikh* (Passing Through History), p. 45, quoted in *Daryouh Homayoun, beh Revayat-e Asnad-e SAVAK* (Daryoush Homayoun, According to SAVAK Documents), Tehran: Ministry of Intelligence, 1999, p. 41.

53 Abrahamian, *Iran between Two Revolutions*, p. 514.

54 Safari, *Qalam va Siyassat*, vol. 3, p. 676.

55 Souroush Publications, *Taqvim-e Tarikh-e Enqelab-e Ealsmi-ye Iran*, p. 130.

56 Abrahamian, *Iran between Two Revolutions*, pp. 514–515.

57 *Kayhan*, 29 August 1978.

58 Abrahamian, *Iran between Two Revolutions*, pp. 515–516.

59 Ibid., p. 517.

60 *The Sunday Times*, 10 September 1978.

61 Safari, *Qalam va Siyassat*, vol. 3, p. 707; BBC Persian Service, 10 September 1978, quoted in *Taqvim-e Tarikh-e Enqelab-e Eslami-ye Iran*, p. 136; Beheshtipour, 'Matbou'at-e Iran dar Dowreh-ye Pahlavi', p. 80.

62 Javanroudi, *Tasskhir-e Kayhan*, p. 55.

63 Ibid., pp. 55–56.

64 Ibid.

65 Abrahamian, *Iran between Two Revolutions*, pp. 517–518; *Taqvim-e Enqelab-e Eslami-ye Iran*, pp. 149–154. At *Kayhan*, the strike was started by print-shop workers (information provided to the author by Dr Hassan Namakdoost-Tehrani).

66 Safari, *Qalam va Siyassat*, vol. 3, pp. 710–714.

67 Ibid., pp. 722–725.

68 Beheshtipour, 'Matbou'at-e Iran dar Dowreh-ye Pahlavi', pp. 83–84.

69 Souroush Publications, *Taqvim-e Tarikh-e Enqelab-e Ealsmi-ye Iran*, p. 170.

70 Abrahamian, *Iran between Two Revolutions*, p. 519.

71 Souroush Publications, *Taqvim-e Tarikh-e Enqelab-e Ealsmi-ye Iran*, pp. 156–175.

72 Ibid., p. 239.

73 For an account of the run-up to the Shah's departure, see Beheshtipour, 'Matbou'at-e Iran dar Dowreh-ye Pahlavi', pp. 84–89. For details of how *Ettela'at*'s headline was prepared see Gholam-Hossein Salehyar, 'Majara-ye yek Titr-e Tarikhi' (The Account of a Historic Headline), *Ettella'at*, 8 February 1991, p. 6, quoted in Sayyed-Farid Qassemi, *Khaterat-e Matbou'ati: Sad Khatereh az Sad Rouydad* (Journalists' Memoirs: One Hundred Memoirs from One Hundred Events), Tehran: Essalat-e Tanshir, 1998, pp. 225–232.

74 Beheshtipour, 'Matbou'at-e Iran dar Dowreh-ye Pahlavi', p. 89.

75 Mohammad-Ali Safari, *Qalam va Siyassat*, vol. 4, Tehran: Namak, 2001, p. 251.

76 *Kayhan*, 17 May 1979, p. 2.

77 Javanroudi, *Tasskhir-e Kayhan*, pp. 138–142; Mohammad Haidari, 'Barressi-ye Sakhtar-e Birouni va Darouni-ye E'tessab-e Matbou'at' (A Review of the External and Internal Structures of the Newspaper Strike), *Gozaresh*, no. 43, August–September 1994, pp. 47–57.

78 Safari, *Qalam va Siyassat*, vol. 4, pp. 289–297.

2 The 'Spring of Freedom' (1979)

1 Youness Javanroudi, *Tasskhir-e Kayhan, Tasskhir-e Kayhan* (The Seizure of Kayhan), Tehran: Hashieh, 1980, pp. 66–69.

2 The author's efforts to establish the precise dates of these meetings have not been successful. The relevant SAVAK records, if any, are not accessible. Some of the named participants have died, and others have given conflicting accounts.

3 Mohammad-Ali Safari, *Qalam va Siyassat* (Pen and Politics), vol. 4, Tehran: Namak, 2001, pp. 284–289. Safari does not give the date of the meeting.

4 Javanroudi, *Tasskhir-e Kayhan*, pp. 69–71.

5 Safari, *Qalam va Siyassat*, vol. 4, pp. 288–289.
6 Javanroudi, *Tasskhir-e Kayhan*, pp. 75–77; Safari, *Qalam va Siyassat* vol. 4, pp. 289–297; Hossein Mahdiyan interviewed by the author, Tehran, 26 August 2002.
7 One member of the delegation, the veteran preacher, Mohammad-Taqi Falsafi, who was a relative of Mr Mahdiyan's, is said to have described the newspapers in the past as a meal 'made up of dried bread and *doogh* [yoghurt drink]', the staple diet of many poor Iranians, especially in the summer. Now, every newspaper was similar to 'a feast with all types of rice and stew and kebabs, chicken, fruits, salad, fruit drinks, so that one does not know where to start' – Gholam-Hossein Salehyar, *Ettela'at*, 10 February 1991, quoted in Safari, ibid.
8 Safari; Javanroudi, *Tasskhir-e Kayhan*, p. 75; Mahdiyan interview.
9 Ibid.
10 *Kayhan*'s front page, reproduced in Javanroudi, *Tasskhir-e Kayhan*, p. 71.
11 Ibid., pp. 71–73.
12 *Kayhan*, 16 January 1979.
13 Ibid.
14 Ibid.
15 Safari, *Qalam va Siyassat*, vol. 4, p. 265.
16 Ibid.
17 Javanroudi, *Tasskhir-e Kayhan*, pp. 81–82.
18 Ibid., pp. 71–73.
19 Safari, *Qalam va Siyassat*, vol. 4, p. 301.
20 *Ettela'at*, 22 January 1979, quoted in Safari, *Qalam va Siyassat*, vol. 4, pp. 323–324.
21 Ibid., pp. 266–269.
22 Soroush publications, *Taqvim-e Tarikh-e Enqelab-e Eslami-ye Iran*, Tehran: Soroush, 1991, pp. 224–244; Baqer, Aqeli, *Rouz-shomar-e Tarikh-e Iran az Mashrouteh ta Enqelab-e Eslami* (Chronology of Iran, 1896–1979), vol. 2, Tehran: Goftar, 1991, pp. 390–399.
23 Ibid.
24 Ne'mat Nazeri, '80 Sa'at Bazdasht-e Panj Rouznamehnegar' (Eighty Hours of Detention of Five Journalists), *Kilk*, no. 84, March 1997, pp. 265–269; Mehdi Beheshtipour, 'Matboua't-e Iran dar Dowreh-ye Pahlavi' (The Iranian Press in the Pahlavi Era), *Rasaneh Quarterly*, vol. 4, no. 4, Winter 1994, pp. 90–91; Safari, *Qalam va Siyassat*, vol. 4, pp. 366–371. The five were: Firouz Gouran and Mass'oud Mohajer from *Ayandegan*, Ne'mat Nazeri and Mehdi Beheshtipour from *Ettela'at* and Jalil Khoshkhu from *Kayhan*.
25 Safari, ibid., p. 369.
26 Nazeri, '80 Sa'at Bazdasht-e Panj Rouznamehnegar'.
27 Safari, *Qalam va Siyassat*, vol. 4, pp. 434–507.
28 Javanroudi, *Tasskhir-e Kayhan*, pp. 65–66.
29 Ibid., pp. 82–83.
30 Ibid., pp. 92–97; Annabelle Sreberny-Mohammadi and Ali Mohammadi, *Small Media, Big Revolution*, Minneapolis, MN and London: University of Minnesota Press, 1994, p. 169.
31 Javanroudi, *Tasskhir-e Kayhan*, pp. 92–97.
32 Sreberny-Mohammadi and Mohammadi, *Small Media, Big Revolution*, pp. 169–174.
33 Aqeli, *Rouz-shomar-e Tarikh-e Iran*, vol. 2, p. 396.
34 *Ettela'at*, 20 February 1979, quoted in Safari, *Qalam va Siyassat*, vol. 4, pp. 554–559. Mr Qotbzadeh later served briefly as foreign minister. He was executed in 1982 for involvement in a coup plot against Ayatollah Khomeini's regime (http://en.wikipedia.org/wiki/Sadegh_Ghotbzadeh, accessed last on 2 August 2006).
35 Ibid., pp. 560–563.
36 Javanroudi, *Tasskhir-e Kayhan*, pp. 103–112.
37 Ibid.
38 Ibid.

39 Ibid., pp. 85–86.
40 Maziar Behrooz, *Rebels with a Cause*, London and New York: I.B. Tauris, 2000, p. 77.
41 Javanroudi, *Tasskhir-e Kayhan*, pp. 85–86, on Assadi, quoting the Tudeh Party's newspaper *Rah-e Mardom* (People's Path).
42 Mehdi Mohsenian-Rad, 'Matbou'at-e Salha-ye Nokhost-e Enqelab-e Eslami' (Press in the First Years of the Islamic Republic), *Kilk*, no. 84, March 1997, pp. 61–91.
43 Safari, *Qalam va Siyassat*, vol. 4, pp. 72–74.
44 Mohsenian-Rad, 'Matbou'at-e Salha-ye Nokhost-e Enqelab-e Eslami'.
45 *Negareshi bar Naqsh-e Matbou'at-e Vabasteh dar Ravand-e Enqelab-e Eslam-e Iran* (A Review of the Role of the Dependent Press in the Course of Iran's Islamic Revolution), hereinafter referred to as *Negareshi bar*, no author's name given, Tehran: Ministry of Islamic Guidance, 1982, vol. 1, pp. 9–11.
46 Ibid.
47 *Ahangar*'s editor, Manouchehr Mahjoubi, who also wrote a satirical column in the daily *Paygham-e Emrouz*, nicknamed the three as 'The BYQ [pronounced *beeq*] triangle', *byq* meaning stupid in Persian slang. The author is grateful to Dr Namakdoost-Tehrani for pointing out Mr Mahjoubi's use of the expression in *Paygham-e Emrouz*.
48 Javanroudi, *Tasskhir-e Kayhan*, p. 111; Hadi Khorsandi, *The Ayatollah and I*, London: Readers International, 1987, pp. 3–5.
49 *Negareshi bar*, p. 119.
50 Ibid., p. 129.
51 Ibid., p. 138.
52 Ibid., p. 144.
53 Javanroudi, *Tasskhir-e Kayhan*, pp. 102–103.
54 Ibid., p. 47.
55 Ibid., pp. 131–133.
56 Ibid., pp. 112–113
57 Safari, *Qalam va Siyassat*, vol. 4, p. 562; Javanroudi, *Tasskhir-e Kayhan*, p. 113.
58 Ibid, p. 113.
59 Ibid., p. 114.
60 Ibid., p. 130.
61 Ibid., pp. 127–128.
62 Beheshtipour, 'Matboua't-e Iran dar Dowreh-ye Pahlavi', p. 89.
63 Javanroudi, *Tasskhir-e Kayhan*, p. 128.
64 Ibid., p. 136.
65 Safari, *Qalam va Siyassat*, vol. 4, pp. 99–104.
66 Ibid., pp. 86–88.
67 Ibid., pp. 562–571.
68 Ibid.
69 Javanroudi, *Tasskhir-e Kayhan*, pp. 156–157.
70 Ibid., pp. 88–91.
71 Ibid., pp. 134–142.
72 Ibid., pp. 143–148.
73 *Kayhan*, 16 May 1979.
74 The author has not been able to establish the date of this meeting, surrounded as it was by even more confusion than the previously mentioned meetings between the journalists and the senior clergy before the overthrow of the Shah's regime.
75 Javanroudi, *Tasskhir-e Kayhan*, pp. 148–154.
76 Ibid., pp. 154–157.
77 Ibid., pp. 116–117.
78 Ibid., p. 152.
79 Ibid., pp. 157–163.
80 Ibid., pp. 114–115.

3 The battle for *Kayhan* and the demise of *Ayandegan*

1 Quoted in Mohammad-Ali Safari, *Qalam va Siyassat* (Pen and Politics), vol. 4, pp. 564–565.
2 Assef Bayat, *Workers & Revolution in Iran*, London: Zed, 1987, pp. 100–141.
3 Safari, *Qalam va Siyassat*, vol. 4, pp. 565–566.
4 Souroush Publications, *Taqvim-e Tarikh-e Enqelab-e Eslami-ye Iran*, pp. 286–287.
5 Safari, *Qalam va Siyassat*, vol. 4, pp. 566–568.
6 Ibid., pp. 569–570.
7 Mohammad Ghaed, *Ayandegan* editorial board member, Tehran, 9 January 2002, unpublished notes made available to the author.
8 *Negareshi bar*, vol. 1. The number of *Ayandegan* items cited as evidence against the paper rises as the revolution develops, putting the paper at the top of the list of offenders for the first six months of the new regime, at the end of which period the paper was closed down.
9 Daryoush Homayoun, 'Sad Sal az Rouznamehnegari beh Siyassat' (One Hundred Years from Journalism to Politics), *Iran Nameh*, vol. 11, nos. 1–2, Spring and Summer 1998, pp. 250–251.
10 Abbas Milani, *The Persian Sphinx: Amir Abbas Hoveryda and the Riddle of the Iranian Revolution*, London and New York: I.B. Tauris, 2000, pp. 224–225.
11 Homayoun, 'Sad sal az Rouznamehnegari beh Siyassat'.
12 Milani, *The Persian Sphinx*, pp. 224–225.
13 *Daryoush Homayoun beh Revayat-e Asnad-e SAVAK* (Daryoush Homayoun, According to SAVAK Documents), Tehran: Ministry of Intelligence, 1999, pp. 26–28.
14 Mohammad Ghaed interviewed by the author, Tehran, 9 January, 2002.
15 *Ayandegan*, 7 May 1978.
16 Ghaed interview.
17 *Ayandegan*, 10 May 1978.
18 Baqer, Aqeli, *Rouz-shomar-e Tarikh-e Iran az Mashrouteh ta Enqelab-e Eslami* (Chronology of Iran, 1896–1979), vol. 2, Tehran: Goftar, 1991, pp. 81–90.
19 Ibid.
20 Ibid., The *Ettela'at* reporter, Gholam-Hossein Rahbar, had been killed on 7 May 1979 (*Kayhan*, 8 May 1979).
21 *Kayhan*, 14 May 1979.
22 Ghaed interview; Javanroudi, *Tasskhir-e Kayhan*, pp. 166–169.
23 Ghaed interview.
24 Javanroudi, *Tasskhir-e Kayhan*, p. 168.
25 *Ayandegan*, 12 May 1979.
26 Javanroudi, *Tasskhir-e Kayhan*, pp. 169–170.
27 *Kayhan*, 12 May 1979.
28 Javanroudi, *Tasskhir-e Kayhan*, pp. 170–171; *Kayhan*, 13 May 1979. Meanwhile, another battle involving the press was being fought by Iranians abroad. The same issue of *Kayhan*, quoting the French news agency (AFP) reported that a day earlier Iranian students in Paris had 'tried' an Iranian journalist, Fereydoun Saheb-jam', for his alleged links with the Shah's regime. The man had been encircled and verbally abused 'in Persian' by 'about one hundred Moslem Iranian students', some of whom had asked for him 'to be punished immediately', while 'the majority believed that he should be given the right to defend himself.' The students, said the report, had accused Saheb-jam' of 'cooperating with the former Shah and the SAVAK', and that he had come to France 'to spy on Iranian students'. He was let off after 'several hours', having denied the charges, and said that 'the former Shah had committed several crimes,' among them 'turning Iran into the West's solid bastion in the Middle East', and 'having left Iran, because when a ship is sinking, the captain must remain on the deck.'
29 *Kayhan*, 14 May 1979.
30 Javanroudi, *Tasskhir-e Kayhan*, pp. 171–176.

31 Ibid., 177–178.
32 *Kayhan*, 15 May 1979.
33 Javanroudi, *Tasskhir-e Kayhan*, pp. 178–179. On 15 May 1979, *Kayhan* carried a statement from Ayatollah Khomeini's office discouraging the public from heading for his residence for the sake of 'every minor matter or outstanding complaint'. Such visits, said the statement, were part of an 'evil plan' by 'the enemies of our holy Islamic movement' to try to stop Ayatollah Khomeini from dealing with the fundamental issues.
34 Baqer Moin, *Khomeini: Life of the Ayatollah*, London and New York: I.B. Tauris, 1999, p. 237.
35 *Kayhan*, 16 May 1979.
36 Ibid.
37 Ibid.
38 Javanroudi, *Tasskhir-e Kayhan*, pp. 181–189.
39 For more on these contacts, see 'Chapter 2: The "Spring of Freedom" (1979)'.
40 Hossein Mahdiyan interviewed by the author, Tehran, 26 August 2002.
41 Javanroudi, *Tasskhir-e Kayhan*, pp. 184–185.
42 Ibid.
43 Mahdiyan interview.
44 Javanroudi, *Tasskhir-e Kayhan*, p. 191.
45 Ibid., pp. 218–224.
46 Ibid., pp. 182–184.
47 Mahdiyan interview.
48 Ibid.
49 Ibid.
50 Safari, *Qalam va Siyassat* (Pen and Politics), vol. 3, Tehran: Namak, 1998, pp. 35–71.
51 Javanroudi, *Tasskhir-e Kayhan*, pp. 189–196.
52 Fereydoun Sediqi, 'Va Shodam Rouznamehnegar' (And I Became a Journalist), *Paojuheshnameh-ye Tarikh-e Matbou'at-e Iran* (Research Document on the History of the Iranian Press), no. 1, 1997, pp. 56–69.
53 Ibid.
54 Ghaed interview; Javanroudi, *Tasskhir-e Kayhan*, p. 99.
55 Ibid., p. 195.
56 Ibid., pp. 194–195.
57 Mahdiyan interview.
58 Ibid.
59 Javanroudi, *Tasskhir-e Kayhan*, pp. 196–197. In the meantime, *Ayandegan*'s assets had been transferred to a new morning newspaper, *Sobh-e Azadegan* (The Morning of the Free), published by Mehdi Moinfar, the brother of Ali-Akbar Moinfar, a member of the Revolutionary Council and the Islamic Republic's first Minister of Oil. One of the most experienced journalists who had left *Kayhan* said the 'errors and shocks' at the paper after it had been taken over by the Islamic Association led Iranian journalism into a 'new era in which there was no room for the techniques that I had learned'. Having joined *Sobh-e Azadegan*, he was to discover other novelties: On hearing that one of Ayatollah Khomeini's speeches had arrived on the telex, the editor asked how long the piece was going to be. Instead of mentioning the number of columns the report was likely to take, the journalist who had received the tape simply said, 'two-and-a-half metres' -Ali-Reza Farahmand, quoted in Sediqi, 'Va Shodam Rouznamehnegar,' *Paojuheshnameh-ye Tarikh-e Matbou'at-e Iran*, p. 27.
60 Mohammad-Ebrahim Ansari-Lari, *Nezarat bar Matbou'at dar Hoqouq-e Iran* (Press Supervision in Iranian Law), Tehran: Soroush, 1996, pp. 116–121.
61 Javanroudi, *Tasskhir-e Kayhan*, p. 195. By now, the paper had been renamed *Azad*, in order not to use the name of '*Kayhan* which is a reminder of many years of work by hundreds of workers, clerical staff and writers.'

62 Javanroudi, *Tasskhir-e Kayhan*, p. 195; Mohsenian-Rad, 'Matbou'at-e Salha-ye Nokhost-e Enqelab-e Eslami', (Press in the First Years of the Islamic Republic), *Kilk*, no. 84, March 1997, p. 80.
63 Ervand Abrahamian, *Radical Islam, the Iranian Mojahedin*, London: I.B. Tauris, 1989, p. 185.
64 Javanroudi, *Tasskhir-e Kayhan*, pp. 98–99.
65 For criticism of the Amouzegar draft law, see *Ettela'at*, 29 June–3 August 1978.
66 Ansari-Lari, *Nezarat bar Matbou'at dar Hoqouq-e Iran*, pp. 116–117.
67 Ibid., pp. 120–121.
68 Dr Mohsen Esma'ili, *Qanoun-e Matbou'at va Seyr-e Tahavol-E An dar Hoqouq-e Iran* (The Press Law and Its Evolution in Iranian Jurisprudence), Tehran: Soroush, 2000, p. 26.
69 Syndicate Treasurer and former *Ayandegan* and *San'at-e Haml-o Naghl* journalist, Mass'oud Mohajer, interviewed by the author, Tehran, 25 August 2002.
70 *Negareshi bar*, vol. 2, pp. 199–224.
71 *Negareshi bar*, vol. 2.
72 Behrouz Turani, former *Bamdad* journalist, interviewed by the author, London, 23 January 2002.
73 *Negareshi bar*, vol. 1, p. 15.
74 Abrahamian, *Radical Islam, the Iranian Mojahedin*, pp. 206–223.
75 Ansari-Lari, *Nezarat bar Matbou'at dar Hoqouq-e Iran*, pp. 117–118.

4 War, reconstruction, and the revival of journalism (1980–96)

1 Figures and political appraisal based on Seyyed-Farid Qassemi, *Rahnema-ye Matbou'at-e Iran 1357–1371* (Directory of Iranian Press 1979–1993), Tehran: Centre for Media Studies and Research, the Ministry of Culture and Islamic Guidance, 1993.
2 Ibid.
3 Syndicate Treasurer and former *Ayandegan* and *San'at-e Haml-o Naghl* journalist, Mass'oud Mohajer interviewed by the author, Tehran, 25 August 2002.
4 Qassemi, *Rahnema-ye Matbou'at-e Iran*.
5 Author's interviews in Tehran with *San'at-e Haml-o Naghl* publisher, Ali Zarghani, 7 February 2005, and *Film* monthly publisher, Mass'oud Mehrabi, 28 February 2005. The first three issues of *Film* monthly were published as *Video*, a guide to the videotaped films that had appeared on the Tehran market in the absence of cinemas and were being distributed by video clubs. Soon, however, the government banned the video clubs, forcing the trade underground, and requiring the renaming of the specialist publication as *Film*.
6 Mohammad Ghaed, 'Mamnou' Ya'ni Qachaq, Qachaq Ya'ni Maskout' (Contraband Means Smuggled, Smuggled Means Hushed), *San'at-e Haml-o Naghl*, no. 86, April 1990, 12–13.
7 Mohammad Ghaed, 'Afsaneh-ye Bazgasht' (The Repatriation Myth), *San'at-e Haml-o Naghl*, no. 87, June 1990, 60–62.
8 Mohammad Ghaed, 'Tali'eh-ye Yek Safkari-e Bonyadi' (The Beginning of a Thorough Facelift), *San'at-e Haml-o Naghl*, no. 117, March 1993, 102–103.
9 Mass'oud Mehrabi, publisher, *Film* monthly, interviewed by the author, Tehran, 18 January 2005.
10 Seyyed-Farid Qassemi, *Rouydadha-ye Matbou'ati-ye Iran 1215–1382* (Iranian Press Events, 1837–2004), Tehran: Ministry of Culture and Islamic Guidance, 2004, pp. 130–136.
11 Two years after the end of the war, Mr Saberi started the Islamic Republic's first satirical paper, the weekly Gol Agha (Mr Flower, a common name in the countryside). He closed down Gol Agha in 2002, at the height of another round of newspaper closures in Iran when his only other options would have been either to publish a tame magazine and see it collapse, or to allow a sharper tone and antagonize his

beloved state, with unforeseeable consequences. Mr Saberi died soon after Gol Agha's closure. Kioumars Saberi-Foumani's website, http://www.golaghaweekly.com/saberi/pages/biography.htm (accessed 17 February 2006).

12 Qassemi, *Rouydadha-ye Matbou'ati-ye Iran*, p. 134. The press laws will be discussed in 'Chapter 10: One hundred years of legal confusion'.

13 The country's Gross National Product at market prices that had risen by 198 per cent during the eight years of war, rose by 728 per cent during Mr Rafsanjani's two terms in office, 1980–88 and 1989–97. The change was remarkable even at constant (1990/1991) prices, from 5 per cent during 1980–88 to 37 per cent during 1989–97 – Central Bank of Iran, *National Accounts of Iran, 1959/60–2000/01*, Tehran: Central Bank of Iran, 2003, www.cbi.ir/publications/PDF/NA3879.pdf (accessed Spring 2005).

14 Ministry of Culture and Islamic Guidance, *Majmou'eh Maqalat-e Nokhostin Seminar-e Barresi-ye Massael-e Mabu'at-e Iran* (Collection of the Papers Presented at the First Seminar to Study the Problems of the Iranian Press), Tehran, 1992, pp. 26–28.

15 Vaihd Pourostad, *Mohakemeh-ye Salam* (The Trial of *Salam*), Tehran, Rouznegar, 2001, pp. 11–12.

16 Mass'oud Barzin, 'Anjomanha-ye Matboua'ti dar Iran ta Sal-e 1357' (Press Associations in Iran until 1978–1979), *Rasaneh Quarterly*, vol. 2, no. 3, Autumn 1991, p. 96.

17 Karim Arghandehpour, *Dowran-e Salam* (Salam Days), Tehran: Negah-e Emrouz, 2001, pp. 115–117.

18 Vahid Pourostad, *Mohakemeh-ye Salam*; Gholam-Reza Kashi, *Matboua't dar Asr-e Khatami, Mordad 76–Mordad 79* (Press in Khatami's Era, August 98–August 2000), Tehran: Selk, 2000, pp. 121–122.

19 Jilla Baniyaghoub, *Rouznamehnegaran* (Journalists), Tehran: Rouznegar, 1997, p. 100.

20 Dr Kazem Mo'tamednejad, 'Barresi-ye Sharayet-e Pishraft-e Nashriyat-e Mostaqel va Kesrat-gera' (A Review of the Conditions for the Development of Independent and Pluralistic Publications), in *Majmou'eh Maqalat-e Dovomin Seminar-e Barresi-ye Massael-e Matbou'at-e Iran* (The Collection of Articles Presented at the Second Seminar to Study the Problems of the Iranian Press), Tehran: Ministry of Culture and Islamic Guidance, 1998, p. 34.

21 The Persian language news site, *Emrooz*, www.emrooz.ws/ShowItem.aspx?ID=2418&p=1 (accessed Spring 2005).

22 Issa Saharkhiz, former Director of Domestic Press at the Ministry of Culture and Islamic Guidance, speaking in Germany, May 2003, reported by the Persian language news site, *Iran Emrooz*, www.iran-emrooz.de/khabar/saharkh820309.html (accessed Spring 2005).

23 Ali Larijani, 'Ghalat-ha-ye Aqa-ye Qouchani' (Mr Qouchanis' Errors), in Mohammad Qouchani, *Pedarkhandeh va Chap-haye Javan* (The Godfather and the Young Leftists), Tehran: Nashr-e Ney, 2000, pp. 198–202. Mr Larijani's comments had been made in a letter to the daily *Asr-e Azadegan*, in response to an article about Mr Larijani on 23 April 2000. The reply was not published because the newspaper was closed down.

24 *Rasaneh Quarterly*, vol. 5, no. 1, Spring 1995, p. 87.

25 Issa Saharkhiz, *Iran Emrooz*, www.iran-emrouz.de/khabar/saharkh820309.html (accessed 12 August 2006).

26 *Adineh* (Friday) monthly, no. 70, April–May 1992, p. 4.

27 Kashi, *Matboua't dar Asr-e Khatami*, pp. 177–178. The jury members' names are given in Table 4.1.

28 Qassemi, *Rouydadha-ye Matbou'ati-ye Iran*, pp. 146–151. *Yassarat-al-Hossein* is commonly, and incorrectly, referred to as *Ya Lessarat*.

29 Mehdi Mohsenian-Rad and colleagues, 'Payam-Afarinan-e Matbou'at-e Iran' (The Message Creators in the Iranian Press), Part 1, *Rasaneh Quarterly*, vol. 4, no. 2,

Summer 1993, pp. 4–17. In 1995, the Minister of Culture and Islamic Guidance, Mr Mir-Salim, reported that more than 80 per cent of Iranian journalists had been in their profession for less than four years – *Hamvatan Salam* (Hello, Compatirot) daily, 27 April 1995.

30 Gholam-HosseinSalehyar, *Chehreh-ye Matbou'at-e Mo'asser* (The Image of the Contemporary Press), Tehran: Press Agent, 1973.

31 The 1992 'free market' rate of exchange of 1,600 rials to the dollar from M. H. Pesaran, 'Economic Trends and Macroeconomic Policies in Post-Revolutionary Iran', Cambridge: Cambridge University, August 1998, Figure 4, p. 22, www.econ.cam.ac.uk/faculty/pesaran/iran98_0.pdf (accessed 11 August 2006).

32 Mohsenian-Rad and colleagues, 'Payam-Afarinan-e Matbou'at-e Iran', part 2, *Rasaneh Quarterly*, vol. 4, no. 3, Autumn 1993, pp. 22–27.

33 Mehdi Mohsenian-Rad, 'Negahi beh Matoub'at-e Iran dar Moqayesehha-ye Jahani' (A Glance at the Iranian Press in the Global Context), *Rasaneh Quarterly*, vol. 4, no. 4, Winter 1994, pp. 22–27.

34 Hossein Moqimi-Esfandabadi and Qassem Roshenas, 'Matbou'at-e Iran va Moshkel-e Bazdehi-ye Sarmayeh' (The Iranian Press and the Problem of Return on Capital), *Rasaneh Quarterly*, vol. 6, no. 1, Spring 1995, pp. 36–52. For a review of the daily newspapers' advertising revenues, see Mehran Sohrabzadeh, 'Matbou'at dar Aineh-ye Tablighat' (The Reflection of the Press in Advertisements), *Rasaneh Quarterly*, vol. 6, no. 3, Autumn 1995, pp. 78–88.

35 *Rasaneh Quarterly*, vol. 2, no. 1, Spring 1991, p. 94. Speakers at the first meeting on 14 May 1991, included Mr Mohammad-Mohsen Sazegara, Mr Mass'oud Behnoud, Ms A'zam Taleqani and Mr Ali-Akbar Qazizadeh. The Cooperative had also been trying to improve the newspaper distribution system in Iran, discussed by Ma'ssoumeh Vatani in his paper, 'Towzi', Vasseteh-ye Towlid va Masraf-e Payam' (Distribution, the Link between the Production and Consumption of the Message), in *Rasaneh Quarterly*, vol. 6, no. 3, Autumn 1995, pp. 58–70.

36 *Rasaneh Quarterly*, vol. 5, no. 2, Summer 1994, pp. 8–13.

37 Akram Didari, 'Sahm-e Rouznameh-haye Sobh az Manabe'-e Khabari' (Morning Dailies' Use of News Sources), *Rasaneh Quarterly*, vol. 6, no. 3, Autumn 1995, pp. 52–57.

38 Mohammad-Mehdi Forqani, 'Matbou'at va Tahavolat-e Ejema'i dar Iran' (The Press and Social Developments in Iran), *Rasaneh Quarterly*, vol. 7, no. 2, Summer 1996, pp. 30–42.

39 *Rasaneh Quarterly*, vol. 5, no. 1, Spring 1994, pp. 50–61.

40 Sohrabzadeh, 'Matbou'at dar Aineh-ye Tablighat', vol. 6, no. 3, Autumn 1995, p. 115.

41 For a selection of criticisms see *Jomhouri-ye Eslami* (Islamic Republic) daily, 6 September 1995, and *Adineh*, no. 102, August 1995, pp. 49–53.

42 Director of Domestic Press at the Ministry of Culture and Islamic Guidance, Hossein Entezami, quoted in Moqimi-Esfandabadi, Hossein, and Roshenas, Qassem, 'Matbou'at-e Iran va Moshkel-e Bazdehi-ye Sarmayeh' (The Iranian Press and the Problem of Return on Capital), *Rasaneh Quarterly*, vol. 6, no. 1, Spring 1995, p. 81.

43 *Rasaneh Quarterly*, vol. 7, no. 1, Spring 1996, pp. 86–92.

44 *Rasaneh Quarterly*, vol. 7, no. 1, Spring 1996, pp. 92–95.

45 Ibid., vol. 7, no. 2, Summer 1996, pp. 48–52. *Payam-e Daneshjou* that had been banned briefly in 1995 was permanently stopped in 1998.

46 Ibid., vol. 7, no. 1, Spring 1996, pp. 2–11.

47 Ibid., vol. 7, no. 2, Summer 1996, p. 1. For details see 'Chapter 9: Organization, education, and training'.

48 Ibid., vol. 7, no. 2, Summer 1996, pp. 93–95.

49 Ibid., vol. 7, no. 3, Autumn 1996, pp. 104–107.

50 Ibid., vol. 7, no. 3, Autumn 1996, pp. 8–9.

51 Ibid., vol. 7, no. 3, Autumn 1996, pp. 13–16.

52 Ibid., vol. 7, no. 3, Autumn 1996, pp. 71–80. For details, see 'Chapter 9: Organization, education, and training'.

53 Hadi Arefi, 'Barresi-ye Noqoush-e Giyahi dar Honar-Hay-ye Eslami' (Review of the Floral Patterns in Islmaic Art), in *Asar-e Bargozideh-ye Chaharomin Jashnvareh-ye Matbou'at* (Selected Works from the Fourth Press Festival), Tehran: Press Festival Secretariat, 1998, pp. 72–80.

54 Dr Gholam-Ali Haddad-Adel, 'Tasir-e Kant bar Tafakor-e Dini-ye Maghreb-zamin' (Kant's Influence on Western Religious Thought), in *Asar-e Bargozideh-ye Chaharomin Jashnvareh Matbou'at* (Selected Works from the Fourth Press Festival), Tehran: Press Festival Secretariat, 1998, pp. 82–97.

55 Ahmad Sha'bani, 'Bala-bordan-e Karai-ye Carbon-e Fa'al Jahat-e Padafand-e Shimiayi' (Raising the Efficiency of Active Carbon for the Purpose of Chemical Defence), in *Asar-e Bargozideh-ye Chaharomin Jashnvareh Matbou'at* (Selected Works from the Fourth Press Festival), Tehran: Press Festival Secretariat, 1998, pp. 98–110.

56 Abdol-Hamid Hosseinnia, 'Dar Kashakesh-e Ab va Sang' (In the Midst of the Battle between Water and Stone), based on the writer's declared experience of drinking plenty of water to treat his kidney stone problem, in *Asar-e Bargozideh-ye Chaharomin Jashnvareh Matbou'at* (Selected Works from the Fourth Press Festival), Tehran: Press Festival Secretariat, 1998, pp. 112–118.

57 Mahin Azar, 'Keifiyat-e Ghazai va Estandard-e Qarch-e Iran' (Nutritional Quality and Standards of Iranian Mushrooms), in *Asar-e Bargozideh-ye Chaharomin Jashnvareh Matbou'at* (Selected Works from the Fourth Press Festival), Tehran: Press Festival Secretariat, 1998, pp. 120–133.

58 Mehdi Mehrizi, 'Negahi Tarikhi beh Mas'aleh-ye Feqh va Zaman' (A Historical View of the Question of Jurisprudence and Time), in *Asar-e Bargozideh-ye Chaharomin Jashnvareh Matbou'at* (Selected Works from the Fourth Press Festival), Tehran: Press Festival Secretariat, 1998, pp. 134–161.

59 Mohammad-Hossein Hosseinzadeh Bahraini, 'Barresi-ye Feqhi va Eqtesadi-ye Soud-e Tazmin-shodeh Alal-Hesab dar System-e Bankdari-ye Bedoun-e Reba' (Review of Advance Guaranteed Profit in Usury-free Banking System), in *Asar-e Bargozideh-ye Chaharomin Jashnvareh Matbou'at* (Selected Works from the Fourth Press Festival), Tehran: Press Festival Secretariat, 1998, pp. 162–190.

60 Majid Razzazi, 'Gozareshi az Vaz'e Control-e Maali dar Sherkat-ha-ye Dowlati' (A Report on the Conditions of Financial Supervision in State-owned Companies), in *Asar-e Bargozideh-ye Chaharomin Jashnvareh Matbou'at* (Selected Works from the Fourth Press Festival), Tehran: Press Festival Secretariat, 1998, pp. 298–314.

61 Hamid-Reza Kaviani, 'Goftogou-ye Shesh-sa'teh ba Mohsen Rafiqdoust' (Six Hour Interview with Mohsen Rafiqdoust), in *Asar-e Bargozideh-ye Chaharomin Jashnvareh Matbou'at* (Selected Works from the Fourth Press Festival), Tehran: Press Festival Secretariat, 1998, pp. 334–352. Morteza Rafiqdoust's co-defendant in the case, Fazel Khodad, was hanged in 1995.

62 Lili Farhadpour Bastani, 'Obour az Gomrok-e Mordegan' (Passing through the Customs House for the Dead), *Daricheh* (Window) monthly, vol. 1, no. 3, reprinted in *Asar-e Bargozideh-ye Chaharomin Jashnvareh Matbou'at* (Selected Works from the Fourth Press Festival), Tehran: Fourth Press Festival Secretariat, 1998, pp. 316–326.

63 Seyyed-Mehdi Shoja'i, 'Shazdeh' (The Prince), in *Asar-e Bargozideh-ye Chaharomin Jashnvareh* (Selected Works from the Fourth Press Festival), pp. 367–371.

64 Ali-Entezari, Fourth Festival Secretary, *Asar-e Bargozideh-ye Chaharomin Jashnvareh Matbou'at*, pp. 10–11. Mr Entezari also said that with the consumption of 29 copies of newspapers per 1,000 heads of population in 1994, Iran still had a long way to go to reach 'the acceptable level of at least 100 copies.'

65 Jury members' biographies, in *Asar-e Bargozideh-ye Chaharomin Jashnvareh Matbou'at*, pp. 14–15.

66 Dr Mohsen Esma'ili, 'Dadgahha-ye Matoub'ati' (Press Courts), *Rasaneh Quarterly*, vol. 8, no. 1, Spring 1997, pp. 100–105.
67 Rahmandoust, Mostafa and Shafi'i, Shahram *Rasaneh Quarterly*, vol. 8, no. 1, Spring 1997, p. 126.

5 The second 'Spring of Freedom' (1997–2000)

1 Kazem Mo'tamednejad, 'Barresi-ye Sharayet-e Pishraft-e Nashriyat-e Mostaqel va Kesrat-gera' (A Review of the Conditions for the Development of Independent and Pluralistic Publications), in *Majmou'eh Maqalat-e Dovomin Seminar-e Barresi-ye Massael-e Matbou'at-e Iran* (The Collection of Articles Presented at the Second Seminar to Study the Problems of the Iranian Press), vol. 1, Tehran: Ministry of Culture and Islamic Guidance, 1998, p. 45.
2 *Rouznamehnegar* (Journalist), organ of the Association of Iranian Journalists, published since August 1999, no. 1, August–September 1999, p. 1.
3 Gholam-Reza Kashi, *Matboua't dar Asr-e Khatami, Mordad 76–Mordad 79* (Press in Khatami's Era, August 1998–August 2000), Tehran: Selk, 2000, p. 178. The jury (named in Table 5.1) were selected by the Minister of Culture and Islamic Guidance, Ataollah Mohajerani, Tehran Mayor, Gholam-Hossein Karbaschi and the Director General of the Justice Ministry, Ali Razini.
4 Mo'tamednejad, 'Barresi-ye Sharayet-e Pishraft', p. 45.
5 Ataollah Mohajerani, *Esteezah* (Censure), Tehran: Ettela'at, 1999, pp. 204–206.
6 *Rasaneh Quarterly*, vol. 8, no. 3, Autumn 1997, p. 130.
7 Baniyaghoub, *Rouznamehnegaran*, pp. 133–138.
8 *Rasaneh Quarterly*, vol. 8, no. 4, Winter 1998, pp. 145–146.
9 Ahmad Zeidabadi, 'Manaafe'-e Melli, Barayand-e Ara-e Mellat' (National Interests, the Vector of People's Votes), in *Asar-e Bargozideh-ye Panjomin Jashnvareh-ye Matbou'at* (Selected Works from the Fifth Press Festival), Tehran: Ministry of Culture and Islamic Guidance, 1999, pp. 26–27.
10 Kazem Mo'tamednejad, 'Gozaresh-e Dabir-e Elmi-ye Seminar' (Report by the Academic Secretary of the Seminar), in *Majmou'eh Maqalat-e Dovomin Seminar-e Barresi-ye Massael-e Matbou'at-e Iran'* (The Collection of Articles Presented at the Second Seminar to Study the Problems of the Iranian Press), Tehran: Ministry of Culture and Islamic Guidance, 1998, vol. 1, pp. 2–3.
11 Mo'tamednejad, 'Gozaresh-e Dabir-e Elmi-ye Seminar', p. 51. Four years later, speaking at the Eighth Press Festival, Dr Mo'tamednejad suggested that state aid to the press had to be studied carefully, because many had started newspapers merely to take advantage of the subsidies that were put in place in 1989, *Rasaneh Quarterly*, vol. 12, no. 1, Spring 2001, p. 22.
12 Hamid-Reza Rezaie, 'Dowlat, Amel-e Asli-ye Bazdarandegi-ye Towse'eh-ye Matbou'at' (The State, the Main Factor Holding Back the Development of the Press), in *Majmou'eh Maqalat-e Dovomin Seminar-e Barresi-ye Massael-e Matbou'at-e Iran'* (The Collection of Articles Presented at the Second Seminar to Study the Problems of the Iranian Press), vol. 1, pp. 131–141.
13 Khosrow Talebzadeh, 'Barressi-ye Mo'zalat-e Chap-e Matbou'at' (Review of the Problems of the Printing of the Press), in *Majmou'eh Maqalat-e Dovomin Seminar-e Barresi-ye Massael-e Matbou'at-e Iran'* (The Collection of Articles Presented at the Second Seminar to Study the Problems of the Iranian Press), Tehran: Ministry of Culture and Islamic Guidance, 1998, vol. 1, pp. 235–245.
14 Ali-Akbar Qazizadeh, 'Zaminehha-ye Sou'-e Tafahom Miyan-e Matbou'at va Massou'lan' (The Background to Misunderstanding between the Press and the Officials), in *Majmou'eh Maqalat-e Dovomin Seminar*, vol. 1, pp. 355–372.
15 Ali-Reza Farahmand, 'Matoub'at-e Jame'ey-ye Madani' (Press in the Civil Society), in *Majmou'eh Maqalat-e Dovomin Seminar-e Barresi-ye Massael-e Matbou'at-e*

Iran' (The Collection of Articles Presented at the Second Seminar to Study the Problems of the Iranian Press), Tehran: 1998, vol. 1, pp. 115–117. Mr Farahmand, with more than twenty years of experience with *Kayhan* before the Revolution, had to leave the paper after its takeover by the Islamic Republic, discussed in Chapter 2, and spent 16 years on the specialist press. He joined the daily *Jameah* that was launched after Mr Khatami's election, but went back to specialist journalism after that paper had been banned.

16 Bijan Zare', 'Barresi-ye Vaz'iyat-e Amouzesh-e Rouznamehnegari dar Iran' (A Review of the State of Journalism Training in Iran), in *Majmou'eh Maqalat-e Dovomin Seminar*, vol. 2, p. 642.

17 Farid Adib-Hasehmi, 'Siyassat-gozari va Amouzesh, Do Massaleh-ye Assassi dar Matbou'at-e Iran' (Policy-Making and Training, Two Fundamental Issues for the Iranian Press), in *Majmou'eh Maqalat-e Dovomin Seminar-e Barresi-ye Massael-e Matbou'at-e Iran'* (The Collection of Articles Presented at the Second Seminar to Study the Problems of the Iranian Press), Tehran: 1998, vol. 2, pp. 612–615. The other side of the problem was that 'because of their political nature, most newspapers would only allow into their offices people whom they know personally' – Chair of Communication Group at Allameh Tabatabaee University, Dr Naiim Badii, quoted in *Rasaneh Quarterly*, vol. 10, no. 1, Spring 1999, p. 18.

18 Mahdokht Boroujerdi-Alavi, 'Pajouheshi dar Mowred-e Vaz'iyat-e Mowjoud-e Amouzesh-e Rouznamehnegari dar Iran' (An Investigation into the Current State of Journalism Training in Iran), in *Majmou'eh Maqalat-e Dovomin Seminar-e Barresi-ye Massael-e Matbou'at-e Iran'* (The Collection of Articles Presented at the Second Seminar to Study the Problems of the Iranian Press), Tehran: 1998, vol. 2, p. 594.

19 Adib-Hasehmi, 'Siyassat-gozari va Amouzesh, Do Mass'aleh-ye Assassi dar Matbou'at-e Iran', vol. 2, p. 617.

20 Article 3 of the Iranian Press Law.

21 Mehdi Mohsenian-Rad, 'Rouznamehnegari-ye Enteqadi!' (Critical Journalism!), in *Majmou'eh Maqalat-e Dovomin Seminar-e Barresi-ye Massael-e Matbou'at-e Iran'* (The Collection of Articles Presented at the Second Seminar to Study the Problems of the Iranian Press), Tehran: 1998, vol. 1, pp. 100–101.

22 Behrouz Geranpayeh, 'Lumpenism ya Bad-akhlaqi-ye Rasanehi dar Matbou'at-e Iran' (Lumpenism or Bad Media Attitude in the Iranian Press), in *Majmou'eh Maqalat-e Dovomin Seminar-e Barresi-ye Massael-e Matbou'at-e Iran'* (The Collection of Articles Presented at the Second Seminar to Study the Problems of the Iranian Press), Tehran: 1998, vol. 2, pp. 733–746.

23 Hamid-Reza Jalaiepour, *Pass az Dovom-e Khordad* (After 22 May), Tehran: Kavir, 1999, pp. 39–46.

24 Vahid Pourostad, *Mohakemeh-ye Jameah* (The Trial of *Jameah*), Tehran: Rouznegar, 2001, pp. 13–15.

25 Ibid., pp. 33–53.

26 Ibid., pp. 19–23.

27 Ibid., pp. 131–135.

28 Ibid., *Mohakemeh-ye Tous* (The Trial of *Tous*), Tehran: Rouznegar, 2002, pp. 17–42.

29 *Rasaneh Quarterly*, vol. 9, no. 2, Summer 1998, pp. 159–160.

30 Hamid Rasai, *Payan-e Dastan-e Ghamangiz: Negahi beh Zaminehhaye Sodour-e Hokm-e Hokoumati-ye Maqam-e Mo'azzam-e Rahbari dar-bareh-ye Qanoun-e Matbou'at* (The End of the Tragic Story: A Glance at the Background to His Excellency the Supreme Leader's Decree on the Press Law), vol. 1, Tehran: Kayhan Publications, 2001, pp. 184–194.

31 Pourostad, *Mohakemeh-ye Tous*, pp. 77–115.

32 Ibid., p. 59.

33 Ibid., p. 46.

34 Ibid., pp. 171–173.

35 Pourostad, *Mohakemeh-ye Tous*, pp. 185–195.

36 Ibid., p. 145.
37 Ibid., pp. 52–53.
38 Ibid., p. 55.
39 Mohajerani, *Esteezah*, p. 215. Pressure on the Ministry continued after the censure. Within weeks, Mr Mohajerani's deputy, Ahmad Bourqani, and a senior aide, Issa Saharkhiz, who had encouraged the growth of the press since Mr Khatami's election, had left the Ministry. IRNA's (Islamic Republic News Agency) director, Fereydoun Verdinejad, was briefly detained on 29 May. He was reported to have faced charges of embezzlement, 'mockery of public organizations' and 'spreading lies, slander and groundless accusations against others', filed by the national television, some 20 members of parliament, the army and the police – BBC World Service reports: http://news.bbc.co.uk/1/hi/world/middle_east/355945.stm (accessed last on 12 August 2006) and http://news.bbc.co.uk/1/hi/world/middle_east/359251.stm (accessed last on 12 August 2006). In the autumn of 2001, Mr Verdinejad was appointed Iran's Ambassador to China (Mr Verdinejad's personal website: www.verdinejad.com/html/History.htm (accessed 12 August 2006), and was succeeded as IRNA's director by Abdollah Nasseri-Taheri.
40 Mohajerani, *Esteezah*, pp. 215–216.
41 Kashi, *Matboua't dar Asr-e Khatami*, pp. 126–127. Jalaie-pour and Shamsolva'ezin moved on to another daily, *Asr-e Azadegan* (The Age of the Free), with a licence by another former member parliament, Ghafour Garshasbi. *Asr-e Azadegan* was closed down, along with 22 other papers, in April 2000. In March 2005, the ban on *Neshat* was reported to have been lifted by the Supreme Court (*Shargh*, 10 March 2005, p. 28), leading to speculation that the paper was expected to support Mr Rafsanjani's potential bid for presidency in the June elections. *Neshat*'s editor, Mr Shamsolva'ezin, said he would prefer to re-launch the paper after the elections to ensure that it would not be 'caught up in electoral bargaining' – *Entekhab* news site, www.entekhab.ir/display/?ID=930&page=1 (accessed last on 12 August 2006). The Head of Tehran's Justice Office, Mr Alizadeh, however, said the Supreme Court had only allowed for the case to be heard again, rather than revoke the ban – Iranian Students News Agency (ISNA) www.isna.ir/Main/NewsView.aspx? ID=News-505976 (accessed last on 12 August 2006).
42 Abbas Assadi, 'Otaq-e Izoleh, Akharin Istgah-e Mobtalayan-e AIDS' (Isolation Room, the Last Stop for AIDS Patients), in *Ketab-e Jashnvareh-ye Sheshom-e Matbou'at* (The Book of the Sixth Press Festival), Tehran: Ministry of Culture and Islamic Guidance, 1999, p. 54.
43 Ibid., p. 60
44 Ibid., p. 68.
45 Ibid., p. 65.
46 Ibid., p. 7.
47 Ibid., p. 74.
48 Ibid., p. 337.
49 Ali Rabi'i, 'Khat-e Nofouz ra Jeddi Begirid' (Take the Infiltration Line Seriously), in *Ketab-e Jashnvareh-ye Sheshom-e Matbou'at* (The Book of the Sixth Press Festival), Tehran: Ministry of Culture and Islamic Guidance, 1999, pp. 91–93. Significantly, the writer also mentioned two other suspected victims of political assassinations, Pirouz Davani and Majid Sharif, whose names had not been included in the list of victims given by the Iranian authorities when it was announced that the killings had been carried out by 'rogue elements' within the Ministry of Intelligence.
50 Mana Neyestani, in *Ketab-e Jashnvareh-ye Sheshom*, p. 287.
51 Javad Montazeri, in *Ketab-e Jashnvareh-ye Sheshom*, p. 203.
52 Sahdi Sadr, 'Ta'me Guilas, Ayeneh, va Hoquq-e Padid-avarandeh' (A Taste of Cherries, the Mirror, and the Creator's Rights), in *Ketab-e Jashnvareh-ye Sheshom-e*

Matbou'at (The Book of the Sixth Press Festival), Tehran: Ministry of Culture and Islamic Guidance, 1999, pp. 97–108.

53 Mohammad-Reza Kamyar, 'Mohakemeh-yi keh dar Khala-e Qanuni bar-pa Shod' (The Trial that was Held in a Legal Vacuum), in *Ketab-e Jashnvareh-ye Sheshom-e Matbou'at* (The Book of the Sixth Press Festival), Tehran: Ministry of Culture and Islamic Guidance, 1999, pp. 153–178.

54 Abbas Assadi, 'Otaq-e Izoleh, Akharin Istgah-e Mobtalayan-e AIDS' (Isolation Room, the Last Stop for AIDS Patients) and other reports, in *Ketab-e Jashnvareh-ye Sheshom*, pp. 227–262.

55 Mehdi Mohsenian-Rad, *Rasaneh Quarterly*, vol. 12, no. 1, Spring 2001, pp. 136–139.

56 Rasai, *Payan-e Dastan-e Ghamangiz*, vol. 1, pp. 96–165.

57 Ibid., pp. 194–200.

58 Ibid., *Payan-e Dastan-e Ghamangiz*, vol. 2, Tehran: Kayhan Publications, 2001, pp. 136–155.

59 Ibid., p. 88.

60 *Salam* front page, 6 July 1999, reproduced in *Mohakemeh-ye Salam*, p. 367.

61 Hamid Kaviani, *Dar Jostojou-ye Mahfel-e Jenayatkaran* (In Search of the Criminal Circle), Tehran: Negah-e Emrouz, 1999, pp. 138–170.

62 Pourostad, *Mohakemeh-ye Salam*, pp. 210–211. The Court later imposed a five year ban on *Salam* for having published a confidential government document, a charge which the paper had denied, saying it had received the report through an anonymous fax – *Mohakemeh-ye Salam*, pp. 68–91.

63 For comments by Ayatollahs Mohammad-Taqi Behjat, Mohammad Fazel-Lankarani, Nasser Makarem-Shirazi, Abdol-Karim Mousavi-Ardebili, Hossein Nouri-Hamadani, and Sheikh Javad Tabrizi, see Rasai, *Payan-e Dastan-e Ghamangiz*, vol. 1, pp. 213–225.

64 Ibid., pp. 200–204.

65 BBC World Service report, 12 March 2000, news.bbc.co.uk/1/hi/world/middle_east/674499.stm (accessed last on 12 August 2006).

66 Rasai, *Payan-e Dastan-e Ghamangiz*, vol. 1, pp. 204–205.

67 BBC World Service report, 17 May 2000, news.bbc.co.uk/1/hi/world/middle_east/752624.stm (accessed 12 August 2006), and BBC Persian Service report, 16 August 2003, www.bbc.co.uk/persian/iran/030816_mf-asgar.shtml (accessed last on 2 August 2006).

68 For details of the conference and its aftermath, see, Mohamad-Ali Zakariaee (ed.), *Conferans-e Berlin: Khedmat ya Khiyant?* (Berlin Conference: Service or Treason), Tehran: Tarh-e Now, 2000. Two translators, Khalil Rostamkhani and Saied Sadr, who had helped the conference organizers interview the guest speakers in Tehran, were given long prison sentences because of their record of imprisonment for left wing political activities a decade earlier.

69 Rasai, *Payan-e Dastan-e Ghamangiz*, vol. 1, pp. 206–209.

70 Association of Iranian Journalists, *Daghdagheh-ye Azadi* (Angst for Freedom), Tehran: Rouznegar, 2003, pp. 201–202.

71 Rasai, *Payan-e Dastan-e Ghamangiz*, vol. 1, p. 209.

72 *Rouznamehnegar*, no. 27, February–March 2001, p. 4.

73 Rasai, *Payan-e Dastan-e Ghamangiz*, vol. 2, p. 247.

74 *Asar-e Bargozideh-ye Haftomin Jashnvareh-ye Matbou'at* (Selected Works from the Seventh Press Festival), Tehran: Ministry of Culture and Islamic Guidance, 2001, p. 7.

75 *Rouznamehnegar*, no. 13, September–October 2000, p. 2.

76 Seyyed-Ebarhim Nabavi, quoted in *Rouznamehnegar*, no. 30, May–June 2002, p. 6.

77 *Asar-e Bargozideh-ye Haftomin Jashnvareh*, p. 27.

78 *Daghdagheh-ye Azadi*, pp. 201–203.

79 *Rasaneh Quarterly*, vol. 11, no. 2, Summer 2000, p. 1.

80 Association of Iranian Journalists' Secretary, Mass'oud Houshmand-e-Razavi, interviewed by the author, Tehran, 4 January 2005.
81 *Asar-e Bargozideh-ye Haftomin Jashnvareh*, p. 24.

6 The second fall (2001–04)

1 BBC Persian Service reports on 28 July 2004 (all accessed last on 2 August 2006). www.bbc.co.uk/persian/iran/story/2004/07/040728_a_mb_mohajerani.shtml,www.bbc.co.uk/persian/iran/story/2004/07/040728_mf_mohajerani01.shtml, and www.bbc.co.uk/persian/iran/story/2004/07/040728_mf_mohajerani.shtml,www.bbc.co.uk/persian/iran/030623_mf-icdac.shtml.
2 *Rouznamehnegar*, no. 33, August–September 2002, 3, and no. 37, February–March 2003, p. 9; *Rasaneh Quarterly*, vol. 11, no. 1, Autumn 2000, p. 1.
3 Head of Tehran Justice Office, Abbas-Ali Alizadeh, quoted in *Rouznamehnegar*, no. 24, October–November 2001, 2. Mr Alizadeh said the same law had earlier been used to close down a newspaper that had been referred to the court by the Ministry of Culture and Islamic Guidance, and the Ministry had not objected at the time.
4 Mr Alizadeh, quoted in *Rouznamehnegar*, no. 16, December 2000–January 2001, 2.
5 *Rouznamehnegar*, no. 23, September–October 2001, 3, named 15 imprisoned journalists: Reza Alijani, Emadeddin Baqi, Mohammad Bastehnegar, Akbar Ganji, Morteza Kazemian, Saied Madani, Nargess Mohammadi, Seyyed-Ebrahim Nabavi, Mohammad Qouchani, Taqi Rahmani, Reza Rais-Tousi, Ali-Reza Rajaie, Hoda Saber, Mashaallah Shamsolva'ezin, and Ahmad Zeidabadi. Two more were named in other issues: Mass'oud Behnoud in no. 13, September–October 2000, 1, and no. 30, May–June 2002, 16 (which said Mr Behonoud had been in prison for five months) and Amid Naini in no. 22, July–September 2001, 2. The journalists' arrests followed trials without a jury since, according to Head of Tehran Justice Office, Abbas-Ali Alizadeh, jury trials had been stipulated in the Press Law only for the publishers, who were legally responsible for the content of their papers. The writers, said Mr Alizadeh, could not be relieved of their personal responsibility for what they had written, but had to be tried on the basis of criminal law, which did not provide for trial with a jury – *Rouznamehnegar*, no. 24, October–November 2001, pp. 1–2.
6 *Rasaneh Quarterly*, vol. 12, no. 1, Spring 2001, pp. 17–18. Addressing the meeting, Mohammad-Mehdi Forqani, Director of the Centre for Media Studies and Research, said professional journalism required safeguarding the national identity, independence, freedom and rule of law; lack of financial, political or cultural dependence; social responsibility and fairness; dealing with national interests without political bias; commitment to shared awareness; and general understanding.
7 Mousa Qorbani, *Rasaneh Quarterly*, vol. 12, no. 1, Spring 2001, pp. 26–27.
8 *Rasaneh*, vol. 12, no. 1, Spring 2001, p. 30.
9 Mohammad Rezaie, *Gozaresh-e Moqayessehiy-e Bargozidegan-e Jashnvareh-ye Haftom va Hashtom-e Matbou'at* (Comparative Report on the Award Winners of the Seventh and Eighth Press Festivals), Tehran: Ministry of Culture and Islamic Guidance, November 2002.
10 *Rasaneh Quarterly*, vol. 12, no. 3, Autumn 2001, p. 1.
11 Ibid., vol. 13, no. 1, Spring 2002, p. 1.
12 Ibid., vol. 12, no. 4, Winter 2002, p. 1.
13 *Daghdagheh-ye Azadi*, pp. 205–206.
14 The daily *Mehr*, published by the Islamic Publicity Organization's Arts Department.
15 The titles were: *Golbang-e Iran* (Iran's Nightingale's Tune), *Nakhl* (Palm), *Ava-ye Varzesh* (Sports Call), *Bazar-e Rouz* (Daily Market), and *Honar-e Haftom* (Seventh Art).
16 The dailies *Mellat* (Nation) and *Akhbar* (News).
17 *Cinema Jahan* (World Cinema) and *Gozaresh-e Film* (Film Report).
18 *Azad* (Free).

19 *Rahiyan-e Feizieh* (Heading for Feizieh), published in Qom, home to the leading Feizieh Seminary.

20 Ayatollah Seyyed-Mahmoud Hashemi-Shahroudi took over as Head of the Judiciary in August 1999, replacing Ayatollah Mohammad Yazdi, who had been widely criticised as having condoned violence against dissidents.

21 For details, see Vahid Pourostad, *Mohakehem-ye Nowrouz* (The Trial of *Nowrouz*), Tehran: Rouznegar, 2002.

22 *Daghdagheh-ye Azadi* (Angst for Freedom), p. 206.

23 *Aineh-ye Jonoub* (Mirror of the South).

24 *Rasaneh Quarterly*, vol. 13, no. 2, Summer 2002, p. 117.

25 *Rouznamehnegar*, no. 32, July–August 2002, 2. Out of 59 awards, eight went to women, the same 13.8 per cent share as the previous year. Women's awards at the Press Festivals will be discussed in 'Chapter 7: Women and journalism'.

26 International Pen, Writers in Prison Committee, 'Half Yearly Caselist to December 2001', www.pen.dk/prison/CaselistJan02.pdf (accessed 3 August 2006).

27 *Rouznamehnegar*, no. 32, July–August 2002, p. 1. The paper reported that 'many participants had expressed their disappointment over the weak performance' of national television broadcasters who had been brought in by the Ministry of Culture and Islamic Guidance to present the Festival's programmes.

28 *Rasaneh Quarterly*, vol. 13, no. 2, Summer 2002, p. 1.

29 *Rasaneh Supplement*, weekly publication of the Office of Deputy Minister for Press and Publicity Affairs, Minstry of Cultre and Islamic Guidance, vol. 1, May 2004, p. 5.

30 Ibid., vol. 1, May 2004, p. 3.

31 Ibid., vol. 1, no. 1, 16 June 2004, p. 4.

32 *Rasaneh Quarterly*, vol. 15, no. 2, Summer 2004, p. 230.

33 Ibid., vol. 13, no. 4, Winter 2003, p. 1.

34 Ali Yousefpour, Secretary General of the Association of Moslem Journalists and managing editor of *Siyassat-e Rouz* (Politics of the Day) daily, quoted in *Rasaneh Quarterly*, vol. 14, no. 1, Spring 2003, p. 7.

35 Kazem Anbarloui, member of the editorial board of *Resalat* (Mission) daily, quoted in *Rasaneh Quarterly*, vol. 14, no. 1, Spring 2003, p. 7.

36 Abbas Salimi-Namin, managing editor of *Tehran Times*, quoted in *Rasaneh Quarterly*, vol. 12, no. 1, Spring 2001, p. 25. The cartoon of Ayatollah Mesbah, who had accused the reformist papers of having been paid by the US, appeared in the daily *Azad* in February 2000. It was drawn by a former Press Festival award winner, Nikahang Kowsar, based on the fact that Ayatollah Mesbah's name rhymes with *temsah*, the Persian word for crocodile. The cartoon led to protests by the clergy in Qom calling for the cartoonist's death. Mr Kowsar was imprisoned, even though under the Press Law at the time, the paper's publisher should have been held accountable. The paper was closed down, along with 22 others, in April 2000. After his release, Mr Kowsar criticized the reformists for not having supported the journalists 'who had taken Khatami's message to the people'. For an account of Mr Kowsar's detention, see Baniyaghoub, *Rouznamehnegaran*, pp. 49–76. He later went to Canada, where in his weblog, http://nikahang.blogspot.com/, he accused the publishers of the reformist press of having exploited him and other journalists for their own political goals.

37 *Rouznamehnegar*, no. 39, May–June 2003, p. 1. The paper named the detainees as: Reza Alijani, Amin Bozorgian, Ensaf-Ali Hedayat, Ali-Reza Jabbari, Taqi Rahmani, Hoda Saber, and Mohammad-Mohsen Sazegara.

38 In July 2004, the judiciary announced that the 'sole defendant' in Zahra Kazemi's case, an Intelligence Ministry agent, had been acquitted and that Zahra Kazemi's death could only have been caused by 'a drop in her blood pressure caused by her hunger strike, thus making her fall from a standing position and get hurt.' Ms Kazemi's family and reformists in Iran said the trial was part of a cover-up to protect a high ranking judiciary official. The ruling was also dismissed by the

Canadian government – BBC World Service, 29 July 2004, http://news.bbc.co.uk/1/hi/
world/middle_east/3936021.stm (accessed 12 August 2006).

39 *Rouznamehnegar*, no. 40, August 2003, pp. 1–6. The names, given by the President
of the Association of Iranian Journalists, Ali Mazru'i, and the Chair of the
Association for the Defence of Press Freedom, Hojjatoleslam Mohsen Kadivar, were
as follows: Abbas Abdi, Reza Alijani, Hashem Aqajeri, Amin Bozorgian, Akbar
Ganji, Abol-Qassem Golbaf, Esma'il Jamshidi, Iraj Jamshidi, Amir Karami, Hossein
Qazian, Taqi Rahmani, Saied Razavi-Faqih, Hoda Saber, Arash Salehi, Mohammad-
Mohsen Sazegara, Amiar Tayarani, Hassan Yousefi-Eshkevari, Nasser Zarafshan, and
Ahmad Zeidabadi.

40 *Rouznamehnegar*, no. 40, July–August 2003, p. 8. The protestors who returned their
awards gave the following reasons: Mohammd Haidari, winner for best political
article: the continued detention of Ganji, Zeidabadi, and Abdi; Bahman Ahmadi-
Amoui, specialist reporting award winner: no reference to imprisoned journalists,
while awards had been given to television reporters, and the fact that there had been
no mention of the photo–journalist, Kaveh Golestan, who had been killed by a mine
in April 2003, while working with a BBC news team covering the invasion of Iraq;
Shadi Sadr, social article award winner, and Azadeh Akbari, the first prize winner in
the children and youth news and interview category: to express the hope for an independent festival in future with a human rights award. Once again, the participants said
they were unhappy with the style in which television presenters had conducted the
ceremony.

41 *Rouznamehnegar*, no. 40, July–August 2003, p. 9.

42 The then Director of Research at the Centre for Media Studies and Research, Ali
Bahrampour, 'Asibha va Masaael-e Herfei-ye Matbou'at' (Professional Failures and
Problems of the Country's Press), *Rasaneh Quarterly*, vol. 14, no. 2, Summer 2003,
pp. 42–49.

43 *Rouznamehnegar*, no. 42, April–May 2004, p. 4.

44 Iranian history web sites, www.parstimes.com/history/press_history.html and www.
iranchamber.com/history/amir_kabir/amir_kabir.php (both accessed 12 August 2006).

45 *Rouznamehnegar*, no. 42, April–May 2004, p. 1. The appearance and closure of
websites marked a new stage in Iranian journalism, discussed in 'Chapter 8: The
electronic media'.

46 *Rouznamehnegar*, no. 44, August–September 2004, p. 8. The eight prisoners were
named as follows: Abbas Abdi, Reza Alijani, Emadeddin Baqi, Akbar Ganji, Hossein
Qazian, Hoda Saber, Hassan Yousefi-Eshkevari, and Nasser Zarafshan.

47 *Rouznamehnegar*, no. 44, August–September 2004, pp. 2–5. Mr Mazru'i said that
under Article 35 of the Press Law a newspaper that had committed an offence for
which no punishment had been stipulated could be closed temporarily – a maximum
of six months for a daily and one year for others – while the case was being examined.
The ceremony was organized and presented by Association of Iranian Journalists
(AOIJ) members.

48 *Rasaneh Supplement*, vol. 1, no. 7, pp. 6–21, September 2004, p. 9.

49 Akbar Safdari, 'Herfeh Rouznamehnegar' (Profession: Journalist), *Rasaneh
Supplement*, vol. 1, no. 5, August 2005, pp. 5–20 and 8–9.

50 *Jahan-e-Football* (World of Football) editor, Ardeshir Laroudi, *Rasaneh Supplement*,
vol. 1, no. 10, 22 October–5 November 2004, pp. 6–7.

51 Lotfollah Maisami, publisher of the political monthly *Cheshmandaz-e Iran* (Iran
Perspective), *Rasaneh Supplement*, vol. 1, no. 1, 16 June 2004, p. 5.

52 Deputy Minister of Culture and Islamic Guidance, Seyyed-Mohammad Sohofi,
Rasaneh Supplement, vol. 1, no. 1, 6 June 2004, p. 2.

53 *Rasaneh Quarterly*, 14, no. 4, Winter 2004, pp. 16–18. 52 of the 90 newspapers
closed down between 1998 and 2004 had received their licenses after Mr Khatami's
election in 1997.

54 Kasra Nouri, editor of *Iran*, the license for which is held by the Ministry of Culture and Islamic Guidance, interviewed by *Rasaneh Supplement*, vol. 1, no. 2, 21 June–5 July 2004, pp. 6–7.

55 *Shargh*'s publisher, Mehdi Rahmanian, interviewed by *Rasaneh Supplement*, vol. 1, no. 1, 6 June 2004, p. 7.

56 Sohofi, *Rasaneh Supplement*, vol. 1, no. 1, 6 June 2004, p. 2.

57 Sohofi, *Rasaneh Supplement*, vol. 1, no. 2, 21 June–5 July 2004, p. 5. Mr Sohofi later announced that the government had provided 600 freelance journalists with insurance cover – *Khabarnameh-ye Deneshjouiy* (University Students' News Bulletin), the news bulletin of the 3rd Seminar to Study the Problems of the Press in Iran, 1 March 2005, p. 1.

58 *Farhang-e Ashti* (Culture of Reconciliation) daily, 26 September 2004.

59 *Rasaneh Supplement*, vol. 1, no. 10, 22 October–5 November 2004, p. 11.

60 Sohofi, *Rasaneh Supplement*, vol. 1, June 2004, p. 5. For more on the four documents, see 'Chapter 10 : One hundred years of legal confusion'.

61 Sohofi, meeting the managers of sports and popular newspapers, *Rasaneh Supplement*, vol. 1, no. 4, 22 July–5 August 2004, p. 4.

62 Director General of Domestic Press and News Agencies, Saied Taqiepour, *Rasaneh Supplement*, vol. 1, no. 2, 21 June–5 July 2004, pp. 4–5.

63 The Director General of the Stock Exchange, Hussein Abdoh-Tabrizi, *Rasaneh Supplement*, vol. 1, no. 3, pp. 6–21 July 2004, pp. 1–2.

64 *Rasaneh Supplement*, vol. 1, no. 12, 21 November–5 December 2004, pp. 1–3.

65 Iraj Babahaji, *Shargh*, 14 October 2004.

66 Mass'oud Kazemi, 'Doshvariha-ye Nashriyat-e Mostaqel dar Barabar-e Gostaresh-e Nashriyat-e Dowlati ya Mowred-e Hemayat-e Dowlat' (The Difficulties Faced by the Independent Publications with Respect to the Expansion of Publications Owned or Supported by the State), *Rasaneh Quarterly*, vol. 14, no. 4, Winter 2004, pp. 18–19.

67 Kasra Nouri, editor of *Iran* daily, *Rasaneh Supplement*, vol. 1, no. 2, 21 June–5 July 2004, pp. 6–7.

68 Kazem Mo'tamednejad, *Shargh*, 19 December 2004, p. 13.

69 Fariborz Rais-dana, in 'Miz-e-gerd-e Towlid-e Melli' (National Production Roundtable), *Naqd-e Now* (New Critique) monthly, no. 4, January–February 2004, p. 8.

70 *Shenasnameh-ye Mowzoui'-ye Matbou'at-e Keshvar* (Subject Catalogue of the Country's Press), Tehran: Ministry of Culture and Islamic Guidance, 2004.

71 Ali Mirzakhani, editor of *Donya-ye-Eqtesad* (The Universe of Economics), interviewed by *Rasaneh Supplement*, vol. 1, no. 6, 22 August–5 September 2004, pp. 8–9.

72 Director General for Domestic Press and News Agencies, Saied Taqiepour, who ran the business daily *Jahan-e Eqtesad* [World of Economics] for 12 years before taking up his post at the Ministry – *Shargh*, 30 November 2004, p. 13.

73 *Rasaneh Supplement*, vol. 1, no. 4, 22 July–5 August 2004, 3. Reporters Without Borders, 3 August 2004, www.rsf.org/article.php3?id_article=10852 (accessed 2 August 2006).

74 *Shenasnameh-ye Mowzoui'-ye Matbou'at-e Keshvar*.

75 For instance, the November 2004 issue of the quarterly *Me'mar* (Architect), had a cover price of 40,000 rials ($4.5), five times greater than the women's monthly Zanan. 33 per cent of Me'mar's glossy, full colour pages carried advertisements for construction material and equipment, fittings, and furniture.

76 Issa Saharkhiz, quoted in *Rouznamehnegar*, no. 42, April–May 2004, p. 12.

77 Sohofi, quoted in *Rouznamehnegar*, no. 42, April–May 2004, p. 12.

78 Ibid., p. 12. By Spring 2005, the eight journalists arrested were still in prison: Abbas Abdi, Reza Alijani, Akbar Ganji, Ensaf-Ali Hedayat, Hossein Qazian, Taqi Rahmani, Hoda Saber, and Arash Sigarchi – Association of Iranian Journalists quoted in *Shargh*, 14 March 2005, p. 28.

7 Women and journalism

1 Hossein Shahidi, 'Women in Iranian Journalism, 1910–1997', in Sarah Ansari and Vanessa Martin (eds), *Women, Religion and Culture in Iran*, London: Royal Asiatic Society and Curzon Press, 2002, pp. 70–71.

2 Ibid., pp. 75–76.

3 *Rasaneh Quarterly in Media Studies and Research*, Ministry of Culture and Islamic Guidance, vol. 1, no. 2, Summer 1980, p. 11.

4 Mass'oud Barzin, 'Anjomanha-ye Matboua'ti dar Iran ta Sal-e 1357' (Press Associations in Iran until 1978–79), *Rasaneh Quarterly*, vol. 2, no. 3, Autumn 1991, pp. 59–60. In Mr Barzin's view, 'the Association's formation and its speed of development' was 'undoubtedly influenced' by the publication of Ms Pari Sheikholeslami's book *Zanan-e Rouznamehnegar va Andishmand-e Iran* (Iran's Women Journalists and Thinkers), Tehran: Tehran University, 1972.

5 Shahidi, 'Women in Iranian Journalism, 1910–1997', pp. 76–79.

6 *Salnema-ye Matbou'at-e Iran* (Almanac of the Iranian Press), Tehran: Ministry of Guidance and Islamic Culture, 1996.

7 *Rasaneh Quarterly*, vol. 6, no. 4, Winter 1996, p. 122.

8 Ibid., vol. 7, no. 3, Autumn 1996, p. 131.

9 *Teenager*'s November 2004 edition included an interview with the Hollywood star, Brad Pitt, and a 'review of the works' of the popular American singer, Johnny Cash – *Rasaneh Supplement*, vol. 1, no. 12, 21 November–5 December 2004, p. 12.

10 For details on *Danestniha*, see Ms Behzadi's interview in *Rasaneh Supplement*, vol. 1, no. 7, pp. 6–21 September 2004, pp. 6–7. Ms Behzadi's father, Ali Behzadi, was one of the most highly regarded journalists before the Revolution.

11 *Shenasnameh-ye Mowzoui'-ye Matbou'at-e Keshvar*.

12 Ibid., pp. 225–234.

13 Afsar Razazifar, *Gozaresh-e Nashriyat-e Zanan va Khanevadeh* (Report on Women and Family Publications), Tehran: Ministry of Culture and Islamic Guidance, Centre for Media Studies and Research, November 2002, pp. 9–57.

14 Shahidi, 'Women in Iranian Journalism, 1910–1997', p. 80.

15 Sadiqeh Babran, *Nashriyat-e Vijeh-ye Zanan* (Specialist Women's Press), Tehran: Roshangaran, 2002, pp. 141–143.

16 *Zan-e Rouz* (Woman of the Day) weekly, no. 1973, 11 December 2004.

17 Babran, *Nashriyat-e Vijeh-ye Zanan*, pp. 195–200.

18 Razazifar, *Gozaresh-e Nashriyat-e Zanan va Khanevadeh*, pp. 25–56. The legal coverage, 9.76 per cent, of the monthly *Zan-e-Jonoub* (Woman of the South), based in the southern port city of Bushehr, was greater than *Zanan*'s and its content was also 100 per cent original. The paper lasted less than two years, one of the women's papers that lost their licenses after failing to appear regularly, as recorded in *Ashnaiy ba Madeh-ye 16 Qanoun-e Matboua'at* (Learning about Article 16 of the Press Law), Tehran: Ministry of Information and Culture, no date, p. 34.

19 BBC Persian Service, 20 Apirl 2004, www.bbc.co.uk/persian/iran/story/2004/04/040420_he-pourzand.shtml (accessed 2 August 2006).

20 *Zanan* (Women) monthly, no. 34, April 1997.

21 The debate surfaced again in 2005, towards the end of President Khatami's second term. On 23 January, the Iranian Women News Agency (IWNA), quoted the Council of Guardians' Spokesman, Gholam-Hossein Elham, as having said that the Council did not regard the word *rejal* a 'gender-based negation' and women could nominate themselves for presidency. www.iwna.ir/shownews.aspx?newsid=410 (accessed 12 August 2006). On the same day, the reformist newspaper *Shargh* quoted Mr Elham as having said that the Council had not offered any new interpretation, and 'the word *rejal* still does not apply to women.'

22 Razazifar, *Gozaresh-e Nashriyat-e Zanan va Khanevadeh*, p. 28.

23 *Zanan*, no. 114, November 2004. Several years earlier, there had been ads for classes in Chinese, Hebrew, and Japanese – *Zanan*, vol. 6, no. 34, April 1997.

24 Vahid Pourostad, *Mohakemeh-ye Zan* (The Trial of *Zan*), Tehran: Rouzengar, 2001, p. 8.

25 Razazifar, *Gozaresh-e Nashriyat-e Zanan va Khanevadeh*, p. 233. The pre-launch advisors included Amid Naini, Jalal Rafi' and Mass'oud Behnoud. Seyyed-Ebrahim Nabavi worked as Ms Hashemi's advisor after the paper had been launched.

26 Nassim Bojnourdi, 'Talaq ba Agahi-ye Rouznameh' (Divorce with a Newspaper Ad), reprinted in *Zan dar Rouzanameh-ye Zan* (Woman in the Newspaper Woman), Tehran: Qolleh, 2000, pp. 605–609.

27 Nazanin Salamat, 'Qatl-e Farzand Tavasot-e Pedar' (Infanticide by the Father), and Mandana Nasser, 'Cheh Kassi Moqasser Ast, Pedar ya Qanoun' (Who is Guilty, the Father or the Law?), reprinted in *Zan dar Rouzanameh-ye Zan* (Woman in the Newspaper Woman), Tehran, Qolleh, 2000, pp. 619–623 and pp. 637–640 respectively.

28 'Hoqouq-e Farzandan' (Children's Rights), interview with Shirin Ebadi, reprinted in *Zan dar Rouzanameh-ye Zan*, pp. 563–569.

29 'Talaq va Hoqouq-e Zanan' (Divorce and Women's Rights), interview with Mehr-Anguiz Kar, reprinted in *Zan dar Rouzanameh-ye Zan*, pp. 579–595.

30 Faezeh Hashemi interviewed by *Zan*, no date given when reprinted in *Zan dar Rouzanameh-ye Zan*, p. 272.

31 Pourostad, *Mohakemeh-ye Zan*, pp. 13–78.

32 Ibid., p. 90 and p. 107.

33 Ibid., pp. 94–97 and pp. 105–106.

34 Dr Nasser Katouzian, quoted in *Mohakemeh-ye Zan*, pp. 111–121.

35 Pourostad, *Mohakemeh-ye Zan*, 2001, p. 103.

36 *Shenasnameh-ye Mowzoui'-ye Matbou'at-e Keshvar*, pp. 641–647.

37 Islamic Women's News Agency (IWNA), 1 June 2005, www.iwna.ir/shownews. aspx?newsid=1330 (accessed 12 August 2006).

38 Razazifar, *Gozaresh-e Nashriyat-e Zanan va Khanevadeh*, pp. 59–92.

39 Horomz Shojai-mehr, publisher of *Khanevadeh-ye Sabz* (Green Family) biweekly, *Rasaneh Supplement*, vol. 1, no. 12, 21 November–5 December 2004, pp. 6–7.

40 *Rasaneh Quarterly*, vol. 5, no. 4, Winter 1995, pp. 92–94.

41 Ma'ssoumeh Kayhani, *Rasaneh Quarterly*, vol. 13, no. 2, Summer 2002, pp. 64–77. The individual coverage figures for the 10 papers, in percentages, were: *Iran* (15.7), *Abrar* (15.1), *Ettela'at* (11.1), *Entekhab* (10.3), *Hamshahri* (9.7), *Kayhan* (9.1), *Resalat* (9.1), *Aftab-e Yazd* (8), *Hayat-e Now* (6.2), *Hambastegi* (5.8).

42 Shadi Sadr, quoted by BBC Persian Service online, 18 July 2004: www.bbc.co.uk/ persian/iran/story/2004/07/040718_la-mb-iranwomen.shtml (accessed 3 August 2006).

43 *Iran* daily, 20 November 2004, p. 13, 11 December 2004, p. 12, 1 January 2005, p. 5 and p. 12.

44 Ibid., 7 November 2004, p. 7.

45 Maryam Jamshidi, *Shargh*, 28 December 2004, p. 6.

46 Mojgan Inanlou, *Shargh*, 28 December 2004, p. 18.

47 Khatereh Vatankhah, *Shargh*, 28 December 2004, p. 10.

48 Iran Hosseini, *Shargh*, 28 December 2004, p. 24.

49 Author's calculations based on *Shargh*'s bylines on 14 and 23 January and 1 and 3 February 2005. *Shargh* has also carried some of the best literary satire in today's Iranian journals, written by one of the early Press Festival award winners, Roya Sadr. Ms Sadr started her career with *Zan-e Rouz*, before moving on the satirical weekly *Gol Agha*. – *Asar-e Bargozideh-ye Chaharomin Jashnvareh-ye Matbou'at* (Selected Works from the Fourth Press Festival), Tehran: Festival Secretariat, 1997, pp. 363–365.

50 Based on figures provided by the AOIJ Secretary, Mass'oud Houshmand-e-Razavi, interviewed by the author, Tehran, 4 January 2005.

51 In November 2004, there were 16 women among 48 business journalists who signed a petition in protest against a competition for selecting the best business journalists. The protestors argued that such competitions were aimed at softening the journalists' approach towards the organizing firms – *Shargh*, 10 November 2004, p. 4.

52 Rouh-Anguiz Mohammadi's interview with Dr Mehadi Akhlaqi-Feizasar, about the discrepancies in unemployment figures given by various government organizations, carried by the Society of Iranian Youth News Agency (SYNA), www.syna.ir/news/news_10193.html (accessed 10 October 2004).

53 Shirin Ebadi, *Hoqouq-e Adabi va Honari* (Literary and Artistic Rights), Tehran: Roshangaran, 1991.

54 *Jameah* (Society), 13 June 1998.

55 Gholam-Hossein Salehyar, *Chehreh-ye Matbou'at-e Mo'asser* (The Image of the Contemporary Press), Tehran: Press Agent, 1973. Mr Salehyar's figures are used here, rather than those of the Association of Iranian Women Journalists cited above, because he also gives men's numbers, making it possible to examine the ratio.

56 AOIJ Secretary, Mr Mass'oud Houshmand-e-Razavi, interviewed by the author, Tehran, 4 January 2005.

57 *Rasaneh Supplement*, vol. 1, no. 6, 22 August–5 September 2004, p. 5.

58 Mohssenian-Rad, op.cit, pp. 2–11, and in *Rasaneh Quarterly*, vol. 5, no. 4, Winter 1994, p. 93.

59 *Rasaneh Supplement*, vol. 1, no. 7, September 2004, pp. 6–21 and p. 9.

60 The daily *Asr-e Rasaneh* (Media Age), with a woman, Maliheh Dehqan, as its licence holder and managing editor, began on 10 February 2005.

61 *Rasaneh Supplement*, vol. 1, no. 1, 6 June 2004, p. 2.

62 *Rasaneh Supplement*, vol. 1, no. 5, pp. 6–21 August 2004, The Iranian Women Journalists' Association publishes a newsletter called *Seday-e Zan* (Woman's Voice).

63 www.womeniniran.com/index.asp (accessed 3 August 2006).

64 www.iftribune.com/ (accessed 12 August 2006).

65 www.badjens.com/ (accessed 12 August 2006)

66 *Rouznamehnegar*, no. 42, April–May 2004, p. 5. For details of the protest, see 'Chapter 8: The electronic media'.

67 www.iwna.ir (accessed 3 August 2006). *Rasaneh Supplement*, vol. 1, no. 12, 21 November–5 December 2004, p. 3. An online database on Iranian women, www.iranwomen.org, (accessed 12 August 2006) was started in 2002, following a directive from the Supreme Cultural Revolution Council, to provide information in Persian and English on '40 groups of prominent women in Iran and around the world'. The women's data centre had been set up in 1999 'to coordinate data collection about women's activities and organizations and deepen and expand women's participation', *Rasaneh Quarterly*, vol. 13, no. 2, Summer 2002, p. 118.

68 For more details on weblogs see 'Chapter 8: The electronic media'. For some of the women's weblogs, see www.persianblog.com (accessed 12 August 2006).

69 Fatemeh Amiri, 'Ehsasat-e Zananeh dar Donya-ye Majazi' (Feminine Feelings in a Virtual World), *Iran* daily, 8 January 2005, p. 7.

70 *Iran* daily, 11 January 2005, p. 1.

71 Ms Abbasqholizadeh was arrested on 1 November and released at the end of the month. She is the director of an orgnaization that specializes in capacity building for non-governmental organizations. Reporters without Borders' site, news item date 1 December 2005, January 2006, www.rsf.org/article.php3?id_article=11793 (accessed 18 February 2007). *Shenasnameh-ye Mowzoui'-ye Matbou'at Keshvar*, p. 230, names her as the editor of the quarterly *Farzaneh* published by Ms Ma'ssoumeh Ebtekar, President Khatami's advisor on the environment. Two male weblog writers, Omid Me'marian and Shahram Rafi'zadeh, who had been arrested on charges of 'acting against the system in illegal internet sites', were released on 1 December 2004 and said later that they had been tortured to sign letters of repentance. For details, see 'Chapter 8: The electronic media'.

8 The electronic media

1 'Tarikhcheh-ye Radio dar Iran' (A Brief History of Radio in Iran), in *Loghatname Dehkhoda*, vol. 7, Tehran, Tehran University Publications, 1993–94, pp. 10289–10290.

2 Mass'oud Mehrabi, *Tarikh-e Cinema-ye Iran* (The History of Iranian Cinema), Tehran: Film Publications, 1988, p. 314.

3 Reza Talachian, 'Major Motion Picture Studios in Iran, 1929–1975', in *A Survey Catalogue and Brief Critical History of Iranian Feature Fim (1896–1975)*, MA dissertation, Department of Cinema and Photography in the Graduate School, Southern Illinois University, December 1980, University of Washington Libraries website: www.lib.washington.edu/neareast/cinemaofiran/intro.html (accessed 12 August 2006).

4 Ibid.

5 *Qanoun-e Assassi-ye Jomhouri-ye Eslami-ye Iran* (The Constitution of the Islamic Republic of Iran), ratified in 1979 and revised in 1989, Tehran: Nashr-e Dowran, 2004, preamble, p. 19.

6 Ibid., p. 93.

7 Majid Mohammadi, *Sima-ye Eqtedargaraiy, Televizion-e Dowlati-ye Iran* (The Authoritarian Vision, Iran's State-owned Television), Tehran: Jameah Iran, 2000, pp. 32–33.

8 Ali Larijani, Islamic Republic of Iran Broadcasting (IRIB) Director, 1994–2004, interviewed by *Shargh* newspaper, 7 February 2005, reproduced by the online news site, *Baztab* (Reflection), www.baztab.com/news/21394.php (accessed 12 August 2006).

9 Ibid.

10 *Rasaneh Quarterly Journal of Media Studies and Research*, Tehran: Ministry of Culture and Islamic Guidance, vol. 5, no. 1, Spring 1994, p. 87.

11 Mohammadi, *Sima-ye Eqtedargaraiy, Televizion-e Dowlati-ye Iran*, p. 67.

12 Ibid., p. 64.

13 *Salnameh-ye Amari-ye Keshvar* (National Statistical Yearbook), Teheran: Statistical Centre of Iran, 2004, p. 613. No figure is given for 2000, but the figures for 1999 and 2001 are, respectively, 296,728 and 295,325.

14 IRIB's 2002–03 budget was Rls159,873,700,000 [$160m], compared to Rls73,074,000,000 [$73m] for the Ministry of Culture and Islamic Guidance and Rls16,388,300,000 [$16m] for the Islamic Culture and Communication Organization – *Novaran* [Innovators] biweekly, no. 3, July 2002, p. 32.

15 *Rasaneh Quarterly*, vol. 5, no. 3, Autumn 1994, p. 89. In October 2004, a Persian language satellite TV station called *Mohajer* (Immigrant), with offices in Germany and Dubai, went on air, backed by the Iranian government and aimed at attracting viewers in Iran away from the US-based stations – Pendar news website, www.pendar.net/83/main1.asp?a_id=607 (accessed Fall 2004).

16 Hojjatoleslam Seyyed-Reza Taqavi, Chairman of Majlis's Culture and Islamic Guidance Committee, quoted in *Rasaneh Quarterly*, vol. 5, no. 3, Autumn 1994, p. 89.

17 Ibid.

18 *Rasaneh Quarterly*, vol. 5, no. 1, Spring 1994, p. 87.

19 Ali Larijani's memoirs for 24 August 1994, *Jam-e Jam* (Jamshid's Goblet) daily, 3 Jaunary 2005, p. 3.

20 *Rasaneh Quarterly*, vol. 7, no. 2, Summer 1996, p. 120.

21 Ali Larijani, interviewed by *Shargh* newspaper, 6–8 February 2005, reproduced by the online news site, *Baztab*, www.baztab.com/news/21394.php (accessed 12 August 2006), *Jam-e Jam*, 21 December 2004.

22 Hadi Khaniki, 'Ertebatat-e Towsse'eh va Massaleh-ye Ertebat dar Iran' (Development Communication and the Problem of Communication in Iran), paper presented at the 3rd Seminar to Study the Problems of the Iranian Press, Tehran, 2 March 2005.

23 Research finding by Dr Naiim Badii, quoted in Mehdi Ahmadi's communication weblog, *Cybercafe* 24 May 2004, http://cc.eprsoft.com/archives/001738.html (accessed 3 August 2006).

24 *Rasaneh Quarterly*, vol. 8, no. 3, Autumn 1998, p. 133.
25 Mr Larijani's interview with *Shargh*, 6–8 February 2005.
26 A survey in 2004 found that 37.7 per cent of the residents of Tehran had access to satellite TV – Behrouz Geranpayeh, speaking at the 3rd Seminar to Study the Problems of the Iranian Press, Tehran, 1 March 2005.
27 *Resalat*, 23 December 2004, *Kayhan*, 4 January 2005, p. 3. *Kayhan* said that 15 of the 21 channels had set up operations in the Persian Gulf emirates, especially in Dubai.
28 *Shargh*, 16 December 2004, p. 13.
29 Akbar Ganji, *Tarikkhaneh-ye Ashabah* (The Dark-House of the Ghosts), 4th impression, Tehran: Tarh-e Now, 1999, pp. 32–33.
30 For more on the Belin Confernece and its aftermath, see Chapter 5 above.
31 BBC Persian Service online report, www.bbc.co.uk/persian/iran/story/2004/05/040517_irib.shtml (accessed 3 August 2006).
32 Mr Larijani's interview with *Shargh*, 6–8 February 2005.
33 www.iran-emrouz.de/khabar/khabar820219.html (accessed 12 August 2006).
34 *Kayhan*, 4 January 2005, p. 2. Also www.iran-emrouz.de/khabar/tahghigh820218.html (accessed 12 August 2006).
35 *Rouznamehnegar*, no. 42, April–May 2004, p. 5. The participants in the protest included Women's Cultural Centre, Iranian Women Journalists' Association, Iranian Women website, Independent Women's Association, Association of New-Thinking Women of Iran, *Zanan* monthly, Zaman Women's Centre, Hasta-Andish Association, *Badjens* website, Centre for Civil Society's New-Thinking Youth, Roshdieh Education and Research Institute, Centre for NGO Productivity, *Farzaneh* magazine, *Zanan-e Iran-e Emrouz* website, and the Association of Young Journalists.
36 Iranian Women's News Agency, 15 January 2005, www.iwna.ir/shownews.aspx?newsid=372 (accessed 12 August 2006).
37 Eshrat Shayeq, *Shargh*, 21 February 2005, p. 2.
38 *Jam-e Jam*, 13 November 2004, p. 6.
39 *Jam-e Jam*, 25 December 2004, p. 3. The meeting was held with Ayatollahs Abdollah Javadi-Amoli, Nasser Makarem-Shirazi and Ja'far Sobhani. The IRIB team included the director of the series, Farajollah Salahshour; advisor to the director, Jamal Shourjeh; planning manager, Hassan Najjarian; acting production manager, Mehdi Kayhani; and Seyyed-Hossein Ja'fari, the young actor playing Joseph's role.
40 *Jam-e Jam*, 2 December 2004, pp. 1–2.
41 Deputy Director for Political Affairs, Iraj Sebqati, *Jam-e Jam*, 11 January 2005, pp. 1–3.
42 *Jam-e Jam*, 9 January 2005, p. 3.
43 Jamal Shourjeh, *Jam-e Jam*, 30 December 2005, p. 3.
44 Hamid Rasai, *Payan-e Dastan-e Ghamangiz: Negahi beh Zaminehhaye Sodour-e Hokm-e Hokoumati-ye Maqam-e Mo'azzam-e Rahbari dar-bareh-ye Qanoun-e Matbou'at* (The End of the Tragic Story: A Glance at the Background to His Excellency the Supreme Leader's Decree on the Press Law), Ayatollah Khamenei addressing the Supreme Cultural Revolution Council, 15 November 1999, vol. 1, Tehran: Kayhan Publications, 2001, p. 204.
45 *Shargh*, 12 October 2004.
46 The Government's representative on the Council, Hojjatoleslam Mohammad Shariati-Dehaqan, quoted in *Iran*, 16 December 2004, p. 2.
47 *Shargh*, 22 December 2004, p. 15.
48 Ibid., 6 November 2004, p. 24. One of the most amusing mispronunciations quoted in the article is 'Arsan Vanjeh', rather than 'Arsène Wenger', for the French manager of the English club, Arsenal, presumably meant to display the broadcaster's knowledge of the French language.
49 *Abrar*, 10 November 2004, p. 5, and Baztab, www.baztab.com/news/21943.php (accessed 12 August 2006).

50 *Jam-e Jam*, 20 December 2004.
51 IRIB's Director General of Music, Seyyed-Mohammad Mirzamani, *Ettela'at*, 2 December 2004, p. 3.
52 Head of IRIB's Music Centre, Mohammad-Hossein Soufi, *Resalat*, 30 December 2004, p. 20.
53 Writer and film-maker, Mohammad Nourizad, *Sharif News*, 29 September 2005, http://sharifnews.com/?544 (accessed 3 August 2006).
54 *Shargh*, 3 March 2005, p. 6.
55 Bulletin of the Syndicate of Iranian Journalists, February 1966, reproduced in Mass'oud Kouhestaninejad, *Asnad va Gozareshha-ye Gorouhha, Anjomanha va Ettehadiehha-ye Matbou'ati* (Documents and Reports on Press Groups, Associations and Unions), Tehran: Centre for Media Studies and Research, 2004, p. 292.
56 Mohammadi, *Sima-ye Eqtedargaraiy, Televizion-e Dowlati-ye Iran*, pp. 83–84.
57 Ibid., pp. 107–108.
58 AOIJ Deputy President, Karim Arghandehpour, *Rouznamehnegar*, no. 32, July–August 2002, p. 4.
59 *Rouznamehnegar*, no. 44, August–September 2005, p. 8.
60 Dr Mehdi Mohsenian-Rad, 'Zarourat-e Tavajoh beh Maqouleh-ye Ertebatat-e Mian-farhangi dar Jame'eh- ye Iran beh Manzour-e Movajeheh-ye Sahih ba Tahavolat-e Jame'eh-ye Ettella'ati' (The Necessity of Paying Attention to the Concept of Inter-cultural Communication in Iran for the Purpose of Correctly Dealing with the Developments in the Information Society), *Rasaneh Quarterly*, vol. 14, no. 1, Spring 2003, pp. 19–26.
61 Ibid.
62 *Shargh*, 31 January 2005, p. 6.
63 Ibid., 24 February 2005, p. 6.
64 *Tehran Times*, 26 February 2005, www.tehrantimes.com/Description.asp?Da=2/26/2005&Cat=14&Num=002 (when accessed 3 August 2006, the page was blank, with a note saying 'No news for this category on February 26, 2005'). Sahar satellite channel has since then been renamed Al-Kawthar (Heavenly River), www.alkawthartv.ir/about.asp (accessed 12 August 2006).
65 *Shargh*, 23 December 2004, p. 13.
66 Chairman of the Board of Directors of Iran's Communications Company, Mass'oud Moqaddas, and the head of the Association of Internet Networks, Hossein Sheikh-Attar, *San'at-e Jahan* daily, 19 December 2004, p. 5.
67 Now named as the Ministry Communication and Information Technology.
68 *Shargh*, 1 February 2005, p. 10. Iran's orbital positions have been set at 26, 34, and 47 degrees of latitude. The Minister of Communication and Information Technology, Seyyed-Ahmad Mo'tamedi, said the purchase of a satellite in 1996 would not have been economical because of higher prices and lower usage. The agreement with Russia also provides for the training of 120 Iranians.
69 *Aftab* (Sunshine), www.aftabnews.ir/vsdd^30632eyih.vylc.html (accessed 15 August 2006).
70 Interview with *Baztab*'s director, Foad Sadeqi, 6 March 2005, www.baztab.com/news/22260.php (accessed 12 August 2006).
71 For instance, see *Baztab*, 10 November 2005, www.baztab.com/news/30239.php (accessed 15 August 2006).
72 www.farsnews.com/aboutus.php (accessed 15 August 2006).
73 *Ghest News Network*, www.ghest.net/framework.jsp?SID=2 (accessed 15 August 2006).
74 *Rasaneh Supplement*, vol. 1. no. 12, 21 November–5 December 2004, p. 8.
75 www.iana.ir/ (accessed 15 August 2006).
76 *Rasaneh Supplement*, vol. 1, no. 1, 6 June 2004, p. 3. The diversity of *Iran Labour News Agency's (ILNA)* output can be demonstrated by a news item carried on 7 January 2005 about the following day being 'the birthday of the American singer,

Elvis Presley, who is knows as the Sultan of Rock and Roll'. The report, complete with a picture from the cover of Presley's album, *Jailhouse Rock*, included a number of details that although informative, may well have also been chosen to minimize any risk of objections on moral grounds. 'Elvis was born to a poor family in Mississippi', said the report, perhaps implying a connection with workers, who are meant to be covered by ILNA. It then went on to say that Presley was believed by the 'Scottish writer, Alan Morrison to have been of Scottish origins', somewhat distancing him from the United States, and that he was 'very religious, had many religious numbers in his albums and won three Grammy awards for his religious songs'. The report did say that Presley had died at the age of 42, but gave no details of its cause – ILNA, 7 January 2005, www.ilna.ir/shownews.asp?code=162381&code1=4 (accessed 12 August 2006).

77 *Rasaneh Supplement*, vol. 1. no. 11, November 2004, pp. 5–20.
78 Budget figure given by ISNA's Director, Dr Fateh, *Rasaneh Supplement*, vol. 1, no. 3, 6–21 July 2004, p. 4.
79 ISNA advertisement, http://www.isna.ir/Main/advertisefiles/journalist.htm# (accessed 3 August 2006).
80 *Rasaneh Supplement*, vol. 1, no. 12, 21 November–5 December 2004, p. 3.
81 www.iribnews.ir/ (accessed 12 August 2006).
82 IRNA, www.irna.ir/fa/content/view/menu-144/id-23/ (accessed 15 August 2006).
83 Pupils Association News Agency (PANA), www.irpana.ir/aboutUs.jsp (accessed 12 August 2006).
84 *Kayhan*, 5 January 2005, p. 11.
85 *Rasaneh Supplement*, vol. 1, no. 10, 22 October–5 November 2004, p. 2.
86 www.shana.ir/AboutUs-html (accessed 15 August 2006).
87 *Sharifnews*, sharifnews.com/?about (accessed 12 August 2006).
88 Managing Director of SYNA, Khosrow Talebzadeh, quoted in *Khabarnameh-ye Deneshjouiy*, p. 3.
89 *E'temad* daily, 14 October 2004.
90 Journalist and journalism lecturer, Fereydoun Sediqi, quoted by Fars news agency, 9 Febaurary 2005, www.farsnews.com/NewsVm.asp?ID = 129819 (accessed 15 August 2006).
91 *Shargh* daily, 14 October 2004.
92 Naiim Badii and Guita Aliabadi, 'A Comparative Analysis of Selected Persian News Websites', paper presented at the 3rd Seminar to Study the Problems of the Iranian Press, Tehran, 3 March 2004.
93 Minister of Communications and Information Technology, Seyyed-Ahmad Mo'tamedi, *Shargh*, 24 January 2005, p. 4.
94 Ibid., 25 December 2004, p. 4.
95 Chairman and Managing Director of Data Communication Iran, Reza Rashidi-Mehrabadi, at the Conference on Global Internet Management, Faculty of Social Sciences, Allameh Tabatabaee University, Tehran, 29 November 2004. Data transfer speed in Iran at the time was in general a few tens of kilobytes per second, at times falling to as low as a few kilobytes – author's own experience.
96 *Shargh* daily, 25 December 2004, p. 4.
97 Gharnabad Conference on Communication and Information Technology for National Development, Conference brochure, March 2005.
98 *Asr-e Ertebatat* (The Age of Communication), 4 December 2004, p. 10.
99 Deputy Minister of Communication and Information Technology, Sadri, interviewed by *Jahan-e San'at* (The World of Industry) daily, 2 March 2005, p. 5.
100 Internet World Stats, Top Twenty Countries, www.internetworldstats.com/top20.htm (accessed 12 August 2006).
101 Internet World Stats, Internet Usage in Asia, www.internetworldstats.com/stats3.htm (accessed 12 August 2006).

102 Internet World Stats, Internet Usage in the Middle East, www.internetworldstats.com/stats5.htm (accessed 12 August 2006).

103 Dr Mohsen Esma'ili, jurist member of the Council of Guardians, 'Jaygah-e Ertebatat dar Qanoun-e Barnameh-ye Chaharom-e Towse'eh' (Status of Communication in the 4th Development Plan), *Rasaneh Quarterly*, vol. 15, no. 2, Summer 2004, p. 82.

104 Deputy Minister of Communication and Information Technology, Sadri, interviewed by *Jahan-e San'at* daily, 2 March 2005, p. 5.

105 The Blog Herald, www.blogherald.com/2005/10/10/the-blog-herald-blog-count-october-2005 (accessed 12 August 2006).

106 en.wikipedia.org/wiki/Persian_weblogs (accessed 12 August 2006).

107 *Badjens* Iranian Feminist Newsletter, September 2004, www.badjens.com/rediscovery.html (accessed 3 August 2006).

108 Persianblog Manager, Mehdi Boutorabi, www.persianblog.com/news/entry.asp?module=press&id=39 (accessed 12 August 2006). Mr Boutorabi said the site had two million visitors per month, 50 per cent of whom lived in Tehran.

109 www.persianblog.com/ (accessed 12 August 2006).

110 Roya Sadr, 'Tanz-e Webloggi' (Weblog Humour), paper prepared for the 3rd Seminar to Study the Problems of the Iranian Press, Tehran, 1–2 March 2005.

111 www.webneveshteha.com/ (accessed 12 August 2006). Mr Abtahi's weblog was started on 24 November 2003, http://en.wikipedia.org/wiki/Iranian_Blogs (accessed 12 August 2006).

112 Reporters Without Borders' website, http://rsf.fr/article.php3?id_article=10733 (accessed 16 January 2005).

113 IRNA, www.irna.ir/?SAB=OK&LANG=PE&PART=_NEWS&TYPE=PP&id=13831022183951Q22 (accessed 11 January 2005). On 9 January, the Minister of Communication and Information Technology, Seyyed-Ahmad Mo'tamedi, told reporters that the Ministry had had nothing to do with the closure of Persianblog and Orkut (*Iran* daily, 10 January 2005, p. 1). The following day, Tehran's General and Revolutionary Prosecutor, the former Press Court Judge, Saied Mortazavi, said the Judiciary would either instruct the Ministry of Communication and Information Technology to block any 'internet sites that publish sacrilegious, atheistic or immoral material', or it would 'take action directly' (*Iran* daily, 11 January 2005, p. 1). The Ministry of Communication and Information Technology has had its own difficulties with the ISPs with respect to telephone calls through the internet, both politically on national security grounds – especially with respect to calls received from abroad – and financially because uncontrolled calls through the internet can take revenues away from the government. For details, see the reply page of the Data Communication Company of Iran (DCI) on its website, www.iranpac.net.ir/answer.html (accessed Spring 2005).

114 Data compiled by the author from various Iranian newspapers.

115 ISNA, 11 December 2004, www.isna.ir/Main/NewsView.aspx?ID=News-454945 (accessed 12 August 2006).

116 Arash Sigarchi, editor of *Guilan-e Emrouz* (Guilan Today), based in Rasht, *Shargh*, 23 February 2005, p. 2. Mr Sigarchi's lawyer said he would lodge an appeal. Mr Sigarchi was arrested in January after using his weblog to criticise the arrest of other online journalists, BBC World Service report, 23 February 2005, http://news.bbc.co.uk/go/pr/fr/-/1/hi/technology/4292399.stm (accessed 12 August 2006).

117 *Shargh*, 2 March 2005, p. 6, quoted Reporters Without Borders as saying that *Webnegar* writer, Mohammad-Reza Abdollahi-Nasab, had been arrested and sent to central prison in Rafsanjan. He had been found guilty of 'publishing lies and insults' and sentenced to six months in prison and payment of 1 million rials [$112]. The sentence was confirmed by the Court of Appeal on 24 February.

118 Omid Me'marian and Shahram Rafi'zadeh, *Iran* daily, 4 December 2004, p. 1.

119 At Tehran's Evin prison, Ms Qazi came across a woman, Akram Qavidel, who had been sentenced to death for killing a man who had tried to rape her. After her release,

Ms Qazi wrote an open letter to President Khatami and the head of the Judicairy to draw their attention to Ms Qavidel's case. Ms Qazi had already highlighted the similar case of Afsaneh Nowrouzi, whose sentence of death was lifted after the court accepted her defence. For Ms Qazi's letter, see the website *Women in Iran*, www.womeniniran.net/archives/FSR/001859.php (accessed 12 August 2006).

120 For details, see Mohammad-Ali Abtahi's weblogs (accessed 3 August 2006): 9 September 2004, webneveshteha.com/weblog/?id=1094731974 2 October 2004, webneveshteha.com/weblog/?id=1096723199 11 October 2004, webneveshteha. com/weblog/?id=-1785452158 26 November 2004, webneveshteha.com/weblog/?id= 1101479209 16 Deccember 2004, webneveshteha.com/weblog/?id=1103205360 4 Jaunary 2005,webneveshteha.com/weblog/?id=1104846403 12 January 2005, webneveshteha.com/weblog/?id=-1723924679

121 Ayatollah Hashemi-Shahroudi's news conference, 9 March 2005, reported in *Shargh*, 10 March 2005, p. 1.

122 The Judiciary Spokesman, Jamal Karimi-Rad, quoted by ISNA, 20 April 2005, www.isna.ir/Main/NewsView.aspx?ID=News-516865 (accessed 12 August 2006).

123 *Baztab* news site, 4 June 2005, www.baztab.com/news/25020.php (accessed 12 August 2006).

124 Reporters Without Frontiers' Julein Pain, quoted by the BBC World Service, 8 March 2005, http://news.bbc.co.uk/1/hi/technology/4327067.stm (accessed 12 August 2006).

125 Peder Are Nøstvold Jensen, 'Blogging Iran', MA dissertation, University of Oslo, Norway, wo.uio.no/as/WebObjects/theses.woa/wa/these?WORKID=21737 (accessed 12 August 2006).

126 www.amontazeri.com/ (accessed 3 August 2006).

127 A few examples of the BBC's coverage of Mr Montazeri's views (all accessed 3 August 2006) include: 2 February 2005, declaring that conversion from Islam to another religion would not necessarily amount to apostasy, which is punishable by death under Islamic law, www.bbc.co.uk/persian/iran/story/2005/02/050202_mj montzari-renegade.shtml 27 December 2004, opposing a referendum on the Constitution, called for by a group of opposition activists, www.bbc.co.uk/ persian/iran/story/2004/12/041227_ amontazeri.shtml 23 December 2004, opposing the call for a referendum on the Islamic Republic's Constitution, www.bbc.co.uk/persian/ iran/story/2004/12/041221_mj-ir-montazeri-referendum.shtml 21 September 2004, describing the occupation of the US Embassy as a mistake, www.bbc.co.uk/ persian/iran/030921_v-saba.shtml.

128 Ahmad Gabel, weblog, http://ghabel.persianblog.com (accessed 12 August 2006).

129 On 13 January 2005, the BBC Persian Service reported Mr Ghabel's views on the relative validity of reason and religious laws, www.bbc.co.uk/persian/iran/story/ 2005/01/050113_mj-qabel-new-approach.shtml, as well as its full text, 'without any alteration', www.bbc.co.uk/persian/iran/story/2005/01/050113_ahmad-qabel-text. shtml. The move could be taken to imply full agreement with the content of the pages, unlike the Corporation's common practice of providing links to related sites, with the disclaimer that the 'The BBC is not responsible for the content of external internet sites.'

130 BBC World Service report, 30 November 2004, http://news.bbc.co.uk/1/hi/ world/middle_east/4056543.stm (accessed 12 August 2006).

131 Reuters, 21 November 2004, carried by MSNBC, www.msnbc.msn.com/id/6548908/ (accessed 3 August 2006).

132 IRNA http://irna.ir/?SAB=OK&LANG=PE&PART=_NEWS&TYPE=IT&id= 13831216143719T16 (accessed 6 March 2005).

133 National Geographic style guide, magma.nationalgeographic.com/ngm/styleguide/ stylemanual.pdf (accessed December 2005).

134 In January 2005, Iran's SMS service already had 1.4 million subscribers – *Hamvatan Salam* daily, 8 January 2005, http://itiran.net/archives/001202.php (accessed 12 August 2006).

135 *Eqbal* daily, 7 March 2005, p. 9.
136 *Shargh*, 2 March 2005, p. 11.
137 Ibid., 25 December 2004, p. 4.

9 Organization, education, and training

1 Bulletin of the Syndicate of Iranian Journalists, February 1966, reproduced in Mass'oud Kouhestaninejad, *Asnaad va Gozareshha-ye Gorouhha, Anjomanha va Ettehadiehha-ye Matbou'ati* (Documents and Reports on Press Groups, Associations and Unions), Tehran: Centre for Media Studies and Research, 2004, p. 296. The book lists documents related to 16 provincial and national journalists' organizations set up in Iran between Reza Shah's abdication in 1941 and his son's overthrow in 1979.

2 Ibid., *Asnaad va Gozareshha-ye Gorouhha*, pp. 309–310.

3 Mohsenian-Rad, 'Matbou'at-e Salha-ye Nokhost-e Enqelab-e Eslami', *Kilk* monthly, special issue on the press, March 1997, p. 220.

4 For more on Mr Homayoun, the article attacking Ayatollah Khomeini, and its aftermath, see 'Chapter 1: The Shah's last years (1977–79)'.

5 For an account of the Syndicate's activities during the Revolution, see 'Chapter 2: The "Spring of Freedom" (1979).'

6 Syndicate members Mohammad Bolouri and Gholam-Hossein Salehyar tell the Kafkaesque tale of the union not being officially recognized by the Islamic Republic's authorities, who would nonetheless communicate with its last elected officials in their capacity as Syndicate leaders. In order to operate under the Islamic Republic, the Syndicate would have had to rename itself an 'association', but it was never allowed to hold a general assembly of its members to make the necessary changes to its constitution. For details, see *Rasaneh Quarterly*, vol. 8, no. 4, Winter 1998, pp. 6–11.

7 Ali-Akbar Qazizadeh, 'Ta'avoni-ye Matbou'at' (The Press Cooperative), *Rasaneh Quarterly*, vol. 3, no. 4, Winter 1992, pp. 37–41. The founding members included Dr Goudarz Eftekhar-Jahromi, managing editor of several legal publications; Mohammad-Mehdi Abd-e-Khodai, publisher of Fadaiyan-e Eslam's weekly, *Manshour-e-Baradari* (Charter of Brotherhood); Ghafour Garshasbi, publisher of the daily *Abrar*; Nader-Kavousi, publisher of the popular weekly, *Setareh Soheil* (Canopus) and Dr Fereydoun Golafra, publisher of the farming weekly, *Keshavarz* (The Farmer). In 1990, Mohammad-Mohsen Sazegara, publisher of the *Ayeneh* (Mirror) group of periodicals, was elected chairman of the board of directors.

8 *Rasaneh Quarterly*, vol. 7, no. 3, Autumn 1996, p. 75.

9 *Rasaneh Quarterly*, vol. 7, no. 3, Autumn 1996, pp. 76–80.

10 *Rasaneh Quarterly*, vol. 8, no. 4, Winter 1998, pp. 12–15. The founding members of the Association included: Ayatollah Khamenei's representative at *Kayhan*, Hossein Shari'atmadari; Ayatollah Khamenei's representative at *Ettella'at*, Mahmoud Do'ai; *Resalat*'s managing editor, Morteza Nabavi; managing editor of *Jomhouri-ye Eslami*, Massih Mohajeri; managing editor of *Abrar*, Seyyed-Mohammad Safizadeh; and managing editor of *Kar-o-Kargar*, Ali Rabi'i.

11 Ibid., pp. 82–83.

12 Article 5 of the Syndicate's Constitution, reproduced in Kouhestaninejad, *Asnaad va Gozareshha-ye Gorouhha*, p. 311.

13 Article 1 of the AOIJ's Constitution, *Rouznamehnegar*, no. 30, June 2002, p. 7, also available at the union's website, www.aoij.org/About-AoijBylaws/Constitution.htm (accessed 4 August 2006).

14 AOIJ Deputy President, Karim Arghandehpour, *Rouznamehnegar*, no. 30, June 2002, p. 1.

15 *Rasaneh Supplement*, vol. 1, no. 12, 21 November–5 December 2004, p. 5.

16 The Association's spokesman, Mashaallah Shamsolva'ezin, quoted in *Khabarnameh-ye Deneshjouiy* (University Students' News Bulletin), the news bulletin of the Third Seminar to Study the Problems of the Press in Iran, 1 March 2005, p. 2.

17 Information provided to the author by a founding member of the Association, Dr Kazem Mo'tamednejad, Tehran, 9 July 2006. The other founding members included Dr Hassan Sadr, Dr Abdol-Hamid Abolhamd, Mehrdad Bahar, Shams Al-Ahmad, and Amid Naini.

18 Information provided to the author by the Association, Tehran, 21 February 2005.

19 *Rasaneh Quarterly*, vol. 8, no. 4, Winter 1998, pp. 22–26.

20 *Rasaneh Supplement*, vol. 1, no. 2, 21 June–5 July 2004, p. 2.

21 Ibid., vol. 1, no. 6, 22 August–5 September 2004, p. 5.

22 *Rasaneh Quarterly*, vol. 8, no. 4, Winter 1998, pp. 22–26.

23 Ibid.

24 The Association's Secretary General, Ali Yousefpour, quoted in *Khabarnameh-ye Deneshjouiy*, 1 March 2005, p. 2.

25 *Rasaneh Quarterly*, vol. 8, no. 3, Autumn 1997, p. 132.

26 Ibid., vol. 8, no. 4, Winter 1998, p. 21.

27 Information provided to the author by the Association of Tehran Freelance Journalists, Tehran, 21 February 2005.

28 Association's Secretary, Fariba Davoudi-Mohajer, quoted in *Rasaneh Supplement*, vol. 1, no. 2, 21 June–5 July 2004, p. 3 and p. 5. The journalists were from the weeklies *Chelcheragh* (Chandelier) and *Soroush*, the daily *Farhang-e Ashti* (Culture of Reconcilation) and the banned dailies *Vaqaye'-e-Ettefaqiye* (Happening Events') and *Yas-e Now* (New Jasmine).

29 Information provided to the author by the Association, Tehran, 26 February 2005.

30 *Rasaneh Quarterly*, vol. 8, no. 4, Winter 1998, pp. 22–26.

31 Ibid., pp. 26–27.

32 Survey by the Ministry of Culture and Islamic Guidance, reported in *Rasaneh Supplement*, vol. 1, no. 7, 6–21 September 2004, p. 9.

33 The Iranian Women Journalists' Association's representative, Ashraf Geramizadegan, and the Association for the Defence of Press Freedom's Deputy President, Ali Hekmat, speaking at the seminar on 1 March 2005.

34 Mohammad Moheet-Tabataie, *Tarikhe- Tahlili-ye Matbou'at-e Iran* (The Analytical History of the Iranian Press), Tehran: Be'that, 1988, pp. 9–10.

35 Dr Mo'tamednejad, interviewed by Mohammad Vahidi, on 21 December 2004, published on the website *Iran va Jame'eh-ye Ettela'ati* (Iran and the Information Society), run by *Markaz-e Pajouheshhay-e Ertebatat* (Centre for Communication Research), an organization set up by Allameh Tabatabaee University and the Ministry of Communication and Information Technology, www.iranwsis/Default.asp?C= IRNW&R=&I=82#BN82 (accessed 18 February 2007).

36 *Rasaneh Quarterly*, vol. 7, no. 3, Autumn 1996, pp. 108–111.

37 Dean of Social Sciences College, Dr Mohammad-Mehdi Forqani, interviewed by *Khabarnameh-ye Deneshjouyi*, 1 March 2005, p. 4.

38 Dr Mehdi Mohsenian-Rad, 'Rouznamehnegaran-e Iran va Amouzesh-e Rouznamehnegari' (Iranian Journalists and Journalism Education), Tehran, Centre for Media Studies and Research, 1994, quoted in *Rasaneh Quarterly*, vol. 5, no. 4, Winter 1995, pp. 5–7.

39 Leyla Rastgar, 'Entekhab-e Daneshjouy-e Rouznamehnegari Azmoun-e Vijeh Mikhahad' (Special Tests are Needed to Select Journalism Students), *Rasaneh Quarterly*, vol. 5, no. 4, Winter 1995, pp. 11–20.

40 *Rasaneh Quarterly*, vol. 10, no. 1, Spring 1999, p. 22.

41 Reza Talachian, 'A Brief Critical History of Iranian Feature Film (1896–1975)', a chapter in *A survey Catalogue and Brief Critical History of Iranian Feature Film (1896–1975)*, MA dissertation, Department of Cinema and Photography in the

Graduate School, Southern Illinois University, December 1980, www.lib.washington. edu/neareast/cinemaofiran/intro.html (accessed 12 August 2006). 'The school', says Talachiah, 'was fully financed and supported by the government through the National Iranian Radio and Television (NIRT). After passing the entrance exam, the students went through a technical training period of two years along with their regular courses of study which related one way or another to film-making. All expenses were paid by the government; included were the use of film equipment, raw stock, processing, animation materials, and the student's housing and board costs, plus a stipend of about $300 a month. In return, students were required to work for the government after their graduation for a period of five years as a cameraperson, soundperson, etc., usually at NIRT in Tehran or its branches in the other cities. The government established this school to train technicians for the expansion of NIRT.

'Later, a graduate school was added, the Graduate School of Television and Cinema. Any Bachelor's degree was accepted, which meant that the Associate degree undergraduates of the School of Television and Cinema could not be considered for the programme. Graduate students of Television and Cinema did not go through the same technical training the undergraduates did. Their curriculum dealt more with theory than practice. After graduation they were employed in government offices and institutions as audio-visual experts and programmers. Most were absorbed by the programming section of NIRT or the Ministry of Education of Iran. These students were treated better financially by the government than the undergraduates both during and after graduation. Most graduate students were married and the number of women was as large as the men, while the undergraduate school was composed of 95 per cent men.'

42 Islamic Republic of Iran Broadcasting (IRIB) College web pages (all accessed 4 August 2006), http://www.irib.ir/education/history11.htm, www.irib.ir/education/ amozeshtolid1.htm, www.irib.ir/education/aertebatat1.htm

43 Soroush catalogue, Tehran, 2004.

44 Centre for Media Studies and Research (CMSR) brochure, Tehran, Ministry of Ministry of Culture and Islamic, 2005; CMSR website, http://www.rasaneh.org/ persian/about.asp (accessed 15 August 2006).

45 The Director of the Centre for Media Studies and Research, Ali Bahrampour, interviewed by *Khabarnameh-ye Deneshjouiy*, 1 March 2005, p. 3.

46 The Islamic Azad University's Chancellor, Dr Abdollah Jassbi, interviewed by *Hambastegi* daily, 19 March 2001, quoted in the educational monthly *Lawh*, no. 11, September 2001, p. 22.

47 Islamic Azad University's website, Information about school of Social Sciences and Psychology, www.iauctb.org/english/Socialpercent20Sciences&Psycologypercent 20.htm (accessed Winter 2005). A brief overview of the University's Faculty of Psychology and Social Sciences, including communications and journalism, can be found on www.iauctb.ac.ir/college/college.aspx?id=6 (accessed 4 August 2006).

48 Information provided to the author by the Faculty, Tehran, 15 March 2005.

49 Faculty announcement, March 2005.

50 *Rasaneh Quarterly*, vol. 5, no. 3, p. 1.

51 Dr Mehdi Mohsenian-Rad, 'Rouznamehnegaran-e Iran va Amouzesh-e Rouznamehnegari' p. 11.

52 *Jam-e-Jam* daily, 27 December 2004, p. 9.

53 See 'Chapter 4: War, reconstruction and the revival of journalism (1980–96)'.

54 *Rasaneh Quarterly*, vol. 7, no. 2, Summer 1996, p. 1.

55 Iran Cartoon House website, www.irancartoon.com/hic/index.htm (accessed March 2005).

56 Information provided by the Cartoon House to the author, Tehran, 5 March 2005.

57 IRNA News College, www.irna.ir/?SAB=OK&LANG=PE&PART=_OTHER& TYPE=_COLLEGE (accessed Spring 2005).

58 AOIJ College, www.aoij.org/About-AoijBylaws/University.htm (accessed 4 August 2006).
59 The Secretary of the Association of Iranian Journalists, Mass'oud Houshmand-e-Razavi, interviewed by the author, Tehran, 4 January 2005.
60 Kasra Nouri, interviewed by *Rasaneh Supplement*, vol. 1, no. 2, 21 June–5 July 2004, pp. 6–7.
61 Mehran Behrooz-Faghani, 'Ghalat-nevissi-ye Herfei-ha' (Professionals' Writing Badly) *Shargh*, 18 January 2005, p. 13.
62 Seminar brochure.
63 Dr Mo'tamednejad, summing up the seminar.
64 Presentation by Hassan Hassanzadeh and Hossein Taheri, from Qazvin.
65 *Shargh*, 6 March 2005, p. 13.

10 One hundred years of legal confusion

1 Article 13 of the 1906 Constitution, reproduced in *Loghatname Dehkohda*, vol. 10, Tehran, Tehran University Publications, 1993–94, p. 15342.
2 Article 20 of the Amendment, quoted in Mohammad-Ebrahim Ansari-Lari, *Nezarat bar Matbou'at dar Hoqouq-e Iran* (Press Supervision in Iranian Law), Tehran, Soroush, 1996, pp. 72–73. The article was based on what is now Article 25 of the Belgian Constitution (1970), available on the University of Berne's website: www.oefre.unibe.ch/law/icl/be00000_.html (accessed 12 August 2006).
3 Ibid., p. 73. Article 79 of the Amendment is based on what is now Article 148 of the 1970 Belgian Constitution.
4 Hamid Moqaddamfar, 'Seyr-e Tarikhi-ye Qavanin-e Matbou'at-e Iran' (The Historical Development of Iran's Press Laws), *Rasaneh Quraterly*, vol. 4, no. 1, Spring 1993, p. 38. The then 'Article 98' is now Article 150 of the 1970 Belgian Constitution, www.oefre.unibe.ch/law/icl/be00000_.html (accessed 12 August 2006).
5 Article 24 of *Qanoun-e Assassi-ye Jomhouri-ye Eslami-ye Iran* (The Constitution of the Islamic Republic of Iran), ratified in 1979 and revised in 1989, Tehran, Nashr-e Dowran, 2004, p. 32.
6 Ibid., p. 90.
7 'Siyassat-ha-ye Farhangi-ye Jomhouri-ye Ealsmi-ye Iran dar Howzeh-ye Matbou'at' (Cultural Policies of the Islamic Republic of Iran in the Domain of the Press), adopted by the Supreme Cultural Revolution Council, chaired by President Khatami, on 2 June 2001, available on the Tehran Justice Office's website, www.ghavanin.ir/detail.asp?id=13692 (accessed 12 August 2006).
8 Malek-o-Sho'ara, Bahar's address reported in *Nowbahar*, no. 203, 11 June 1915, reproduced in Mass'oud Kouhestani-nejad, *Asnad-e Dadgahha va Hey'at-ha-ye Monsefeh-ye Matbou'ati az Enqelab-e Mashrouteh ta Enqelab-e Eslami* (Documents on the Press Courts and Juries from the Constitutional Revolution to the Islamic Revolution), Tehran: Centre for Media Studies and Research, 2001, pp. 234–235.
9 *Iran* had begun life as a Qajar court newspaper in 1871 but had gone through several changes of management and for a while had been edited by Malek-o-Sho'ara Bahar himself. In 1918, the paper was edited by Mirza Ali-Akbar Khan Khorassani – Mohammad Sadr-Hashemi, *Tarikh-e Jarayed va Majallat-e Iran* (The History of Iranian Newspapers and Magazines), Isfahan: Kamal, 1984, vol. 1, pp. 305–313.
10 'Vazi'yat-e Taassof-anguiz-e Matbou'at-e Ma' (The Sorry State of our Press), *Iran*, 25 March 1918, p. 1, reproduced in Kouhestani-nejad *Asnad-e Dadgahha va Hey'at-ha-ye Monsefeh-ye Matbou'ati az Enqelab-e Mashrouteh ta Enqelab-e Eslami*, pp. 238–239.
11 Dr Kazem Mo'tamednejad, *Hoqouq-e Matbou'at* (Press Law), vol. 1, Tehran: Centre for Media Studies and Research, 2000, pp. 101–110.

12 Article 12, 1986 Press Law, available on the Tehran Justice Office's website, www.ghavanin.ir/detail.asp?id=5429 (accessed 12 August 2006).
13 Ibid.
14 Hamid Moqadamfar, 'Matbou'at, Hoqouq, Hodoud, Jara'em' (The Press, Rights, Limits, Offences), *Rasaneh Quarterly Journal of Media Studies and Research*, Tehran, Ministry of Culture and Islamic Guidance, vol. 1, no. 3, Autumn 1990, pp. 59–63.
15 The 2000 Press Law provides for six months to two years' suspension from government service for such officials, to be raised to permanent suspension in case of repetition (Article 3, Note 1).
16 *Rasaneh Quarterly*, vol. 10, no. 2, Summer 1999, p. 1.
17 Kouhestani-nejad, *Asnad-e Dadgahha va Hey'at-ha-ye Monsefeh-ye Matbou'ati*, pp. 22–77.
18 Ibid.
19 Mohsen Esma'ili, 'Dadgahha-ye Matoub'ati' (Press Courts), *Rasaneh Quarterly*, vol. 8, no. 1, Spring 1997, pp. 69–72.
20 The trial of Hojjatoleslam Moussavian, publisher of the daily *Khorasan*. *Rasaneh Quarterly*, vol. 2, no. 3, Autumn 1991, p. 97.
21 Vahid Pourostad, *Mohakemeh-ye Salam* (The Trial of *Salam*), Tehran: Rouznegar, 2001, pp. 27–35. The cleric jury members were: Hojjatoleslams Amid-Zanjani, Aboutorabi, Mohammadi-Araqi, Seyyed-Mahmoud Do'ai, Nezatmzadeh and Taqavi.
22 Ibid., pp. 87–91. For details of the closure and its aftermath, see 'Chapter 5: The second "Spring of Freedom" (1977–2000)'.
23 *Rasaneh Quarterly*, vol. 2, no. 3, Autumn 1991, p. 97.
24 Kashi, *Matboua't dar Asr-e Khatami*, pp. 177–178. For the jourors' names, see 'Chapter 4: War, reconstruction and the revival of journalism (1980–96)'. Advice on the jury's political composition provided by Dr Hassan Namakdoost-Tehrani.
25 Kashi, *Matboua't dar Asr-e Khatami*, p. 136.
26 Ibid., p. 178. For the jourors' names, see 'Chapter 5: The second "Spring of Freedom" (1997–2000)'. Advice on the jury's political composition provided by Dr Hassan Namakdoost-Tehrani.
27 Kashi, *Matboua't dar Asr-e Khatami*, pp. 115–116.
28 Vahid Pourostad, *Mohakemeh-ye Adineh* (The Trial of *Adineh*), Tehran: Rouznegar, 2002, p. 57. The five were Hadi Khaniki, Ali Khoshru, Mehdi Hojjat, Kambiz Nowrouzi, and Ms A'zam Nouri.
29 Mr Nowrouzi said the judge had spent '16 minutes' to take the decision to dismiss the jury members, whereas the trial of a serial killer known as the 'Vampire of the Night' had lasted two months – Mr Nowrouzi quoted in *Ketab-e Jashnvareh-ye Sheshom-e Matbou'at* (The Book of the Sixth Press Festival), Tehran: Ministry of Culture and Islamic Guidance, 1999, p. 37.
30 Text of the Press Law reproduced in Rasai, *Payan-e Dastan-e Ghamangiz: Negahi beh Zaminehha-ye Sodour-e Hokm-e Hokoumati-ye Maqam-e Mo'azzam-e Rahbari dar-bareh-ye Qanoun-e Matbou'at* (The End of the Tragic Story: A Glance at the Background to His Excellency the Supreme Leader's Decree on the Press Law), vol. 2, Tehran: Kayhan Publications, 2001, pp. 392–413.
31 For details of the 2000 Press Law's Ratification, see 'Chapter 5: The second "Spring of Freedom" (1997–2000)'.
32 For details, see 'Chapter 7: Women and journalism'.
33 Head of Tehran Justice Office, Hojjatoleslam Abbas-Ali Alizadeh, quoted in *Daghdagheh-ye Azadi* (Angst for Freedom), Tehran: Association of Iranian Journalists, 2003, pp. 111–112 and 163–164.
34 *Daghdagheh-ye Azadi*, p. 112.
35 Kambiz Nowrouzi, 'Azadi-ye Matbou'at az Akhlaq ta Hoqouq' (Freedom of the Press from Ethics to Rights), in *Majmou'eh Maqalat-e Dovomin Seminar-e Barresi-ye Massael-e Matbou'at-e Iran'* (The Collection of Articles Presented at the Second

Seminar to Study the Problems of the Iranian Press), vol. 1, Tehran: Ministry of Culture and Islamic Guidance, 1998, pp. 287–288.

36 Minister of Culture and Islamic Guidance, Ahmad Masjed-Jame'i, quoted in *Rasaneh Quarterly*, vol. 12, no. 1, Spring 2001, p. 17.

37 Dr Kazem Mo'tamednejad, quoted in *Rasaneh Quarterly*, vol. 12, no. 2, Summer 2001, p. 151.

38 Amir Hosseinabadi, lawyer, quoted in *Rasaneh Quarterly*, vol. 12, no. 1, Spring 2001, p. 28.

39 Kambiz Nowrouzi, quoted in *Rasaneh Quarterly*, vol. 12, no. 1, Spring 2001, p. 28.

40 Mousa Qorbani, member of the Majlis Judicial Committee, quoted in *Rasaneh Quarterly*, vol. 12, no. 1, Spring 2001, p. 28.

41 *Resalat* daily's editor, Mohamamd-Kazem Anbarloui, quoted in *Rasaneh Quarterly*, vol. 12, no. 1, Spring 2001, pp. 106–111.

42 *Rasaneh Supplement*, vol. 1, June 2004, p. 5.

43 Dr Kazem Mo'tamednejad, *Pishneviss-e Layeheh-ye Qanouni-ye Shora-ye Matbou'at* (Draft Bill on the Press Council), Tehran, no date.

44 Ibid., *Pishneviss-e Missaq-e Osoul-e Akhlaqi-ye Herfeh-ye Rouznamehnegari* (Draft Convention on the Ethical Principles of Professional Journalism), Tehran: March 2004, pp. 3–12.

45 Ibid., *Pishneviss-e Qanoun-e Nezam-e Hoqouqi-ye Herfeh-ye Rouznamehnegari* (Draft Convention on the Legal System of Professional Journalism), Tehran: June 2004.

46 Ibid., *Pishneviss-e Peyman-e Jam'i-e Kare-ye Rouznamehnegaran* (Draft Collective Employment Contract for Journalists), Tehran: June 2004.

47 *Rasaneh Supplement*, vol. 1, no. 1, 6 June 2004, p. 4. A 'media system' is called for in the Islamic Republic's 4th Development Plan –in Esma'ili, 'Jaygah-e Ertebatat dar Qanoun-e Barnameh-ye Chaharom-e Towse'eh', p. 82.

48 *Rasaneh Quarterly*, vol. 14, no. 4, Winter 2004, p. 1.

49 The Organization of the Mojahedin of Islamic Revolution, quoted by the Iranian Labour News Agency, ILNA, 22 December 2004, www.ilna.ir/shownews.asp?code=157793&code1=1 (accessed 12 August 2006).

50 *Resalat*, 23 December 2005, p. 22.

51 The deputy head of the Majlis' Culture and Islamic Guidance Committee, Mohammad-Reza Mir-Tajeddini, quoted by ISNA, http://science.isna.ir/news/NewsPrint.asp?id=463851 (accessed 3 December 2004).

52 The head of the Majlis' Judiciary Committee, Ezatollah Yousefian-Molla, quoted by the Judiciary news site, *Ghest*, www.ghest.net/framework.jsp?SID=2 (accessed 15 August 2006).

53 Ayatollah Hashemi-Shahroudi's news conference, ISNA, 9 March 2005, www.isna.ir/Main/NewsView.aspx?ID=News-503795 (accessed 12 August 2006).

54 *Eqabl* daily, 7 March 2005, p. 4.

55 ISNA: 1 March 2005, www.isna.ir/Main/NewsView.aspx?ID=News-500036 (accessed 12 August 2006), and 2 March 2005, www.isna.ir/Main/ NewsView.aspx?ID=News-500089 (accessed 12 August 2006).

56 *Khabarnameh-ye Deneshjouiy*, p. 2.

57 Esma'ili, 'Jaygah-e Ertebatat dar Qanoun-e Barnameh-ye Chaharom-e Towse'eh', p. 84.

58 Kambiz Nowrouzi, 'Me'yarha-ye Azadi-ye Matbou'at' (The Standards of Freedom of the Press), paper presented at the Third Seminar to Study the Problems of the Iranian Press, Faculty of Social Sciences, Allameh Tabatabaee University, Tehran, 2 March 2005.

59 Mohammad Ghaed, 'Taqaddos va Ebtezal-e Sotounha-ye Chapi' (The Sanctity and Vulgarity of Printed Columns), the introduction to *Qodrat-ha-ye Jahan-e Matbou'at*, Persian tralslation of Martin Walker, *The Powers of the Press*, Tehran: Nashr-e Markaz, 1993, pp. 10–11.

60 Mohammad Qouchani quoted by the Iranian Students News Agency (ISNA), reproduced by the German-based Persian language news site, *Iran-e Emrouz*, 3 August 2004, http://news.iran-emrooz.de/more.php?id=6792_0_21_0_M (accessed 12 August 2006).

11 Conclusion

1 For the definition and elaboration of the concept of Iran as a 'short-term' society, see Homa Katouzian, *Iranian History and Politics*: *The Dialectic of State and Society*, London: RoutledgeCurzon, 2002.

Bibliography

A Books and articles

Abrahamian, Ervand, *Iran between Two Revolutions*, Princeton, NJ: Princeton University Press, 1982.

——, *Radical Islam, the Iranian Mojahedin*, London: I.B. Tauris, 1989.

Adib-Hasehmi, Farid, 'Siyassat-gozari va Amouzesh, Do Massaleh-ye Assassi dar Matbou'at-e Iran' (Policy-making and Training, Two Fundamental Issues for the Iranian Press), in *Majmou'eh Maqalat-e Dovomin Seminar-e Barresi-ye Massael-e Matbou'at-e Iran'* (The Collection of Articles Presented at the Second Seminar to Study the Problems of the Iranian Press), 2 vols, Tehran: 1998.

Amiri, Fatemeh, 'Ehsasat-e Zananeh dar Donya-ye Majazi' (Feminine Feelings in a Virtual World), *Iran* daily, 8 January 2005.

Ansari-Lari, Mohammad-Ebrahim, *Nezarat bar Matbou'at dar Hoqouq-e Iran* (Press Supervision in Iranian Law), Tehran: Soroush, 1996.

Aqeli, Baqer, *Rouz-shomar-e Tarikh-e Iran az Mashrouteh ta Enqelab-e Eslami* (Chronology of Iran, 1906–79), 2 vols, Tehran: Goftar, 1991.

Arefi, Hadi, 'Barresi-ye Noqoush-e Giyahi dar Honar-Hay-ye Eslami' (Review of the Floral Patterns in Islmaic Art), in *Asar-e Bargozideh-ye Chaharomin Jashnvareh-ye Matbou'at* (Selected Works from the Fourth Press Festival), Tehran: Press Festival Secretariat, 1998.

Aryani, Assefnia, 'Negahi beh Qanoun-e Matbou'at az Aghaz ta Emrouz' (A Glance at the Press Law from the Beginning Until Today), Part 12, *Ettela'at*, 2 August 1978.

Assadi, Abbas, 'Otaq-e Izoleh, Akharin Istgah-e Mobtalayan-e AIDS' (Isolation Room, the Last Stop for AIDS Patients), in *Ketab-e Jashnvareh-ye Sheshom-e Matbou'at* (The Book of the Sixth Press Festival), Tehran: Ministry of Culture and Islamic Guidance, 1999.

Association of Iranian Journalists, *Daghdagheh-ye Azadi* (Angst for Freedom), Tehran: Rouznegar, 2003.

Azar, Mahin, 'Keifiyat-e Ghazai va Estandard-e Qarch-e Iran' (Nutritional Quality and Standards of Iranian Mushrooms), in *Asar-e Bargozideh-ye Chaharomin Jashnvareh-ye Matbou'at* (Selected Works from the Fourth Press Festival), Tehran: Press Festival Secretariat, 1998.

Babahaji, Iraj, *Shargh*, 14 October 2004.

Babran, Sadiqeh, *Nashriyat-e Vijeh-ye Zanan* (Specialist Women's Press), Tehran: Roshangaran, 2002.

Badii, Naiim and Aliabadi, Guita, 'A Comparative Analysis of Selected Persian News Websites', paper presented at the Third Seminar on the Problems of the Iranian Press, Tehran, 3 March 2004.

Bahar, Malek-o-Sho'ara Mohammad-Taqi, address to the Majlis, reported in *Nowbahar*, no. 203, 11 June 1915, reproduced in 'Mass'oud Kouhestaninejad', *Asnad-e Dadgahha va Hey'at-ha-ye Monsefeh-ye Matbou'ati az Enqelab-e Mashrouteh ta Enqelab-e Eslami* (Documents on the Press Courts and Juries from the Constitutional Revolution to the Islamic Revolution), Tehran: Centre for Media Studies and Research, 2001.

Bahrampour, Ali, 'Asibha va Masaael-e Herfei-ye Matbou'at' (Professional Failures and Problems of the Country's Press), in *Rasaneh Quarterly*, vol. 14, no. 2, Summer 2003.

——, *Khabarnameh-ye Daneshjouiy*, 1 March 2005.

Baniyaghoub, Jilla, *Rouznamehnegaran* (Journalists), Tehran: Rouznegar, 1997.

Barzin, Mass'oud, *Seiri dar Matbou'at-e Iran* (A Survey of the Iranian Press), Tehran: Behjat, 1966.

——, *Matbou'at-e Iran 1343–53* (The Iranian Press, 1965–75), Tehran: Behjat, 1976.

——, 'Anjomanha-ye Matboua'ti dar Iran ta Sal-e 1357' (Press Associations in Iran until 1978–79), *Rasaneh Quarterly*, vol. 2, no. 3, Autumn 1991.

Bayat, Assef, *Workers and Revolution in Iran*, London: Zed, 1987.

Beheshtipour, Mehdi, *Tashakkolha-ye Senfi-ye Matbou'at* (Journalists' Trade Organizations), *Kilk* monthly, no. 84, March 1987.

——, 'Matbou'at-e Iran dar Dowreh-ye Pahlavi' (The Iranian Press in the Pahlavi Era), in *Rasaneh Quarterly*, vol. 4, no. 4, Winter 1994.

Behrooz, Maziar, *Rebels with a Cause*, London and New York: I.B. Tauris, 2000.

Behrooz-Faghani, Mehran, 'Ghalat-nevissi-ye Herfei-ha' (Professionals' Writing Badly) *Shargh*, 18 January 2005.

Behzadi, Ali, *Shebhe Khaterat* (Pseudo Memoirs), Tehran: Zarrin, 1997.

Bharier, Julian, *Economic Development in Iran, 1900–1970* (Persian Translation), Tehran: Planning Organization, 1984.

Bojnourdi, Nassim, 'Talaq ba Agahi-ye Rouznameh' (Divorce by a Newspaper Ad.), in *Zan dar Rouzanameh-ye Zan* (Woman in the Newspaper Woman), Tehran: Qolleh, 2000.

Boroujerdi-Alavi, Mahdokht, 'Pajouheshi dar Mowred-e Vaz'iyat-e Mowjoud-e Amouzesh-e Rouznamehnegari dar Iran' (An Investigation into the Current State of Journalism Training in Iran), in *Majmou'eh Maqalat-e Dovomin Seminar-e Barresi-ye Massael-e Matbou'at-e Iran'* (The Collection of Articles Presented at the Second Seminar to Study the Problems of the Iranian Press), 2 vols, Tehran: 1998.

Didari, Akram, 'Sahm-e Rouznamehha-ye Sobh az Manabe'-e Khabari' (Morning Dailies' Use of News Sources), in *Rasaneh Quarterly*, vol. 6, no. 3, Autumn 1995.

Ebadi, Shirin, *Hoqouq-e Adabi va Honari* (Literary and Artistic Rights), Tehran: Roshangaran, 1991.

——, 'Hoqouq-e Farzandan' (Children's Rights), in *Zan dar Rouzanmeh-ye Zan* (Woman in the Newspaper Woman), Tehran: Qolleh, 2000.

Esma'ili, Mohsen, 'Dadgahha-ye Matoub'ati' (Press Courts), in *Rasaneh Quarterly*, vol. 8, no. 1, Spring 1997.

——, *Qanoun-e Matbou'at va Seyr-e Tahavol-e an dar Hoqouq-e Iran* (The Press Law and its Evolution in Iranian Jurisprudence), Tehran: Soroush, 2000.

——, 'Jaygah-e Ertebatat dar Qanoun-e Barnameh-ye Chaharom-e Towse'eh' (Status of Communication in the 4th Development Plan), in *Rasaneh Quarterly*, vol. 15, no. 2, Summer 2004.

Farahmand, Ali-Reza, 'Matbou'at-e Jame'ey-ye Madani' (Press in the Civil Society), in *Majmou'eh Maqalat-e Dovomin Seminar-e Barresi-ye Massael-e Matbou'at-e Iran'* (The Collection of Articles Presented at the Second Seminar to Study the Problems of the Iranian Press), 2 vols, Tehran: 1998.

Farhadpour-Bastani, Lili, 'Obour az Gomrok-e Mordegan' (Passing Through the Customs House for the Dead), in *Daricheh* (Window) monthly, vol. 1, no. 3, reprinted in *Asar-e Bargozideh-ye Chaharomin Jashnvareh-ye Matbou'at* (Selected Works from the Fourth Press Festival), Tehran: Press Festival Secretariat, 1998.

Forqani, Mohammad-Mehdi, 'Matbou'at va Tahavolat-e Ejema'i dar Iran' (The Press and Social Developments in Iran), in *Rasaneh Quarterly*, vol. 7, no. 2, Summer 1996.

Fourth Press Festival Secretariat, *Asar-e Bargozideh-ye Chaharomin Jashnvareh-ye Matbou'at* (Selected Works from the Fourth Press Festival), Tehran: 1998.

Ganji, Akbar, *Tarikkhaneh-ye Ashabah* (The Dark-house of the Ghosts), 4th impression, Tehran: Tarh-e Now, 1999.

Geranpayeh, Behrouz, 'Lumpenism ya Bad-akhlaqi-ye Rasanehi dar Matbou'at-e Iran' (Lumpenism or Bad Media Attitude in the Iranian Press), in *Majmou'eh Maqalat-e Dovomin Seminar-e Barresi-ye Massael-e Matbou'at-e Iran'* (The Collection of Articles Presented at the Second Seminar to Study the Problems of the Iranian Press), 2 vols, Tehran: Ministry of Culture and Islamic Guidance, 1998.

——, addressing the Third Seminar to Study the Problems of the Iranian Press, Tehran, 1 March 2005.

Ghaed, Mohammad, 'Mamnou' Ya'ni Qachaq, Qachaq Ya'ni Maskout' (Contraband Means Smuggled, Smuggled Means Hushed), in *San'at-e Haml-o Naghl*, no. 86, April 1990.

——, 'Afsaneh-ye Bazgasht' (The Myth of Return), in *San'at-e Haml-o Naghl*, no. 87, June 1990.

——, 'Tali'eh-ye yek Safkari-e Bonyadi' (The Beginning of a Complete Facelift) *San'at-e Haml-o Naghl*, no. 117, March 1993.

——, 'Taqaddos va Ebtezal-e Sotoun-ha-ye Chapi' (The Sanctity and Vulgarity of Printed Columns), the introduction to *Qodrat-ha-ye Jahan-e Matbou'at*, Persian translation of Martin Walker, *The Powers of the Press*, Tehran: Nashr-e Markaz, 1993, pp. 10–11.

——, unpublished notes on *Ayandegan*.

Gharnabad Conference on Communication and Information Technology for National Development, Conference brochure, March 2005.

Haddad-Adel, Dr Gholam-Ali, 'Ta'sir-e Kant bar Tafakor-e Dini-ye Maghreb-zamin' (Kant's Influence on Western Religious Thought), in *Asar-e Bargozideh-ye Chaharomin Jashnvareh-ye Matbou'at* (Selected Works from the Fourth Press Festival), Tehran: Press Festival Secretariat, 1998.

Haidari, Mohammad, 'Barressi-ye Sakhtar-e Birouni va Darouni-ye E'tessab-e Matbou'at' (A Review of the External and Internal Structures of the Newspaper Strike), in *Gozaresh*, no. 43, August–September 1994.

Homayoun, Daryoush, 'Sad Sal az Rouznamehnegari beh Siyassat' (One Hundred Years from Journalism to Politics), in *Iran Nameh*, vol. XI, nos. 1–2, Spring and Summer 1998.

Hosseinnia, Abdol-Hamid, 'Dar Kashakesh-e Ab va Sang' (In the Midst of the Battle between Water and Stone), in *Asar-e Bargozideh-ye Chaharomin Jashnvareh-ye Matbou'at* (Selected Works from the Fourth Press Festival), Tehran: Press Festival Secretariat, 1998.

Hosseinzadeh Bahraini, Mohammad-Hossein, 'Barresi-ye Feqhi va Eqtesadi-ye Soud-e Tazmin-shodeh Alal-Hesab dar System-e Bankdari-ye Bedoun-e Reba' (Review of Advance Guaranteed Profit in Usury-free Banking System), in *Asar-e Bargozideh-ye Chaharomin Jashnvareh-ye Matbou'at* (Selected Works from the Fourth Press Festival), Tehran: Press Festival Secretariat, 1998.

Jalaiepour, Hamid-Reza, *Pass az Dovom-e Khordad* (After 22 May), Tehran: Kavir, 1999.

Jassbi, Abdollah, interviewed by *Hambastegi* daily, 19 March 2001, quoted in the educational monthly *Lawh*, no. 11, September 2001, p. 22.

Javanroudi, Youness, *Tasskhir-e Kayhan* (The Seizure of Kayhan), Tehran: Hashieh, 1980.

Kamyar, Mohammad-Reza, 'Mohakemeh-yi keh dar Khala'-e Qanuni bar-pa Shod' (The Trial that was Held in a Legal Vacuum), in *Ketab-e Jashnvareh-ye Sheshom-e Matbou'at* (The Book of the Sixth Press Festival), Tehran: Ministry of Culture and Islamic Guidance, 1999.

Kar, Mehr-Anguiz, 'Talaq va Hoqouq-e Zanan' (Divorce and Women's Rights), *Zan dar Rouzanameh-ye Zan* (Woman in the Newspaper Woman), Tehran: Qolleh, 2000.

Kashi, Gholam-Reza, *Matboua't dar Asr-e Khatami, Mordad 76–Mordad 79* (Press in Khatami's Era, August 1997–August 2000), Tehran: Selk, 2000.

Katouzian, Homa, *The Political Economy of Modern Iran*, Persian translation by Mohammd-Reza Nafissi and Kambiz Azizi, Tehran: Markaz, 1993.

——, 'The Pahlavi Regime in Iran', in H. E. Chehabi and J. Linz (eds), *Sultanistic Regimes*, Baltimore, MD: Johns Hopkins Press, 1997.

——, *Iranian History and Politics: The Dialectic of State and Society*, London: Routledge-Curzon, 2002.

Kaviani, Hamid, *Dar Jostojou-ye Mahfel-e Jenayatkaran* (In Search of the Criminal Circle), Tehran: Negah-e Emrouz, 1999.

Kaviani, Hamid-Reza, 'Goftogouy-e Shesh-sa'teh ba Mohsen Rafiqdoust' (Six-Hour Conversation with Mohsen Rafiqdoust), in *Asar-e Bargozideh-ye Chaharomin Jashnvareh-ye Matbou'at* (Selected Works from the Fourth Press Festival), Tehran: Press Festival Secretariat, 1998.

Kazemi, Mass'oud, 'Doshvariha-ye Nashriyat-e Mostaqel dar Barabar-e Gostaresh-e Nashriyat-e Dowlati ya Mowred-e Hemayat-e Dowlat' (The Difficulties Faced by the Independent Publications with Respect to the Expansion of Publications Owned or Supported by the State), in *Rasaneh Quarterly*, vol. 14, no. 4, Winter 2004.

Khaniki, Hadi, 'Ertebatat-e Towsse'eh va Massaleh-ye Ertebat dar Iran' (Development of Communication and the Problem of Communication in Iran), paper presented at the Third Seminar to Study the Problems of the Iranian Press, Tehran, 2 March 2005.

Khorsandi, Hadi, *The Ayatollah and I*, London: Readers International, 1987.

Kouhestani-nejad, Mass'oud, *Asnad-e Dadgahha va Hey'at-ha-ye Monsefeh-ye Matbou'ati az Enqelab-e Mashrouteh ta Enqelab-e Eslami* (Documents on the Press Courts and Juries from the Constitutional Revolution to the Islamic Revolution), Tehran: Centre for Media Studies and Research, 2001.

——, *Asnad va Gozareshha-ye Gorouhha, Anjomanha va Ettehadiehha-ye Matbou'ati* (Documents and Reports on Press Groups, Associations and Unions), Tehran: Centre for Media Studies and Research, 2004.

Larijani, Ali, 'Ghalat-ha-ye Aqa-ye Qouchani' (Mr Qouchanis' Errors), in Mohammad Qouchani, *Pedarkhandeh va Chap-haye Javan* (The Godfather and the Young Leftists), Tehran: Nashr-e Ney, 2000.

Loghatname Dehkhoda, vol. 7, Tehran: Tehran University Publications, 1993–94.

——, vol. 10, Tehran: Tehran University Publications, 1993–94.

Mehrabi, Mass'oud, *Tarikh-e Cinema-ye Iran* (The History of Iranian Cinema), Tehran: Film Publications, 1988.

Mehrizi, Mehdi, 'Negahi Tarikhi beh Massaleh-ye Feqh va Zaman' (A Historical View of the Question of Jurisprudence and Time), in *Asar-e Bargozideh-ye Chaharomin Jashnvareh-ye Matbou'at* (Selected Works from the Fourth Press Festival), Tehran: Press Festival Secretariat, 1998.

Milani, Abbas, *The Persian Sphinx: Amir Abbas Hoveryda and the Riddle of the Iranian Revolution*, London and New York: I.B. Tauris, 2000.

Ministry of Culture and Islamic Guidance, *Negareshi bar Naqsh-e Matbou'at-e Vabasteh dar Ravand-e Enqelab-e Eslam-e Iran* (A Review of the Role of the Dependent Press in the Course of Iran's Islamic Revolution), Tehran, 1982.

——, *Rasaneh Quarterly Journal of Media Studies and Research*, vols. 1 –15, 1990–2004.

——, *Majmou'eh Maqalat-e Nokhostin Seminar-e Barresi-ye Massael-e Matbou'at-e Iran* (Collection of the Papers Presented at the First Seminar to Study the Problems of the Iranian Press), Tehran, 1992.

——, *Salnema-ye Matbou'at-e Iran* (Almanac of the Iranian Press), Tehran, 1996.

——, *Majmou'eh Maqalat-e Dovomin Seminar-e Barresi-ye Massael-e Matbou'at-e Iran'* (The Collection of Articles Presented at the Second Seminar to Study the Problems of the Iranian Press), Tehran, 1998.

——, *Ketab-e Jashnvareh-ye Sheshom-e Matbou'at* (The Book of the Sixth Press Festival), Tehran, 1999.

——, *Asar-e Bargozideh-ye Haftomin Jashnvareh-ye Matbou'at* (Selected Works from the Seventh Press Festival), Tehran, 2001.

——, *Matbou'at az Negah-e Amar* (Press Through the Statistical Viewpoint), Tehran, August 2004.

——, *Shenasnameh-ye Mowzoui'-ye Matbou'at-e Keshvar* (Subject Catalogue of the Country's Press), Tehran, 2004.

——, Centre for Media Studies and Research, brochure on training courses, March 2005.

Ministry of Information and Culture, Tehran, *Ashnaiyba Madey-ye 16 Qanoun-e Matboua'at*, Learning about Article 16 of the Press Law, no date, p. 34.

Ministry of Intelligence, *Daryoush Homayoun beh Revayat-e Asnad-e SAVAK* (Daryoush Homayoun According to SAVAK Documents), Tehran, 1999.

Mirzakhani, Ali, interviewed by *Rasaneh Supplement*, vol. 1, no. 6, 22 August–5 September 2004, pp. 8–9.

Mohajerani, Ataollah, *Esteezah* (Censure), Tehran: Ettela'at, 1999.

Mohammadi, Majid, *Sima-ye Eqtedargaraiy, Televizion-e Dowlati-ye Iran* (The Authoritarian Vision, Iran's State-owned Television), Tehran: Jameah Iran, 2000.

Moheet-Tabataie, Mohammad, *Tarikh-e Tahlili-ye Matbou'at-e Iran* (The Analytical History of the Iranian Press), Tehran: Be'that, 1988.

Mohsenian-Rad, Mehdi, 'Rouznamehnegaran-e Iran va Amouzesh-e Rouznamehnegari' (Iranian Journalists and Journalism Education), Tehran: Centre for Media Studies and Research, 1994, quoted in *Rasaneh Quarterly*, vol. 5, no. 4, Winter 1995.

——, 'Matbou'at-e Salha-ye Nokhost-e Enqelab-e Eslami' (Press in the First Years of the Islamic Republic), *Kilk*, no. 84, March 1997.

——, 'Rouznamehnegari-ye Enteqadi!' (Critical Journalism!), in *Majmou'eh Maqalat-e Dovomin Seminar-e Barresi-ye Massael-e Matbou'at-e Iran'* (The Collection of Articles Presented at the Second Seminar to Study the Problems of the Iranian Press), 2 vols, Tehran: 1998.

——, 'Zarourat-e Tavajoh beh Maqouleh-ye Ertebatat-e Mian-farhangi dar Jame'eh- ye Iran beh Manzour-e Movajeheh-ye Sahih ba Tahavolat-e Jame'eh-ye Ettella'ati' (The Necessity of Paying Attention to the Concept of Inter-cultural Communication in Iran for the Purpose of Correctly Dealing with the Developments in the Information Society), in *Rasaneh Quarterly*, vol. 14, no. 1, Spring 2003.

Mohsenian-Rad, Mehdi and colleagues 'Payam-Afarinan-e Matbou'at-e Iran' (The Message Creators in the Iranian Press', Part 1, in *Rasaneh Quarterly*, vol. 4, no. 2, Summer 1993, pp. 4–17.

——, 'Negahi beh Matoub'at-e Iran dar Moqayesehha-ye Jahani' (A Glance at the Iranian Press in the Global Context), in *Rasaneh Quarterly*, vol. 4, no. 4, Winter 1994.

Moin, Baqer, *Khomeini: Life of the Ayatollah*, London and New York: I.B. Tauris, 1999.

Molana, Hamid, *Journalism in Iran – A History and Interpretation*, PhD dissertation, Evanston, IL: Northwestern University, 1963.

Moqadamfar, Hamid, 'Matbou'at, Hoqouq, Hodoud, Jara'em' (The Press, Rights, Limits, Offences), in *Rasaneh Quarterly Journal of Media Studies and Research*, Tehran: Ministry of Culture and Islamic Guidance, vol. 1, no. 3, Autumn 1990.

——, 'Seyr-e Tarikhi-ye Qavanin-e Matbou'at-e Iran' (The Historical Development of Iran's Press Laws), in *Rasaneh Quraterly*, vol. 4, no. 1, Spring 1993.

Moqimi-Esfandabadi, Hossein and Roshenas, Qassem 'Matbou'at-e Iran va Moshkel-e Bazdehi-ye Sarmayeh' (The Iranian Press and the Problem of Return on Capital), in *Rasaneh Quarterly*, vol. 6, no. 1, Spring 1995.

Mo'tamednejad, Kazem, 'Barresi-ye Sharayet-e Pishraft-e Nashriyat-e Mostaqel va Kesrat-gera' (A Review of the Conditions for the Development of Independent and Pluralistic Publications), in *Majmou'eh Maqalat-e Dovomin Seminar-e Barresi-ye Massael-e Matbou'at-e Iran'* (The Collection of Articles Presented at the Second Seminar to Study the Problems of the Iranian Press), vol. 1, Tehran: Ministry of Culture and Islamic Guidance, 1998, vol. 1, p. 51.

——, 'Gozaresh-e Dabir-e Elmi-ye Seminar' (Report by the Academic Secretary of the Seminar), in *Majmou'eh Maqalat-e Dovomin Seminar-e Barresi-ye Massael-e Matbou'at-e Iran'* (The Collection of Articles Presented at the Second Seminar to Study the Problems of the Iranian Press), Tehran: Ministry of Culture and Islamic Guidance, 1998.

——, *Hoqouq-e Matbou'at* (Press Law), vol. 1, Tehran: Centre for Media Studies and Research, 2000.

——, *Pishneviss-e Missaq-e Osul-e Akhlaqi-ye Herfeh-ye Rouznamehnegari* (Draft Convention on the Ethical Principles of Professional Journalism), Tehran: typescript, March 2004.

——, *Pishneviss-e Peyman-e Jam'i-e Kare-ye Rouznamehnegaran* (Draft Collective Employment Contract for Journalists), Tehran: typescript, June 2004.

——, *Pishneviss-e Qanoun-e Nezam-e Hoqouqi-ye Herfeh-ye Rouznamehnegari* (Draft Convention on the Legal System of Professional Journalism), Tehran: typescript, June 2004.

——, *Rasaneh Quarterly*, vol. 12, no. 1, Spring 2001, p. 22.

——, *Shargh*, 19 December 2004, p. 13

——, *Pishneviss-e Layeheh-ye Qanouni-ye Shora-ye Matbou'at* (Draft Bill on the Press Council), Tehran: typescript, no date.

Nabavi, Seyyed-Ebarhim, quoted in *Rouznamehnegar*, no. 30, May–June 2002, p. 6.

Nazeri, Ne'mat, '80 Sa'at Bazdasht-e Panj Rouznamehnegar' (Eighty Hours of Detention of Five Journalists), *Kilk*, no. 84, March 1997, pp. 265–269.

(No author's or editor's name) *Zan dar Rouzanameh-ye Zan* (Woman in the Daily Zan), Tehran: Qolleh, 2000.

Nowrouzi, Kambiz, 'Azadi-ye Matbou'at az Akhlaq ta Hoqouq' (Freedom of the Press from Ethics to Rights), in *Majmou'eh Maqalat-e Dovomin Seminar-e Barresi-ye Massael-e Matbou'at-e Iran'* (The Collection of Articles Presented at the Second Seminar to Study the Problems of the Iranian Press), vol. 1, Tehran: Ministry of Culture and Islamic Guidance, 1998.

Nowrouzi, Kambiz, 'Me'yarha-ye Azadi-ye Matbou'at' (The Standards of Freedom of the Press), paper presented at the Third Seminar to Study the Problems of the Iranian Press, Faculty of Social Sciences, Allameh Tabatabaee University, Tehran, 2 March 2005.

Pourostad, Vahid, *Mohakemeh-ye Jameah* (The Trial of *Jameah*), Tehran: Rouznegar, 2001.

——, *Mohakemeh-ye Salam* (The Trial of *Salam*), Tehran: Rouznegar, 2001.

——, *Mohakemeh-ye Zan* (The Trial of *Zan*), Tehran: Rouzengar, 2001.

——, *Mohakemeh-ye Adineh* (The Trial of *Adineh*), Tehran: Rouznegar, 2002.

——, *Mohakehem-ye Nowrouz* (The Trial of *Nowrouz*), Tehran: Rouznegar, 2002.

——, *Mohakemeh-ye Tous* (The Trial of *Tous*), Tehran: Rouznegar, 2002.

Qanoun-e Assassi-ye Jomhouri-ye Eslami-ye Iran (The Constitution of the Islamic Republic of Iran), ratified in 1979 and revised in 1989, Tehran: Nashr-e Dowran, 2004.

Qassemi, Seyyed-Farid, *Rahnema-ye Matbou'at-e Iran 1357–1371* (Directory of Iranian Press 1979–1993), Tehran: Centre for Media Studies and Research, the Ministry of Culture and Islamic Guidance, 1993.

——, *Khaterat-e Matbou'ati, vol. 1: Sad Khatereh az Sad Rouydad* (Journalists' Memoirs: One Hundred Memoirs from One Hundred Events), Tehran: Essalat-e Tanshir, 1998.

——, *Rouydadha-ye Matbou'ati-ye Iran 1215–1382* (Iranian Press Events, 1837–2004), Tehran: Ministry of Culture and Islamic Guidance, 2004.

Qazizadeh, Ali-Akbar, 'Ta'avoni-ye Matbou'at' (The Press Cooperative), in *Rasaneh Quarterly Journal of Media Studies and Research*, Ministry of Culture and Islamic Guidance, vol. 3, no. 4, Winter 1992, pp. 37–41.

——, 'Zaminehha-ye Sou'-e Tafahom Miyan-e Maboua't va Massoulan' (The Background to the Misunderstanding Between the Press and the Officials), in *Majmou'eh Maqalat-e Dovomin Seminar-e Barresi-ye Massael-e Matbou'at-e Iran'* (The Collection of Articles Presented at the Second Seminar to Study the Problems of the Iranian Press), 2 vols, Tehran: 1998.

Qouchani, Mohammad, *Pedarkhandeh va Chapha-ye Javan* (The Godfather and the Young Leftists), Tehran: Nashr-e Ney, 2000.

Rabi'i, Ali, 'Khat-e Nofouz ra Jeddi Begirid' (Take the Infiltration Line Seriously), in *Ketab-e Jashnvareh-ye Sheshom-e Matbou'at* (The Book of the Sixth Press Festival), pp. 91–93.

Rais-dana, Fariborz, 'Miz-e-gerd-e Towlid-e Melli' (National Production Roundtable), *Naqd-e Now* (New Critique) monthly, no. 4, January–February 2004, p. 8.

Rasai, Hamid, *Payan-e Dastan-e Ghamangiz: Negahi beh Zaminehha-ye Sodour-e Hokm-e Hokoumati-ye Maqam-e Mo'azzam-e Rahbari dar-bareh-ye Qanoun-e Matbou'at* (The End of the Tragic Story: A Glance at the Background to His Excellency the Supreme Leader's Decree on the Press Law), vol. 2, Tehran: Kayhan Publications, 2001.

Rastgar, Leyla, 'Entekhab-e Daneshjouy-e Rouznamehnegari Azmoun-e Vijeh Mikhahad' (Special Tests are Needed to Select Journalism Students), in *Rasaneh Quarterly*, vol. 5, no. 4, Winter 1995, pp. 11–20.

Razazifar, Afsar, *Gozaresh-e Nashriyat-e Zanan va Khanevadeh* (Report on Women and Family Publications), Tehran, Ministry of Culture and Islamic Guidance, Center for Media Studies and Research, November 2002.

Razzazi, Majid, 'Gozareshi az Vaz'e Control-e Maali dar Sherkat-ha-ye Dowlati' (A Report on the Conditions of Financial Supervision in State-owned Companies), in *Asar-e Bargozideh-ye Chaharomin Jashnvareh-ye Matbou'at* (Selected Works from the Fourth Press Festival), Tehran: Press Festival Secretariat, 1998.

Rezaie, Hamid-Reza, 'Dowlat, Amel-e Asli-ye Bazdarandegi-ye Towsse'eh-ye Matbou'at', (The State, the Main Factor Holding Back the Development of the Press), in *Majmou'eh Maqalat-e Dovomin Seminar-e Barressi-ye Massael-e Matbou'at-e Iran'* (The

Collection of Articles Presented at the Second Seminar to Study the Problems of the Iranian Press), 2 vols, Tehran: 1998.

Sadr, Roya, 'Tanz-e Webloggi' (Weblog Humour), paper prepared for the Third Seminar to Study the Problems of the Iranian Press, Tehran, 1–2 March 2005.

Sadr, Shadi, 'Ta'me Gilas, Ayeneh, va Hoquq-e Padid-avarandeh' (A Taste of Cherries, The Mirror, and The Creator's Rights), in *Ketab-e Jashnvareh-ye Sheshom-e Matbou'at* (The Book of the Sixth Press Festival), Tehran: Ministry of Culture and Islamic Guidance, 1999.

Sadr-Hashemi, Mohammad, *Tarikh-e Jarayed va Majallat-e Iran* (The History of Iranian Newspapers and Magazines), Isfahan: Kamal, 1984.

Safari, Mohammad-Ali, *Qalam va Siyassat* (Pen and Politics), vol. 1, Tehran: Namak, 1998.

——, *Qalam va Siyassat* (Pen and Politics), vol. 3, Tehran: Namak, 1998.

——, *Qalam va Siyassat* (Pen and Politics), vol. 4, Tehran: Namak, 2001.

Safdari, Akbar 'Herfeh Rouznamehnegar' (Profession, Journalist), in *Rasaneh Supplement*, vol. 1, no. 5, 5–20 August 2005, pp. 8–9.

Saharkhiz, Issa, quoted in *Rouznamehnegar*, no. 42, April–May 2004, p. 12.

Salamat, Nazanin, 'Qatl-e Farzand Tavasot-e Pedar' (Infanticide by the Father), and Mandana Nasser, 'Cheh Kassi Moqasser Ast, Pedar ya Qanoun' (Who is Guilty, the Father or the Law?), reprinted in *Zan dar Rouzanameh-ye Zan* (Woman in the Newspaper Woman), Tehran: Qolleh, 2000.

Salehyar, Gholam-Hossein, *Chehreh-ye Matbou'at-e Mo'asser* (The Image of the Contemporary Press), Tehran: Press Agent, 1973.

——, *Vijegiha-ye Irani-ye Matbou'at* (Iranian Features of the Press), Tehran: Ministry of Information and Tourism, 1976.

——, 'Majara-ye yek Titr-e Tarikhi' (The Story of a Historic Headline), in *Ettella'at*, 8 February 1991, p. 6, quoted in Sayyed-Farid Qassemi, *Khaterat-e Matbou'ati: Sad Khatereh az Sad Rouydad* (Journalists' Memoirs: One Hundred Memoirs from One Hundred Events), vol. 1, Tehran: Essalat-e Tanshir, 1998.

Sebqati, Iraj, *Jam-e Jam*, 11 January 2005, pp. 1–3.

Sediqi, Fereydoun, 'Va Shodam Rouznamehnegar' (And I Became a Journalist', *Paojuheshnameh-ye Tarikh-e Matbou'at-e Iran* (Research Document on the History of the Iranian Press), no. 1, 1997.

Sha'bani, Ahmad, 'Bala-bordan-e Karai-ye Carbon-e Fa'al Jahat-e Padafand-e Shimiayi' (Raising the Efficiency of Active Carbon for the Purpose of Chemical Defence), in *Asar-e Bargozideh-ye Chaharomin Jashnvareh-ye Matbou'at* (Selected Works from the Fourth Press Festival), Tehran: Press Festival Secretariat, 1998.

Shahidi, Hossein 'Women in Iranian Journalism, 1910–1997', in Sarah Ansari and Vanessa Martin (eds), *Women, Religion and Culture in Iran*, London: Royal Asiatic Society and Curzon Press, 2002.

Shamsolva'ezin, Mashaallah, *Yaddasht-ha-ye Sardabir* (Editor's Notes), Tehran: Jameah Iran, 2001.

Sheikholeslami, Pari, *Zanan-e Rouznamehnegar va Andishmand-e Iran* (Iran's Women Journalists and Thinkers), Tehran: Tehran University, 1972.

Shoja'i, Seyyed-Mehdi, 'Shazdeh' (The Prince), in *Asar-e Bargozideh-ye Chaharomin Jashnvareh-ye Matbou'at* (Selected Works from the Fourth Press Festival), Tehran: Press Festival Secretariat, 1998.

Sohrabzadeh, Mehran, 'Matbou'at dar Aineh-ye Tablighat' (The Reflection of the Press in Advertisements), in *Rasaneh Quarterly*, vol. 6, no. 3, Autumn 1995.

Soroush publications, *Taqvim-e Tarikh-e Enqelab-e Eslami-ye Iran* (*Journal of the Islamic Revolution of Iran*), Tehran: Soroush, 1991.

Soroush publications catalogue, Islamic Republic of Iran Broadcasting, Tehran, 2004.

Sreberny-Mohammadi, Annabelle and Mohammadi, Ali, *Small Media, Big Revolution*, Minneapolis, MN and London: University of Minnesota Press, 1994.

Statistical Centre of Iran, *Natayej-e Moqaddamti-ye Sarshomari az Kargahha-ye Bozorg-e San'ati, 1355* (Preliminary Results from the Census of Large Industrial Firms, 1976), Tehran, 1978.

——, *Nemagarha-ye Jam'iyati-ye Iran (Iran Population Index)*, Tehran, 1999.

——, *Salnameh-ye Amari-ye Keshvar* (The National Statistical Yearbook), various years.

Talebzadeh, Khosrow, 'Barressi-ye Mo'zalat-e Chap-e Matbou'at' (Review of the Problems of the Printing of the Press), in *Majmou'eh Maqalat-e Dovomin Seminar-e Barresi-ye Massael-e Matbou'at-e Iran'* (The Collection of Articles Presented at the Second Seminar to Study the Problems of the Iranian Press), 2 vols, Tehran: Ministry of Culture and Islamic Guidance, 1998. Towfiq, Abbas, *Ketab-e Hafteh* (The Book Weekly), no. 455, 22 June 2002.

Taqiepour, Saied, *Shargh*, 30 November 2004, p. 13

Vatani, Ma'ssoumeh, ' "Towzi", Vasseteh-ye Towlid va Masraf-e Payam' (Distribution, the Link Between the Production and Consumption of the Message), in *Rasaneh Quarterly*, vol. 6, no. 3, Autumn 1995.

Yousefpour, Ali quoted in *Rasaneh Quarterly*, vol. 14, no. 1, Spring 2003, p. 7.

Zakariaee, Mohamad-Ali, (ed.), *Conferans-e Berlin: Khedmat ya Khiyant?* (Berlin Conference: Service or Treason), Tehran: Tarh-e Now, 2000.

Zare', Bijan, 'Barresi-ye Vaz'iyat-e Amouzesh-e Rouznamehnegari dar Iran' (A Review of the State of Journalism Training in Iran), in *Majmou'eh Maqalat-e Dovomin Seminar-e Barresi-ye Massael-e Matbou'at-e Iran* (The Collection of Articles Presented at the Second Seminar to Study the Problems of the Iranian Press), Tehran: Ministry of Culture and Islamic Guidance, 1998, vol. 2, p. 642.

Zeidabadi, Ahmad, 'Manaafe'-e Melli, Barayand-e Aara-e Mellat' (National Interests, the Vector of People's Votes), in *Asar-e Bargozideh-ye Panjomin Jashnvareh-ye Matbou'at* (Selected Works from the Fifth Press Festival), Tehran: Ministry of Culture and Islamic Guidance, 1999, pp. 26–27.

B   Interviews and direct communications

Association of Children and Youths' Writers, Tehran, 21 February 2005.
Association of Graphic Artists, Tehran, 22 February 2005.
Association of Iranian Journalists,
    Vice President, Dr Karim Arghandehpour, Tehran, 8 January 2002.
    Secretary, Mr Mass'oud Houshmand-e-Razavi, Tehran, 4 January 2005.
Association of Iranian Press Photographers, Tehran, 22 February 2005.
Association of Tehran Freelance Journalists, Tehran, 21 February 2005.
Association of Young Iranian Journalists, Tehran, 26 February 2005.
Ghaed, Mohammad, former *Ayandegan* editorial board member, Tehran, 9 January 2002.
Hashemi, Faezeh, interviewed by the daily *Zan*, no date given, reprinted in *Zan dar Rouzanameh-ye Zan* (Woman in the Newspaper Woman), Tehran: Qolleh, 2000, p. 272.
Iran Cartoon House, Tehran, 5 March 2005.
Iranian Women Journalists' Association, Tehran, 26 February 2005.
Khorsandi, Hadi, former *Ettela'at* columnist, London, 26 February 2002.

Mahdiyan, Hossein, businessman, publisher and temporary owner of *Kayhan* in 1979, Tehran, 26 August 2002.

Mehrabi, Mass'oud, *Film* monthly publisher, Tehran, 28 February 2005.

Mohajer, Mass'oud, former *Ayandegan* and *San'at-e Haml-o Naghl* journalist, Tehran, 25 August 2002.

Namakdoost-Tehrani, Dr Hassan, Tehran, 3 July 2006.

Rahmanian, Mehdi, interviewed by Rasaneh Supplement, vol. 1, no. 1, 6 June 2004.

Taheri, Ali-Reza, former *Ettela'at* journalist, London, 26 February 2002.

Tehran University's Faculty of Social Sciences, Education Affairs Officer, 15 March 2005.

Turani, Behrouz, former *Bamdad* journalist, London, 23 January 2002.

Zarghani, Ali, publisher of *San'at-e Haml-o Naghl*, Tehran, 7 February 2005.

C   Newspapers and periodicals

Abrar (The Free) daily.

Adineh (Friday) monthly.

Asr-e Ertebatat (Age of Communication) daily.

Ayandegan (Posterity) daily.

Asr-e Rasaneh (Media Age) daily.

Eqbal (Fortune) daily.

E'temad (Trust) daily.

Ettela'at (Information) daily.

Farhang-e Ashti (Culture of Reconciliation) daily.

Film monthly.

Hamvatan Salam (Hello, Compatriot) daily.

Haubastegi (Solidarity) daily

Iran daily.

Jahan-e San'at (World of Industry) daily.

Jam-e Jam (Jamshid's Goblet) daily.

Jomhouri-ye Eslami (Islamic Republic) daily.

Kayhan (Universe) daily.

Keshavarz (Farmer) monthly.

Khabarnameh-ye Daneshjouyi (University Students' News Bulletin), the news bulletin of the Third Seminar on the Problems of the Press is Iran, 2 March 2005.

Khanevadeh-ye Sabz (Green Family) biweekly.

Kilk (Plume) monthly.

Lawh (Tablet) monthly.

Me'mar (Architect) quarterly.

Naqd-e Now (New Critique) monthly.

Novaran (Innovators) biweekly.

Rasaneh (Medium) *Quarterly Journal of Media Studies and Research*, Centre for Media Studies and Research, Ministry of Culture and Islamic Guidance, published since Summer 1990.

Rasaneh Supplement, weekly publication of the office of Deputy Minister for Press and Publicity Affairs, Ministry of Culture and Islamic Guidance, published since May 2005.

Resalat (Mission) daily.

Rouznamehnegar (Journalist), organ of the Association of Iranian Journalists published since August 1999.

San'at-e Haml-o Naghl (Transport Industry) monthly.

Seday-e Zan (Woman's Voice), newsletter of the Iranian Women Journalists' Association.

Shargh (East) daily.

Sunday Times.
Zanan (Women) monthly.
Zan-e Rouz (Woman of the Day) weekly.

D   Online news and information sites

Abtahi, Mohammad-Ali, weblog, www.webneveshteha.com/ (accessed 12 August 2006).

Aftab (Sunshine) news site www.aftabnews.ir/ (accessed 15 August 2006).

Ahmadi, Mehdi, communication weblog, Cyber-Café, http://cc.eprsoft.com/archives/ 001738.html (accessed 18 February 2007).

Al-Kawthar, Iranian Arabic television channel, www.alkawthartv.ir/about.asp (accessed 3 August 2006).

Association of Iranin Journalists, http://rooznamenegar.ir/index.php (accessed 12 August 2006).

Association of Iranian Journalists (AOIJ) College, www.aoij.org/About-AoijBylaws/ University.htm (accessed 4 August 2006)

Ayatollah Hossein-Ali Montazeri's website, www.amontazeri.com/ (accessed 3 August 2006)

Badjens Iranian Feminist Newsletter, www.badjens.com/ (accessed 12 August 2006).

Baztab news site, www.baztab.com/ (accessed 12 August 2006).

BBC Persian Service, www.bbc.co.uk/persian/index.shtml (accessed 12 August 2006).

BBC World Service news, http://news.bbc.co.uk/ (accessed 12 August 2006).

Belgian Constitution, University of Berne website, www.oefre.unibe.ch/law/icl/ be00000_.html (accessed 12 August 2006).

Central Bank of Iran, 'National Accounts of Iran, 1959/60–2000/01', www.cbi.ir/publications/ PDF/NA3879.pdf (accessed Spring 2005).

Centre for Media Studies and Research, www.rasaneh.org/persian/index.asp?b=01 (accessed 15 August 2006).

Data Communication Company of Iran (DCI) website, www.iranpac.net.ir/ (accessed Spring 2005).

Entekhab news site, www.entekhab.ir/ (accessed 12 August 2006).

e-Public Relations Software Group's website, www.eprsoft.com/home/information/doc3. htm (16 February 2007)

Fars news agency, www.farsnews.com/ (accessed 15 August 2006).

Ghabel, Ahmad, weblog, http://ghabel.persianblog.com/ (accessed 12 August 2006).

http://en.wikipedia.org/wiki/Iranian_Blogs (accessed 12 August 2006).

International Pen, Writers in Prison Committee, 'Half Yearly Caselist to December 2001', www.pen.dk/prison/CaselistJan02.pdf (accessed 3 August 2006).

Internet World Stats, Internet Usage in Asia, www.internetworldstats.com/stats3.htm (accessed 15 August 2006).

——, Internet Usage in the Middle East, www.internetworldstats.com/ stats5.htm (accessed 12 August 2006).

——, Top Twenty Countries, www.internetworldstats.com/top20.htm (accessed 12 August 2006).

Iran Agriculture News Agency, IANA, www.iana.ir/ (accessed 15 August 2006).

Iran and Information Society website, www.iranwsis.ir/Default.asp?C=IRNW&R=&I=82 #BN82 (accessed 18 February 2007).

Iran Cartoon House website, www.irancartoon.com/hic/index.htm (accessed March 2005).

Iran Chamber Society, www.iranchamber.com/ (accessed 12 August 2006).

Iran Emroz Persian language news site based in Germany, www.iran-emrooz.net/ (accessed 12 August 2006).

Iranian Feminist Tribune, www.iftribune.com/ (accessed 12 August 2006).

Iranian history website, Parstimes, www.parstimes.com/history/press_history.html (accessed 12 August 2006).

Iranian Judiciary's news site, Ghest, www.ghest.net/news.jsp/ (accessed 15 August 2006).

Iranian Labour News Agency, ILNA, www.ilna.ir/ (accessed 12 August 2006).

Iranian Students News Agency (ISNA), www.isna.ir/ (accessed 12 August 2006).

Iranian Women News Agency (IWNA), www.iwna.ir/ (accessed 13 August 2006).

Islamic Azad University, journalism students' enrolment numbers, www.iauctb.org/english/ Social per cent20Sciences&Psycology per cent20.htm (accessed Winter 2005).

Islamic Republic of Iran Broadcasting (IRIB) College, www.irib.ir/education/ univer111.htm (accessed 12 August 2006).

Islamic Republic of Iran Broadcasting News, www.iribnews.ir/ (accessed 12 August 2006).

Islamic Republic News Agency, IRNA, www.irna.ir/fa/content/view/menu-144/id-23/ (accessed 15 August 2006).

IT Iran, http://itiran.net/ (accessed 12 August 2006).

Jensen, Peder Are Nøtvold, 'Blogging Iran', MA dissertation, University of Oslo, Norway, http://wo.uio.no/as/WebObjects/theses.woa/wa/these?WORKID=21737 (accessed 12 August 2006).

Kioumars Saberi-Foumani's website, http://www.golaghaweekly.com/saberi/pages/biography. htm (17 February 2006).

Larijani, Ali, interviewed by Shargh newspaper, 7 February 2005, reproduced by the online news site, *Baztab*, www.baztab.com/news/21394.php (accessed 12 August 2006).

Mir-Tajeddini, Mohammad-Reza, quoted by the Iranian Students News Agency, ISNA, <http://science.isna.ir/news/NewsPrint.asp?id=463851> (accessed 3 December 2004).

Mohammadi, Rouh-Anguiz, interview with Dr Mehadi Akhlaqi-Feizasar, about the discrepancies in unemployment figures given by various government organizations, carried by the Society of Iranian Youth News Agency (SYNA), 10 October 2004, www.syna.ir/ news/news_10193.html (accessed 10 October 2004).

Montazeri, Ayatollah Hossein-Ali, website, www.montazeri.com/ (accessed 12 August 2006).

National Geographic style guide, http://magma.nationalgeographic.com/ngm/ styleguide/ stylemanual.pdf (accessed December 2005).

New Statesman online, www.newstatesman.com/ (accessed 12 August 2006).

Nikahang Kowsar's weblog, http://nikahang.blogspot.com/ (accessed 12 August 2006).

Pendar, English language Iranian news website based in the US: www.pendar.net/ (accessed 12 August 2006).

Persianblog, www.persianblog.com (accessed 12 August 2006).

Pesaran, M. H., 'Economic Trends and Macroeconomic Policies in Post-Revolutionary Iran,' August 1998, Cambridge University, Cambridge, www.econ.cam.ac.uk/faculty/ pesaran/iran98_0.pdf (accessed 12 August 2006).

Petroleum Information Network, SHANA, www.shana.ir/aboutus-fa.html (accessed 15 August 2007).

Pupils News Agency of Iran (PANA), www.irpana.ir/ (accessed 12 August 2006).

Reporters Without Borders, www.rsf.org/ (accessed 18 February 2007).

Reuters news agency report, 21 November 2004, carried by MSNBC, www.msnbc.msn. com/id/6548908/(accessed 3 August 2006).

Saharkhiz, Issa, Iran-e Emrouz, www.iran-emrouz.de/khabar/saharkh820309.html (accessed 12 August 2006).

Sharif News, http://sharifnews.com/ (accessed 12 August 2006).

Society of Iranian Youth News Agency (SYNA), www.syna.ir/ (accessed Fall 2005).

Supreme Cultural Revolution Council, 'Siyassat-haye Farhangi-ye Jomhouri-ye Ealsmi-ye Iran dar Howzeh-ye Matbou'at' (Cultural Policies of the Islamic Republic of Iran in the Domain of the Press), www.ghavanin.ir/detail.asp?id=13692 (accessed 12 August 2006).

Supreme Cultural Revolution Council's women's website, www.iranwomen.org/ (accessed 12 August 2006).

Talachian, Reza, 'A Brief Critical History of Iranian Feature Film (1896–1975)', a chapter in *A Survey Catalogue and Brief Critical History of Iranian Feature Film (1896–1975)*, MA dissertation, Department of Cinema and Photography in the Graduate School, Southern Illinois University, December 1980, University of Washington Libraries website, www.lib.washington.edu/ neareast/cinemaofiran/intro.html (accessed 12 August 2006).

——, 'Major Motion Picture Studios in Iran, 1929–1975', in *A Survey Catalogue and Brief Critical History of Iranian Feature Fim (1896–1975)*, MA dissertation, Department of Cinema and Photography in the Graduate School, Southern Illinois University, December 1980, University of Washington Libraries website, www.lib.washington.edu/neareast/cinemaofiran/intro.html (accessed 12 August 2006).

Tehran Times online, www.tehrantimes.com/ (accessed 12 August 2006).

The Persian language news site, *Emrooz*, www.emrooz.ws/ShowItem.aspx?ID=2418&p=1 (accessed Spring 2005).

Verdinejad, Fereydoun, personal website, www.verdinejad.com/html/History.htm (accessed 12 August 2006).

Women in Iran news site, www.womeniniran.net/ (accessed 12 August 2006).

Index

Lightning Source UK Ltd.
Milton Keynes UK
171848UK00001B/41/P